Japanese Policymaking

Japanese Policymaking

The Politics Behind Politics
Informal Mechanisms and the Making of China Policy

Quansheng Zhao

PRAEGER

Westport, Connecticut
London

Library of Congress Cataloging-in-Publication Data

Zhao, Quansheng.
    Japanese policymaking : the politics behind politics : informal
mechanisms and the making of China policy / Quansheng Zhao.
      p. cm.
    Includes bibliographical references and index.
    ISBN 0–275–94449–2 (alk. paper)
    1. Political culture—Japan. 2. Japan—Politics and
government—1945– 3. Pluralism (Social sciences)—Japan. 4. Japan
—Economic policy—1945–1989. 5. Japan—Economic policy—1989– .
I. Title. II. Title: Japanese policy making.
JQ1681.Z43   1993
306.2′0952—dc20   92–20052

British Library Cataloguing in Publication Data is available.

Library of Congress Catalog Card Number: 92–20052
ISBN: 0–275–94449–2

First published in 1993

Praeger Publishers, 88 Post Road West, Westport, CT 06881
An imprint of Greenwood Publishing Group, Inc.

Printed in the United States of America

The paper used in this book complies with the
Permanent Paper Standard issued by the National
Information Standards Organization (Z39.48-1984).

10 9 8 7 6 5 4 3 2 1

Copyright Acknowledgments

John Quansheng Zhao, "The Making of Public Policy in Japan: Protectionism in Raw Silk
Importation" © 1988 by The Regents of the University of California. Reprinted from *Asian
Survey*, Vol. 28, No. 9, pp. 926–44, by permission of the Regents.

John Quansheng Zhao, "Informal Pluralism and Japanese Politics: Sino-Japanese Rapprochement
Revisited," *Journal of Northeast Asian Studies* 8, no. 2 (Summer 1989): 65–83, by permission
of Transaction Publishers.

John Quansheng Zhao, "Politics of Japan-China Trade Negotiations," *Asian Profile* 18, no. 2
(April 1990): 97–115, by permission of the Asian Research Service.

To My Parents and My Wife

Contents

Foreword

In contrast to a number of East Asian societies, Japan has appeared to be a nation that has successfully synthesized stability and development. No one doubts the extraordinary economic accomplishments of this country in the past four decades. Meanwhile, one political party has held national power since its formation in 1955. The bureaucracy has remained highly professional, relatively honest, and self-confident in its role. Its authority—and legitimacy—continue to be high. Protest in the forms familiar in other societies are barely visible in Japan, and generally center around a very specific issue. And political continuity is symbolized by the large number of children and other relatives of former Diet members who "inherit" their positions.

In recent years, analysts of the Japanese scene have sketched two seemingly contradictory images of this society and more particularly, its decision-making process. Their short-hand descriptions are "Japan, Inc." and "the rudderless ship."

The first image is one of a close, government-directed integration of economic policies with officials and the private sector cooperating to this end. Further, a series of tight, interlocking directorates bind the financial-industrial structure together. This situation yields a highly focused set of objectives, rigorously pursued, and a relatively exclusivist system, difficult to penetrate from the outside.

The second image is that of highly competitive units in and out of government, and the absence of any supreme coordinating authority. Hence, no one is prepared to take responsibility for decisions that are initiated bottom up. Further, only after much delay is a consensus murkily achieved. To employ Gertrude Stein's description of Oakland, "There's no there there."

These two images capture a portion of reality, at least in "pure" form, but the evidence increasingly indicates that Japanese society and its politics are currently both more complex and more fluid than these relatively simple, static images indicate. In recent times, the role of such critically important governmental agencies as the Ministry of International Trade and Industry (MITI) has been changing. Administrative *guidance* partakes increasingly of administrative *suggestion*, with its potency dependent in considerable degree on whether the private sector toward which it is directed agrees.

The growing independence of the Japanese industrial community from governmental authority has in considerable degree paralleled the process of economic internationalization. Few nations have gone as far as Japan in seeking less expensive, more plentiful labor, the requisite natural resources, and a haven from foreign protectionist measures through internationalization. And the process has provided new leverage as well as new challenges for both the private sector and the government.

One should not depreciate the role of the Japanese bureaucracy. Officialdom is still the source of policy in major degree, especially in its details, and on occasion, the bureaucracy still thwarts political leaders even after they have publicly enunciated a policy. The extent to which this differs from other parliamentary systems, especially those of West Europe, can be debated. In any case, however, as several of the specific studies in this volume make clear, increasingly, politicians are setting the broad guidelines within which bureaucrats must work, especially in the realm of foreign policy. In this respect, the influence of the Policy Affairs Research Council of the dominant Liberal Democratic Party (LDP) has steadily increased.

Policy coordination remains a problem, and this is scarcely unique to Japan. Historically, the bureaucratization of the dominant conservative party—the process whereby ex-bureaucrats assumed high positions in that party—smoothed the path for party-bureaucratic cooperation. And personal connections were all-important in this, as in other aspects of Japanese politics. In recent years, the external influences that influence decision making have been stronger and more varied: a widening range of private interest groups, a more involved media, and a growing number of private "think-tanks." Nor can one ignore the role of pressures external to Japan. In some cases, indeed, foreign pressures—or policies—have been of critical importance.

Thus, political changes, quite possibly of a substantial nature, are enroute. The only questions relate to their timing and extent. The antiquated electoral system which heavily favors the rural voters is long overdue for reform. The recurrent scandals involving money and politics have increased cynicism and apathy among an electorate long known for its conservativism. And a younger, post-war generation is rapidly rising in the political world, a generation likely to be more independent and assertive. Many observers expect a political realignment in the not too distant future, with a new party or parties being formed. Whatever may be the course of events, there is a ferment in Japanese politics that has not been seen since the early postwar era.

Yet whatever the changes, Japanese politics will continue to be strongly shaped by those procedures born out of Japan's political culture, signalled by terms like *kuromaku* (black veil), *nemawashi* (root-building), *tatemae* (public position) versus *honne* (true intention), *tsukiai* (social activity and networks). These policy-making instruments and behavior patterns, elucidated in the case studies of this work, are critical to an understanding of Japanese decision making as well as other aspects of the Japanese scene. The interplay between tradition and innovation, with the relative weight of each constantly changing, makes a study of modern Japan at once fascinating and enormously difficult.

In this work, Quansheng Zhao has selected four case studies through which to illustrate what he calls "politics behind politics," namely, those informal procedures and behavior patterns crucial to the policies ultimately pursued. Each of the studies involves some aspect of Japan's China policy and collectively they cover some four decades, from the early 1950s to recent times.

In his study of the protectionist policies applied to raw silk, Zhao explores the intimate social and organizational connections between the silk producers and the Liberal Democratic Party. Like most other rural constituents, the cocoon farmers pledged loyalty in exchange for LDP support. Within the party, an agricultural *zoku* (literally, tribe) dedicated to the interest of their rural supporters entrenched itself in power. Through it, the LDP gave "instructions" to the appropriate ministry, and the desired policy resulted. As Zhao makes clear, however, Japanese society has now entered a more pluralistic stage when conflicting interests make it impossible for any single social group to control the society.

In his second case study, dealing with the process of Sino-Japanese normaliza-tion, the author emphasizes the importance of informal or behind-the-scenes channels involving those who wore the "black veil." Among these, none were more important than the intra-party groups set up specifically to influence Japan's decisions on China policy. In the final analysis, he argues, China policy was altered by the decisions of a factional coalition of three LDP leaders rather than either the bureaucracy or the LDP formal organizations.

However, as Zhao makes clear, it is extremely important to understand that the Chinese leaders of the 1960s and 1970s understood the game that they were playing with Japan, and played it well. Moreover, the shifting policies of the United States were another external factor of critical importance.

Meanwhile, the independent activities of individual Diet members, opposition parties, corporations, and the media provided a multiplicity of channels to test policy options as well as a set of diverse pressures upon policy makers. Even the intellectuals, through "think-tanks" and in the capacity of advisors, played a role, albeit a relatively modest one.

The picture that Zhao draws is one of great complexity, with China policies far from being under the exclusive control of the bureaucracy (itself divided and competitive) or the formal party organs. Yet at the same time, when the formal shift came, it took place under an approving leadership and the preliminary steps had all been taken. And once the government recovered from the shock of having not been consulted by President Nixon prior to his opening to Beijing, it moved swiftly with wide (although not unanimous) support.

Zhao then moves to examine the economic agreements reached with China in the initial period after diplomatic relations had been established. He uses the achievement of these agreements to explore the extensive consultation process (*nemawashi*) that took place prior to the consummation of the accords, and by this means, he illustrates the vital importance of personal relations as manifested in "groupism" and leader–follower clusters in all aspects of Japanese society. His analysis of these accords takes him into the field of political culture, including the intricate relation between one's outward expressions and inner beliefs and intentions as well as the issue of trust. These and other aspects of Japanese culture are invariably a powerful factor in every bargaining situation, and it might be added, connect Japan with a number of other Asian societies.

Finally, the issue of Japanese assistance to China—pre- and post-Tiananmen— is studied. Once PRC economic reforms had begun, economic assistance to China was widely regarded as being in Japan's national interest. Thus, the Tiananmen incident posed the most serious dilemma: how to support the West, and most particularly, the United States in its condemnation of the Chinese government's actions and at the same time, prevent a prolonged disruption of Sino-Japanese relations. Japan's policies were crafted to accept sanctions while striving to avoid isolating China—thereby placing it close to (but not identical with) the Bush administration. High level visits were begun at a relatively early time, informal channels were kept open, and behind-the-scenes discussions were initiated. Thus, by the time of the G-7 Houston meeting of July 1990, Japan was prepared to apply modest pressure upon the industrial nations (with Washington's "understanding") to soften the punishment being applied to China.

Throughout this work, Zhao displays a familiarity with a wide range of theoretical works dealing with such subjects as international relations theory, the policymaking process, and political culture, and employs them selectively. The combination of theory, the available literature dealing with the specific data, and in-depth interviews provide a stimulating approach. Moreover, although the focus is kept on Japan, the fact that the author grew up in China and had his undergraduate education at Peking University make his selection of four policy studies dealing with aspects of Sino-Japanese relations most appropriate. This is a work well worth a close examination, representing a step forward in research on one of the world's most important nations.

Robert A. Scalapino

Preface

There are various approaches to the study of comparative politics and international relations. The realm of empirical analysis, for example, tests hypotheses about what *is* the case—a conceptual framework that provides for the orderly arrangement and examination of data. On the other hand, propositions in normative theory deal with what *should* be the case, with an emphasis on value considerations.[1] This book is a blend of the two.

The primary emphasis of this book is on empirical analysis. It examines and analyzes several important policymaking mechanisms in Japan, involving a broad range of social elements at different levels such as the social environment and structures, political institutions, and personal connections. By identifying several intuitive Japanese ways of policymaking, such as the social network, informal political actors and organizations, and behind-the-scenes consensus-building, it argues that informal mechanisms are distinguished characteristics of Japanese politics and policymaking.

This study is based on a thorough examination of four case studies on Japan's China policy and Sino-Japanese relations. Therefore, in addition to a fresh and analytical framework in the study of Japanese policymaking, the reader may also learn some important aspects of Japanese foreign policy toward China and the evolution of political and economic relations between China and Japan.

In 1991 five specialists of Japanese politics—Scott Flanagan, Shinsaku Kohei, Ichirō Miyake, Bradley Richardson, and Jōji Watanuki—published their book *The Japanese Voter*, making a superb contribution to the fields of Japan studies and comparative politics. The authors have not only produced a comprehensive analysis of formal political institutions, but have also conducted extensive research on extragovernmental factors in Japan's political life, such as social structure, informal social network, and political culture. It is significant in that it brings Japanese political research, as Warren Miller says in the book's foreword, "into the intellectual mainstream in a comprehensive treatment commensurate with the established tradition of the national election studies of the Atlantic community." By following a similar line, I examine and analyze the characteristics of Japanese policymaking in a comprehensive way, connecting them to concepts in Western social science and prior studies on Japan.

Formal practice of policymaking in Japan has been thoroughly examined in a series of general studies on Japanese politics, such as Robert Scalapino and Junnosuke Masumi's *Parties and Politics in Contemporary Japan* (1962), Haruhiro Fukui's *Party in Power: The Japanese Liberal-Democrats and Policymaking* (1970), J.A.A. Stockwin's *Japan: Divided Politics in a Growth Economy* (1982), T. J. Pempel's *Policy and Politics in Japan: Creative Conservatism* (1982), and Gerald Curtis' *The Japanese Way of Politics* (1988). Although the present book focuses on the informal aspect of Japanese politics that has been less examined before, it is not intended to downplay the importance of formal political structures. Rather, it argues that informal practice is at least as important as formal practice in Japan's political life. In this sense, this book is a supplement (not a replacement) to the above-mentioned excellent accounts of Japanese politics and policymaking.

This study also has a normative side. The political implication of the Japanese model of policymaking is one of the main concerns here. In the middle of the nineteenth century, the Frenchman Alexis de Tocqueville conducted a study of American democracy, which became a milestone. The urgency for advancing to democratization is reflected in a statement made by Tocqueville (1969: 58). It may also be used to express a similar sentiment in East Asia today.

> [I]f we do not succeed in gradually introducing democratic institutions among us, . . . there will be no independence left for anybody, neither for the middle classes nor for the nobility, neither for the poor nor for the rich, but only an equal tyranny for all; and I foresee that if the peaceful dominion of the majority is not established among us in good time, we shall sooner or later fall under the *unlimited* authority of a single man. [emphasis by Tocqueville]

This sense of urgency for democracy in East Asia has increased the importance of the Japanese experience. Even though some traditional Japanese thinkers such as Yukichi Fukuzawa advocated *datsu-a*, or out of Asia (literally, "shed Asia," as a snake sheds its skin) about a century ago, Japan has always been a vital player in the region (B. Hashikawa 1980). As an economic superpower and a democracy in the region, Japan may provide not only a successful model for economic modernization, but also a possible alternative for political development for other East Asian societies.

In this study, I have been motivated by a similar desire to examine the political development and policymaking of Japan, one of the first non-Western democracies. The Japanese experiences are valuable not only to the Japanese, but also to other nations, East and West alike. It is my hope that this kind of study will ultimately help other East Asian societies explore useful models for democratization and modernization.

Finally, the object of this study is not to determine whether one system is better than another, nor does this study suggest that other countries should copy Japan's example. As Kōzō Yamamura (1982: 106) argues, for example, "most of Japan's policies and managerial practices that once contributed to rapid growth cannot serve as a guide to U.S. economic policy or business executives." Rather, the purpose is to enhance our knowledge of Japanese politics and policymaking, which in turn may promote a better mutual understanding between East and West.

A list of acknowledgments, even a long one, will not be adequate to express my gratitude to the many individuals and institutions that were involved in the long process of research and writing this book.

My thanks should go first to my teachers at the University of California, Berkeley. I owe a great deal to Robert A. Scalapino, who was the principal adviser at the early stage of this project. During and after the Berkeley period, Scalapino has always been an enlightened teacher, a solid supporter, and an understanding friend. This project could not have been completed without his consistent guidance and support. During the same period at Berkeley, Richard Holton, Chalmers Johnson, Kenneth Waltz, and Aaron Wildavsky provided precious advice in various aspects and encouragement to this project. My intellectual development also benefited from Vinod Aggarwal, Lowell Dittmer, Thomas Gold, Ernst Haas, Martin Landau, William Muir, Nelson Polsby, Carl Rosberg, the late Paul Seabury, and Raymond Wolfinger. I appreciate the institutional support at the Berkeley campus—the Department of Political Science, the Institute of East Asian Studies, the Institute of Governmental Studies, and the Institute of International Studies. I also thank Peking University where I received my undergraduate education in international politics.

I gratefully acknowledge academic support from the following three Japanese institutions that made my one-year field research (1985–86) in Japan rewarding: the University of Tokyo which provided an excellent intellectual environment, the International House of Japan where many stimulating presentations were conducted and the Japan–China Economic Association which provided valuable primary research materials. I greatly appreciate the kindness and guidance I received from the following: Kenichiro Hirano and Takashi Inoguchi who were my sponsors during my affiliation with the University of Tokyo; Mikio Katō who creatively supported me and others to establish the Chinese Forum for Social Science Studies at the International House of Japan; Shinkichi Etō, Junnosuke Masumi, and Seizaburō Satō, who gave me constructive advice during my field research and in the years since; Sumiko Itō, Kiyotaka Katō, Tadao Kimura, Yoshio Uchida, and many unnamed Japanese friends and colleagues, who enriched, in various ways, my understanding of Japanese society and politics.

I extend my deep appreciation to the following people who made thoughtful comments, at different phases of the project, on either portions of earlier papers or the final manuscript: Hans Baerwald, Thomas Burkman, Haruhiro Fukui, Alexander George, Michael Halderman, Fumiko Halloran, Donald Hellmann, Hidenori Ijiri, Young Kim, Bruce Koppel, Ellis Kraus, Yasumasa Kuroda, Takie Lebra, Chae-Jin Lee, Tingjiang Li, Edward Lincoln, Gerard Mare, Jing Mei, Sadako Ogata, Robert Orr, Susan Pharr, Lucian Pye, the late Edwin Reischauer, Robert Sakai, Patricia Steinhoff, Christopher Szpilman, Nathaniel Thayer, Allen Whiting, and several anonymous reviewers. For example, Fumiko Halloran read the entire manuscript word by word and provided much needed comments from the Japanese perspective. Another memorable example is Edwin Reischauer, who sent me a two-page encouraging comment in July 1989 after reading an early version of a case study. Reischauer's second letter reached me in May 1990, several months prior to his passing away. He stated that he was too sick to read my manuscript but nevertheless wished me "success in preparing the manuscript for publication." All these intellectual supports have indeed been crucial to improvement of the manuscript. Research assistance or proofreading from Elaine Dawson, Sharee Groves, Mieko Ishibasi, Savitri Krishnamurty, Hinako Watanabe, David Wolff, Martha Yamamoto, and Peter Yuen are also appreciated. I wish to thank all interviewed individuals who took time out to see me and to try to enlighten me in various aspects of Japanese politics and policymaking.

I would especially like to thank the Japan Foundation, the University of California at Berkeley, Old Dominion University, the Earhart Foundation, and the Masayoshi Ōhira Memorial Foundation for providing research grants and fellowships to this project; and to the East-West Center and Charles Morrison, who helped to arrange a fellowship (1989–90) for me, conducting thorough revisions of the manuscript at the Center.

A special expression of gratitude goes to my wife, my son, and daughter for their warmhearted support and understanding during the years of research and writing. I dedicate this book to my parents and my wife, who remain an enduring source of spiritual support.

I remain solely responsible for the analysis and conclusions expressed in this book.

NOTE

1. There are many discussions on empirical and normative approaches in the field of international relations. See, for example, J. Dougherty and R. Pfaltzgraff (1990: 17), and P. Viotti and M. Kauppi (1987: 519–20).

Abbreviations

AAB	Asian Affairs Bureau
ADB	Asian Development Bank
CAAC	Civil Aviation Administration of China
CCP	Chinese Communist Party
CCPIT	China Council for the Promotion of International Trade
CGP	Clean Government Party (Kōmeitō)
CHINCOM	China Committee of the Consultative Group
COCOM	Coordinating Committee of the Consultative Group (Paris Group)
CSRSSP	Corporation on the Stabilization of Raw Silk and Sugar Prices
DAC	Development Assistance Committee
DSP	Democratic Socialist Party
EPA	Economic Planning Agency
FLS	Forum of Liberal Society
GATT	General Agreement on Tariffs and Trade
JCEA	Japan-China Economic Association
JCP	Japanese Communist Party
JCPIT	Japan Council for the Promotion of International Trade
JETRO	Japan External Trade Organization
JSP	Japanese Socialist Party
KMT	Kuomintang (Nationalist Party)

LDP	Liberal Democratic Party
MAFF	Ministry of Agriculture, Forestry, and Fisheries
MFN	most-favored-nation (treatment)
MITI	Ministry of International Trade and Industry
MOF	Ministry of Finance
MOFA	Ministry of Foreign Affairs
MOJ	Ministry of Justice
ODA	Official development assistance
OECD	Organization of Economic Cooperation and Development
PARC	Policy Affairs Research Council
PRC	People's Republic of China
SCAP	Supreme Commander for the Allied Powers
SFT	special favor treatment

Japanese Terms

ahiru gaikō	duck diplomacy
amakudari	descent from heaven, referring to a typical method for Japanese bureaucrats to have second careers after mandatory retirement
gakubatsu	school clique
giri	a feeling of obligation
gyōkai	industrial groups
haragei	stomach art (implicit mutual understanding)
honne	true intention, one's real feelings
Keidanren	(Japanese) Federation of Economic Organizations
kigyō	individual corporations
kōenkai	association of supporters for individual Diet members
kuromaku	black veils (informal political organizations)
nemawashi	root-building (behind-the-scenes preparations)
Nōkyō	agricultural cooperatives
ringisei	to ask from below, referring to a decision-making system that starts at lower levels
seikei bunri	differentiation of economic activities from political ones
shinkutanku	think-tanks or research institutions
tatemae	public statement or behavior

Japanese names are placed in the Western order, given name first and family name second.

tsukiai	social activities, such as after-work entertaining (social networks)
yatō gaikō	opposition party diplomacy
zaibatsu	financial clique
zaikai	leaders of major economic corporations
zoku	tribes (senior Diet members who are specialized in certain policy areas)

PART I

Introduction

1

Japanese Policymaking

This study examines and analyzes Japan's behind-the-scenes policymaking mechanisms, or politics behind politics. The mechanisms in Japanese policymaking often appear, as Glen Fisher (1980: 34) suggests, hidden from outsiders; or as M. Y. Yoshino and Thomas Lifson (1986: 6) note, they are usually invisible. In his discussion on political style in Japan, Edwin Reischauer (1988: 289) argues that Japan's democracy operates in ways "unfamiliar to Westerners," with "vast amounts of behind-the-scenes negotiations among political allies and with opponents." The policymaking mechanisms in Japan involve a broad range of social phenomena, including social system and structures, political institutions, and personal connections. The subtle and elusive nature of these policymaking mechanisms in the ever-changing dynamics of Japanese politics deserves closer examination. The main theme of this study is the notion of informal mechanisms, an important characteristic of the Japanese policymaking process.

Conventional analyses of policymaking in Japan have often seen the Japanese variant as distinctive in being more "patterned" (Krauss and Muramatsu 1988) or "channeled" (S. Satō and T. Matsuzaki 1986), which actually means somewhat more formal structure than in a Western democratic society. (These models are discussed later in Part II.) In contrast, this book emphasizes that policymaking in Japan has a distinguished informal aspect. By identifying several intuitive Japanese ways of conducting Japan's foreign policy and international activities, it argues that informal channels and practice are at least as important as formal ones in the policymaking process of Japanese politics. It is important to first look at what are the central issues of this study, for choosing a mode of analysis, as John Campbell points out (1992: 379), "first depends on what questions one wishes to answer."

CENTRAL ISSUES AND THE CONCEPT OF
INFORMAL MECHANISMS

The following questions are given special attention throughout the book:

- Does Japan have its own patterns and characteristics in the policymaking process?

- If there are such patterns and characteristics, what are the mechanisms for policy input and political influence that often appear behind-the-scenes and are difficult for "outsiders" to observe?

- How does Japan's foreign policymaking process interrelate to its domestic political, social, and cultural environments?

- What differences and similarities in the policymaking process can be identified when comparing Japan to other East Asian societies and Western democracies such as the United States?

In his classic study *Man, the State and War*, Kenneth Waltz (1959) developed a systemic approach on the theory of international relations, analyzing world systems from three levels: individual, state, and international systems. This innovative method of analysis has had an enormous impact on the study of international affairs and related theories. With a different subject of study, this book attempts to adopt a similar pattern where the method of levels of analysis will be applied.

This book analyzes the Japanese policymaking process from three different levels: (1) the societal level—social system and environment, (2) the institutional level—political actors and organizations, and (3) the individual level—personal connections and consensus-building. It examines not only regular political institutions, but also the social and cultural environments, and it differs from the standard, single-faceted treatment of the internal workings of Japanese politics and policymaking. This study is not a general introduction to Japan's political system with an institutional approach, nor is it a standard stereotype of the "Japan as unique" perception using a cultural perspective. And it is certainly not a simple (or more elaborate) restatement of old notions on Japanese politics and society. Rather, it is a multifocused perception, derived from a comprehensive study of various political mechanisms, thereby providing a fresh and an analytical framework in looking into a more complex and sophisticated picture of Japanese policymaking.

The term *informal* means "not formal; irregular; without ceremony or formality" (Hornby 1963: 548). In a more specific sense, informal practice refers to a set of informal political activities that take place outside the formal state structures (such as legislative, executive, and judiciary branches). Therefore, it may also be called extragovernmental activities.

The concept of policymaking mechanisms means a set of arrangements, actions, norms, values, and behavior patterns and styles that effectively affect policy inputs and outputs. These mechanisms may influence or even control the actions of decision-makers and the policymaking process. They are products of social environment, political structure, and cultural values. These variables can be examined at different levels with various theoretical notions, such as pluralism and social network, organizational theory, and political culture.

Throughout the book, these approaches are applied individually or collectively to four case studies on a series of foreign policy issues, particularly Japanese foreign policy toward China. Special attention is paid to three components: social environment and network (*tsukiai*), informal political actors and organizations (*kuromaku*), and behind-the-scenes consensus-building activities (*nemawashi*).

The use of fairly common Japanese terms in this book, such as *tsukiai*, *kuromaku*, and *nemawashi*, is to give the reader some direct "Japanese flavor," thereby enlivening the illustrations and analyses. These terms and their imputed meanings are intriguing and, to some extent, useful to an understanding of Japanese politics and policymaking. However, these Japanese words are not used as analytical concepts; therefore, they cannot be overused. In addition, the reader may notice that on many occasions the use of these Japanese terms is rather specific, whereas the English equivalents can have much broader and less concrete meaning. To avoid confusion, especially in the theoretical parts, the reader may ultimately look into and depend on English definitions (which are more accurate in explaining the concepts) for a better and correct understanding.

The relationship between formal authority and informal activities in Asian societies has long been regarded as an important topic among scholars. In *Asian Power and Politics*, Lucian Pye (1985: 285) claims: "To uncover the actual flow of power, it is necessary to look through the formal arrangements of authority to the dynamics of the informal relationships." The informal relationships in Asian societies often "generate the substance of power that is ultimately decisive in determining political developments." In a study on status conflict in Japan, Susan Pharr (1984: 238) discovered that there is "an extraordinary amount of informal background activity that smoothed the way"; Pharr particularly noticed the importance of behind-the-scenes preparatory work (*nemawashi*) in Japanese negotiating behavior. Donald Hellmann (1988: 351) also emphasized extra-institutional practices in Japan that "surround and sustain the formal policymaking of the government." Hellmann claimed that the success of Japan's economic foreign policies "can be understood only by placing the formal governmental processes within the context of this broader, informal, personalized" system. Pye's observation of the actual flow of power through "the dynamics of the informal relationships," Pharr's analysis on "informal background activity," and Hellmann's emphasis of the "extra-institutional practices" are, I believe, some of the most intuitive studies on policymaking mechanisms in Japanese politics.

Anthropologists, sociologists, and legal specialists have also studied informal social settings and informal behavior in Japanese society. In *Political Anthropology*, Ted Lewellen (1983: 124–125) argues that anthropologists have focused on two elements in Japanese society. The first comprises the informal groups, based on class interests, age, and education, that function within formal organizations. The second involves the relationship between the organization, the individuals that comprise it, and the wider environment. Legal specialist Frank Upham (1987: 166–204) claims that "social conflict in Japan is characterized by informality and verticality" and that "informality is preferred by every level of government and in all areas of government-citizen contact." According to Joy Hendry (1987: 42), informality in Japan may also reflect Japan's traditional values that show differences in behavior, corresponding to the difference between *tatemae* or public behavior, and *honne*, or one's real feelings. Chie Nakane (1986: 177), a sociologist, explains that Japan's industrialization has produced a new type of organization, the formal structure of which may be closely akin to that found in modern Western societies. However, this does not necessarily accord with changes in the informal structure in which, as in the case of Japan, the traditional structure survived in large measure.

Personal relationships and informal aspects in Japan's political life have also drawn attention from some Japan specialists. In a study on Japan's political parties, Bradley Richardson and Scott Flanagan (1984: 100) argue that informal relationships and groups are at times possibly more important than formal structures. Gerald Curtis (1975: 46) believes that, although not as crucial as many writers contend, "informal contact" between top political and business leaders in Japan" obviously plays a part in structuring business-government communication." In his study on Japanese budget politics, John Campbell (1977: 118–121) argues that activities of the "unofficial groups" within the ruling Liberal Democratic party are "important as one among several pressure-generating mechanisms."

Although the informal (or extragovernmental) aspects of Japanese politics have drawn attention from a variety of scholars, they have not often been, as Richard Samuels (1983: 13–16) suggests, "the objects of empirical research" and systematic study. Moreover, they have not been examined by putting them into the theoretical context of policymaking mechanisms in Japanese politics. There are reasons for this neglect. In a recent study of Japanese voting behavior, Scott Flanagan (1991: 144–145) argues that social environment (such as social network) and interpersonal relationship have been "neglected" in the studies of Japanese politics (such as election politics) and policymaking. He cites three reasons for the inattention: The first reason is a methodological one—when large-scale nationwide survey samples are conducted, the effect of the individual's social context becomes obscured. The second reason comes from the influence of traditional democratic theory, which emphasizes individual decision-making and self-interested choices; external social influence has often been viewed as a negative or less important element. Third, research on political behavior (voting behavior in particular) in the West has historically been dominated by "models that minimize the role of interpersonal influences." Thus, a study like this one may naturally be regarded as an attempt to bridge these theoretical and empirical gaps.

I would like to emphasize that the above statement is not meant to downplay the importance of formal practice and that informal practice is only one characteristic in Japan's political life. Policymaking in Japan has its decidedly "formal" aspects, and the Japanese process of policy input is in some important respects wide open to public view. It is wrong to argue that only informal channels deserve attention and that postwar Japanese politics and policymaking take place only at the informal level. Instead, this book examines organizations, process, norms, and activities that have heretofore received inadequate attention in policy analysis and highlights their significance. It attempts to demonstrate that the informal process is a critical factor in Japan's policymaking process and is at least as important as the formal process. It argues that it is more difficult to examine informal mechanisms since they often appear behind-the-scenes. Therefore, formal procedures and institutions in the policymaking process, which have been amply examined in many other books, will not be a focus of analysis in this book, although time and again they may be discussed in comparison with informal practice.

An interdisciplinary approach is needed to study informal mechanisms in Japan. This approach seems more important for political scientists since, as Lewellen (1983: 124–125) points out, it has been less emphasized in the field. More than four decades ago, pioneering research, using a variety of disciplinary approaches, was conducted on a Japanese village. The investigation was the product of the combined efforts of three members of the University of Michigan's Center for Japanese Studies: Richard Beardsley, an anthropologist; John Hall, a historian; and Robert Ward, a political scientist (1959). Their interdisciplinary research on community associations has set up a remarkable model for Japan studies. Taking that as a model, this book focuses on comparative politics, but it also incorporates research efforts from other fields such as sociology, anthropology, and legal studies.

In *Community Power and Political Theory*, Nelson Polsby (1980: 4) has tried to use three types of data to distinguish decision-making, which serve as indices of the power of actions. His three categories are: "(1) who participates in decision-making, (2) who gains and who loses from alternative possible outcomes, and (3) who prevails in decision-making." Polsby suggests that identifying the last group would be "the best way to determine which individuals and groups have 'more' power in social life." In order to investigate "who prevails in decision-making," there needs to be an understanding of political influence and the mechanisms of policy input in the decision-making process.

The study of policymaking is closely related to the study of democratic societies. T. J. Pempel (1990: 14–15) argues that the real key to understanding and differentiating among the industrialized democracies would appear to lie more in locating the collective intersection among political parties and other factors. Pempel asks two questions for further research: "In what ways do political parties and the party system connect, either causally or consequentially, to the other state and societal forces that shape and differentiate public policies within the industrialized democracies? In what way are parties and the party system nested in a country's power structure?" To answer these questions, we have to examine not only political institutions as most political scientists do, but also the influence of the social environment.

This study may also be placed in a broader context—modernization and development, which is a major research topic in comparative politics. According to Lucian Pye (1990: 7), the modernization theory predicted that "such developments as economic growth, the spread of science and technology, the acceleration and spread of communications, and the establishment of educational systems would all contribute to political changes." In studying non-Western societies, such as Japan, emphasis has been placed on making a distinction between modernization and Westernization. An increasing number of scholars have begun to believe that, as Samuel Huntington states (1987: 26–27), "The partnership between modernization and Westernization has been broken."

Indeed, the relationship between modernization and Westernization needs to be addressed when we examine most non-Western societies that have embarked on modernization. These societies have been brought into closer contact with the West, and with each other, for more than a century by Western colonial expansion and cultural influence. As a major non-Western country, Japan's path to modernization has been examined carefully by a number of social scientists and Japan specialists. Since the beginning of the 1980s, having already achieved an economic "miracle," Japan has been striving to become a global political power. The issue of Japan's modernization vis-à-vis Westernization and the nature of Japanese politics and policymaking has become a focus of study among many scholars in international relations and comparative politics. It has also drawn interest from policymakers, the business community, and the general public.

In the mid-1970s Japan historian W. G. Beasley (1975: 23) raised a fundamental question: do the differences between non-Western societies chiefly reflect location at different stages along a single path of modern development, or are they primarily to be taken as evidence that variant premodern traditions react differently with—and in the end contribute differently to—an entity identifiable as "modern"? Beasley argues that the Japanese were already asking the question as early as the Meiji period, and it is now "being posed again by the character of Japanese society." Clearly, the key question here is how modernization relates to traditional values, and how this interrelationship influences the direction of modernization in non-Western societies.

With regard to how tradition has influenced Japanese society today, there are different, and often contradictory, perceptions. One school of thought believes that the Japanese "absorb the new rather than struggle to keep the old; therefore, there is a lack of persistence or stubbornness to Japan's tradition" (T. Kuwabara 1983: 81). On the other hand, others make the opposite comments that Japan has maintained its own "Eastern spirit" in terms of traditional values (K. Kamei 1958: 906), or that despite an outstanding economic performance, "Japan lags behind in its social and cultural modernization, since it retains many traditional elements" (H. Befu 1986: 168–169).

Generally speaking, there has been a remarkable combination of modernization and tradition in Japan. This combination has produced a series of fascinating questions and explorations on Japanese society and politics for foreigners as well as for the Japanese themselves. In his presidential address to the Association of Asian Studies, Robert Smith (1989: 715) pointed out, "The history of the study of Japan in the West is in very large part the history of a running debate over the nature and content of tradition and the relative importance of culture, history, and institutions." Along the same line, this study should be regarded as part of this continuing process of intellectual inquiry.

Modernization has made today's formal political and economic systems in Japan essentially similar to those in Western societies. But the influence of political development and traditional social and cultural values has enabled Japan to maintain its own way of political operation in political institutions, social environments, and working styles, in comparison to the West.

As John W. Hall (1965: 36) pointed out, the study of the modernization of Japan is that of the interplay of external and indigenous events. In conducting case studies on Japanese politics within a framework of the making of China policy and Sino-Japanese relations, this book may also be regarded as an effort to explore the Japanese way of political development and modernization.

A series of systemic studies on Japanese politics received acclaim in the 1960s and early 1970s. During this period, several major works on Japan's contemporary political system and society were published.[1] From the mid-1970s, research on Japanese politics began to diversify. Attention has been paid not only to political institutions, but also to various subfields, including the political economy, social studies, and local politics. These studies have become more specialized.[2] All these works have significantly enlarged our understanding of a broad range of issues in contemporary Japanese politics. At the same time, Japanese foreign policy and its policymaking process have also been given close attention by Japan specialists. A number of significant studies have been published representing different research methodologies and approaches.[3] The variety of studies on Japanese politics and its foreign relations has provided a useful analytical framework, as well as rich background materials, which has laid the foundation for later studies.

CASE STUDIES AND THEORY BUILDING

This study has selected the formation of Japan's China policy as the basis for examining its foreign policymaking process and the dynamics of Japanese politics. Four case studies have been chosen:

1. Japan's protectionism of raw silk importation
2. The 1972 Sino-Japanese rapprochement
3. Negotiations for the four Sino-Japanese economic agreements (trade, aviation, navigation, and fisheries)

  4. Japan's foreign aid policy toward China before and after the Tiananmen
     incident of 1989

The examination of these case studies, starting from the Japan-China trade which can be traced back to the 1950s, will cover more than four decades: from the immediate post–World War II period to the early 1990s. The case of Japan's aid policy toward China before and after Tiananmen is one of the most recent studies in Sino-Japanese relations.

In a general study of foreign policy and the policymaking process as a whole, Bernard Cohen and Scott Harris (1975: 388–391) analyze various theoretical frameworks in the field of foreign policy. In particular, they illustrate the evolution from the traditional "state-as-actor" or "rational model" approach[4] to "an approach to foreign-policy analysis which focuses on the conversion process, on mechanisms of transforming inputs into policies." Through this development, the study of foreign policymaking has been broadened and deepened. Foreign policy and domestic structures are treated as closely linked entities.

There are countless cases in Japanese policymaking, in both domestic and foreign policy issues. The reader may naturally wonder why this study has chosen foreign policy issues, and the China policy in particular, as case studies. The study of foreign policymaking and domestic political structures leads to the question of relationships among political parties, the government bureaucracy, and various interest groups. Foreign policymaking in Japan has long been regarded as a field dominated by the government bureaucracy, particularly the Ministry of Foreign Affairs (MOFA) and the Ministry of International Trade and Industry (MITI).[5] Examining the issue of informal mechanisms in foreign policy will be more convincing and demonstrative, because in this area one may expect more formal mechanisms and the lowest levels of interest group politics. To identify high levels of informal mechanisms in Japanese foreign policy makes a good case for the likelihood of finding it throughout the entire political system in Japan.

Now let us look at the issue of Japan's China policy. Japan's policy toward China and Sino-Japanese relations have been studied by a number of political scientists and historians. Several studies covering historical background (M. Jansen 1975), overall Sino-Japanese relations (Chae-Jin Lee 1976 and 1984, and A. Whiting 1989), or a single diplomatic event such as the Sino-Japanese rapprochement in 1972 (S. Ogata 1977 and 1988, and H. Fukui 1977) have provided detailed empirical data and excellent analyses of various aspects of Sino-Japanese relations. Nevertheless, none of these studies has tested the hypotheses that emerged from recent research on the informal mechanisms in Japanese policymaking process, and it will be useful to examine the making of Japan's China policy in this context.

Japan's China policy has been selected as part of the case studies because the formation of the China policy has involved a complicated network of intertwining political forces in the Japanese policymaking system. Against the background of regional and global international environments, this study probes the dynamics of interactions among many groups in Japanese society which participate in, or seek to influence, the process of policymaking. In addition to Japan's traditionally powerful political "tripod,"[6]—the longtime ruling Liberal Democratic Party (LDP), the government bureaucracy,[7] and organized business—the formation of the China policy also involved opposition parties, the National Diet, the news media, the intellectual community, and such interest groups as organized farmers and small- and medium-sized businesses. The extensive involvement of these political forces in the policymaking process can be easily found in the four case studies, thereby making it easier to answer such questions as where and when crucial decisions were made and by whom, and to those forces and policymaking mechanisms that were outside of the previous decision-making models such as the bureaucratic-dominance school. Therefore, the making of Japan's China policy can be regarded as providing a clear means for understanding Japanese foreign policymaking process in general, for it provides rich empirical data for the study.

The case study approach constitutes what Theodore Lowi (1964: 677) called "one of the more important methods of political science analysis." In his case study on the Soviet-Japanese Peace Agreement, Donald Hellmann (1969: 4–5) found that the case study approach "permits specific and systematic examination of each component" of Japanese foreign policymaking. Through this approach, the interrelations between these components can be analyzed and their effective influence on the decision more readily gauged. More importantly, case studies, as Harry Eckstein (1975: 79–86) indicates, are often used "in theory building," and "comparative study is simply the study of numerous cases along the same lines, with a view to reporting and interpreting numerous measures on the same variables of different 'individuals'." Case studies are particularly useful in the theory-building process. To develop the notion of informal mechanisms, the case study approach seems valuable and appropriate.

Nevertheless, the case study approach has an inherent limitation. One debilitating handicap of all case studies is "the problem of uniqueness" (Lowi 1964: 686–688). Any case, no matter how carefully chosen, can only contribute in part to theory building and will have its own limitations. One cannot draw unqualified general conclusions from a single case or from several cases. The case studies in this book, namely, the making of Japan's China policy, are no exception. Therefore, this study does not attempt to interpret the Japanese political system as a whole. Rather, it focuses on informal practice as an important aspect of the formation of Japan's China policy, which will have significant implications for an understanding of Japanese politics and policymaking.

The four case studies used for this book include three foreign economic policies, agricultural protectionism, the negotiations for the four economic agreements, and the official development assistance (ODA) policy. Economics has been one of the most dynamic and active fields in Sino-Japanese relations, and in many cases the formation of economic policy has involved broader social forces, especially interest groups. Political maneuvering of interest groups, such as organized farmers and small- to medium-sized businesses, may be more easily identified by examining cases on the formation of economic policies.

The first case looks at Japan's protectionism of raw silk importation and the establishment of the Statute on Centralized Control of Importation of Raw Silk. It examines interest groups, such as silkworm farmers and small- to medium-sized businesses, and how they act and interact with the ruling LDP and the bureaucracy. The raw silk case looks at the *zoku* phenomenon (longtime Diet members become influential in certain policy areas) within the LDP, especially within the policymaking organ PARC (the Policy Affairs Research Council), and the "old boy connection" of *gakubatsu* (school clique) evident in the government bureaucracy. This case study illustrates the pluralistic nature of the Japanese political system, and how social network works as a mechanism for policy formation and political influence in Japanese society.

The second case study examines the process of Sino-Japanese rapprochement, which is a classic example showing the interrelationship between foreign policy and domestic politics in Japan. For the Japanese, the decision in 1972 to normalize relations with Beijing and to cut off relations with Taipei was highly political and controversial. The process of normalization involved individuals in both official and private capacities, as well as formal and informal political institutions in Japan's political life. In this study, particular attention is paid to the importance of informal political actors and organizations that share power with formal structures and institutions. Some of the informal organizations include the ruling LDP's internal factions, "study groups" and ad hoc committees, the official and unofficial opinions of the government bureaucracy, *yatō gaikō* (opposition party diplomacy), and the prime minister's "duck diplomacy," intellectuals' think-tanks, the news media's political influence, and the business community's "freedom of action."

The negotiations for the first set of Sino-Japanese economic agreements (trade, aviation, navigation, and fisheries during the period 1972–75) is the focus of the third case study. This case touches on several controversial issues, such as the Taiwan issue, COCOM (Coordinating Committee of the Consultative Group designed to make export control regulations toward communist countries), and MFN (most-favored-nation) treatment. By applying the perspective of political culture, Japan's *nemawashi* working styles (root-building and behind-the-scenes consensus-building) receive special attention. The emphasis is on political trust and internal understanding reached through *nemawashi* activities within, and outside of, the LDP/bureaucracy apparatus.

The last case study is that of Japan's aid policy toward China before and after the 1989 Tiananmen Square incident. As the most recent development of Sino-Japanese relations, this study attempts to combine all three levels of analyses that are treated separately in the previous cases—social networks, informal political organizations, and personal connections—to summarize informal mechanisms in Japan's foreign policymaking process. This case shows us how the Japanese have utilized their economic strength to serve political and strategic purposes.

Special attention is paid to the practice of informal mechanisms in Japan's dealing with international crisis—Japan's diplomatic dilemma in its post-Tiananmen China policy.

Each case study includes brief discussions on the historical background, the international environment, and China's positions and reactions. Although this study is not on Chinese politics, discussions also involve the evolution of China's foreign policy and the evolving process of China's perceptions toward the outside world.

There is an imbalance among the four case studies in terms of primary materials and documents. The cases of Japan's protectionism of raw silk importation and the negotiation processes for the Sino-Japanese economic agreements have been less fully examined before; therefore, they involved extensive field research, including taking interviews and checking the validity of original materials. The studies on Japan's decision to normalize relations with China in 1972 and the evolution of Sino-Japanese economic ties are well documented diplomatic events, which have already been thoroughly studied.[8] Therefore, in these cases I have relied heavily on secondary sources. The sources for the study on Japan's aid policy during the Tiananmen incident in 1989, the most recent example in this book, are mainly published journal articles and a few interviews.

I would like to make two points clear. First, even though the four cases on Sino-Japanese relations are significant enough in their own right, the primary purpose of this book is not to discuss these cases per se. Rather, it attempts to provide a fresh, analytical framework for a better understanding of Japanese policymaking and its distinct characteristic—informal mechanisms. The four case studies are used to provide an empirical base to support this concept. While acknowledging the valuable studies related to some cases in this book done by previous scholars, especially the case of Japan's decision to normalize relations with China, I nevertheless bear all responsibility for analyses and conclusions based on these case studies, particularly the concept of informal mechanisms and its implications.

Second, the methodology used in this book is that each of the first three case studies concentrates on only one level of analysis—the levels of societal, institutional, and individual—whereas the fourth case shows all three levels of interplay. Separate analysis of the different levels is made through different case studies not only because each of the case studies can better illuminate the corresponding level of analysis, but also for the sake of making the theoretical notion more precise and clear. This arrangement of case studies, of course, does not mean that each element would singlehandedly influence the policymaking process. Rather, all three elements of informal mechanisms often collectively exercise influence in Japan's political life as demonstrated in the fourth case study.

This study is comparative in nature. While emphasizing Japan's political development as an individual case, the study has also made international comparisons: comparing Japan and the United States, and Japan and its East Asian neighbors.

The concluding chapter focuses on the theory and practice of informal mechanisms, as well as making international comparisons.

NOTES

1. Such as Robert Scalapino and Junnosuke Masumi's study of political parties (1962), Ezra Vogel's analysis of the new middle class (1963), Nathaniel Thayer's work on Japan's conservative rule (1969), Haruhiro Fukui's study of the ruling LDP (1970), Chie Nakane's examination of Japanese society (1970), Gerard Curtis' research on election campaigning (1971), and Nobutaka Ike's book on patron-client democracy (1972). These pioneering works have become classics.

2. Research on Japanese politics and society has covered a variety of topics such as Japan's Parliament (H. Baerwald 1974), political culture (B. Richardson 1974), Japanese radicals (E. Krauss 1974), community power structure (Y. Kuroda 1974), budget politics (J. Campbell 1977), policymaking (T. Pempel, ed. 1977), the bureaucratic system (M. Muramatsu 1981), journalists and the press (Y. Kim 1981), bureaucracy and industrial policy (C. Johnson 1982), politics and economic growth (J. Stockwin 1982), regional policy (R. Samuels 1983), tradition and social order (R. Smith 1983), social protest (D. Apter and N. Sawa 1984), bureaucrats and ministers (Y. Park 1986), the LDP regime (S. Satō and T. Matsuzaki 1986), economic structural adjustment (R. Dore 1986), prefectural politics (S. Reed 1986), *zoku* Diet members (T. Inoguchi and T. Iwai 1987), law and social change (F. Upham 1987), crisis and compensation (K. Calder 1988), civil service system (P. Kim 1988), financial politics (F. Rosenbluth 1989), government intervention in the computer industry (M. Anchordoguy 1989), the enigma of power (K. van Wolferen 1989), the urban society (T. Bestor 1989), status politics (S. Pharr 1990), the voting behavior (S. Flanagan, etc. 1991), and failure of economic policy (R. Angel 1991). There are many more books on contemporary Japanese politics and society, but they cannot be listed here owing to limited space. For example, many of the above-mentioned authors have two or more books on various aspects of Japan's political or social life, but I listed only one from each author that I feel is the most representative of his or her works.

3. For example, Donald Hellmann (1969) examined Japanese foreign policy and its link to domestic policy by conducting a case study on the 1956 Soviet-Japanese peace settlement. Michael Blaker (1977) studied Japan's international negotiating style by looking into eighteen historical prewar examples. In a collective volume, Robert Scalapino (1977) and his colleagues analyzed Japanese foreign policy from four different perspectives: decision-making, public and private interests, foreign economic policy, and security issues. More recently, a similar effort on Japan's political economy in the changing international context has been made through a comprehensive study edited by Takashi Inoguchi and Daniel Okimoto (1988). Robert Orr (1990) studied Japan as a newly emerging power of foreign aid. Gilbert Rozman (1992) examined Japan's response to the former Soviet Union in the Gorbachev era. There are also works concentrating on bilateral relations or Japan's regional role, including Japan-U.S. relation (P. Clapp and M. Halperin, ed. 1974; T. McCraw, ed. 1986; J. Makin and D. Hellmann, ed. 1989; A. Iriye and W. Cohen, ed. 1989, D. Encarnation 1992), Sino-Japanese relations (C. J. Lee 1976 and 1984; A Iriye, ed. 1980; A. Whiting 1989), Japan-Korea relations (C. S. Lee 1985), Japan-Canada relations (F. Langdon 1983), and Japan and East Asia (H. Ellison, ed. 1987; and E. Lincoln 1987). There also have been considerable efforts in comparing

Japan with other countries, such as such the United States (C. Hosoya and J. Watanuki, ed. 1977; F. Valeo and C. Morrison, ed. 1983; and S. Kernell, ed. 1991), or with other nations (B. Szajkowski, ed. 1986; and T. Pempel, ed. 1990).

4. According to this approach, the motives of policymakers stem primarily from a concern with preserving or enhancing the security of the state, and the mechanism of choice has been assumed to be rational calculation. Therefore, little room is provided for consideration of domestic factors, organizational structures, or processes of choice that are other than analytic (see Allison 1971, and Steinbruner 1974).

5. See, for example, Chalmers Johnson (1982), among others.

6. See Chihiro Hosoya, "Taigai seisaku kettei katei ni okeru tokushitsu" (The Nature of Formation of Foreign Policies of Japan and the United States), in Chihiro Hosoya and Jōji Watanuki, eds. (1977: 5–8), *Taigai seisaku kettei katei no nichi-bei hikaku*.

7. Some friends have suggested that the words "bureaucracy" or "bureaucrat" should be replaced by "official," since "bureaucracy" may have different perceptions in Japan and in the United States. (In Japan, for example, bureaucracy has enjoyed a much higher social status than in the United States.) But since "bureaucracy" has been widely used in the academic publications, and many people do understand the differences, I decided to keep the words.

8. See, for example, books and articles on these subjects written by Chae-Jin Lee (1976 and 1984), Sadako Ogata (1977 and 1988), and Haruhiro Fukui (1977).

PART II

Social Environment and the Notion of Pluralism

Case Study: Japan's Protectionism of Raw Silk

2

Social Environment and Informal Network

In Japan, there is a social phenomenon known as *tsukiai*: after-hours entertaining and socializing among managers and workers in companies and manufacturing enterprises. This widespread social activity involves some four or five hours of daily socializing with other employees after work. The group may go to a bar or two, then to a restaurant, and finally to a coffee shop or another bar. The practice of *tsukiai* is quite different from such activities in Western societies, where people tend to go home right after a day's work to be with family or friends outside of their working circles. In this sense, Japan's *tsukiai* is an intriguing pattern of social interrelations. The literal translation of *tsukiai* in Japanese is "social network," or "treat with courtesy."

Many social scientists have studied Japan's social relations. The importance of social environment in terms of understanding the Japanese society has long been studied by anthropologists.[1] Robert Smith (1983: 65–67), for example, has paid special attention to *tsukiai*, which he called "an indispensable technique designed to make affairs of the firm run more smoothly." His definition is an appropriate one, for to make a firm "run more smoothly" is exactly the function that *tsukiai* activities intend to play. In Smith's study (1983: 66), the definition of *tsukiai* is rather limited and refers only to one's "work relationships" and "after-hours association and entertainment."[2] Some other Japan specialists tend to apply the notion of *tsukiai* in a broader sense, applying it to social interaction (B. Moeran 1986: 65).

The impact of social activities on Japanese politics has also been studied by political scientists. Social environment has been recognized as an important variable for studies of the policymaking process and political system. Social relations are "unavoidable in many, perhaps most, work situations" (Almond and Verba 1965: 209). For instance, Takako Kishima (1991: 26–27) examines the informal social activities of the Finance Committee in the Japanese Diet, contending that "the political elite's informal, nonpolitical behavior and the activities that are commonly observed in ordinary people's daily lives have as much significant political potential as their conscious, calculated political actions do." These informal social activities, according to Kishima, can create conditions in which politicians can "transcend party lines, boundaries of roles and statuses and laws."

Part II (Chapters 2 and 3) studies informal mechanisms in Japan's policy-making process from the first level of analysis—the social system and environment, including social groups and informal networks. It examines the way various social groups operate and their interrelations with the state under Japan's political system and social environment. The notions of pluralism and social network are applied to the study of extragovernmental political activities in Japan's policymaking process. A case study of Japan's protectionist policy on raw silk importation is conducted, taking into account social groups such as organized farmers and business groups and, more specifically, the way these interest groups interact with the ruling LDP and the central bureaucracy in the formation of Japan's protectionist policy.

The social network approach is important to the study of Japanese politics. This approach, according to Scott Flanagan (1991: 146), "highlights the role of both formal organizational networks and informal small group networks in the transmission of political opinions, voting cues, and other influence communications." It is important to notice that, although social network may be useful in any kind of regime—democratic and authoritarian alike—a pluralistic political setting, where there is more access for policy input, will provide better environments for social networks and social groups to operate. Thus, we need to look first into pluralism as an important school of thought, its basic function, theoretical development, and its application and implication to the study of Japanese politics and policymaking.

THE NOTION OF PLURALISM

Now let us turn to the theoretical background by examining how the notion of pluralism has developed and its relationship to the study of Japanese politics. By using the term *pluralism* I mean (1) there is no single source of authority and, as a result, there is no concentration of power in the sense of the absolutist state; (2) there is a legitimate right for nonpolitical as well as political groups to exist and to influence the state; and (3) these groups must be, as Philippe Schmitter (1979: 15) points out, "organized into an unspecified number of multiple, voluntary, competitive, non-hierarchically ordered and self-determined categories."

Originating in England, the concept of pluralism was initially developed as a philosophical idea challenging Hegelian monism, but it was quickly accepted and developed by English and American political scientists as a core part of democracy theories. The development of political studies since the 1950s has demonstrated the prevailing position of the notion of pluralism in the field of American politics. It is believed that the study of pluralism can help illuminate fundamental issues of American politics. The heated debate, for example, between the school of pluralism and the school of stratification on the issue of community power has sparked keen interest in the notion of pluralism among political scientists in the United States.[3] The central theme of pluralism is, as Robert Dahl (1956: 137) points out, the evolution of a political system in which various political activities and interest groups in the population "can make themselves heard at some crucial stage in the process of decision." We can conclude that pluralism emphasizes conflict and resolution of conflict through bargaining among groups and coalitions organized around shared interests (T. Lowi 1964: 680). Many political scientists have paid close attention to the relationship among groups, society, and the state.

Some U.S. political scientists have made a continuing effort to apply existing theories that have been popular in the field of American politics to non-Western societies. Japan, as a major democracy in East Asia, has become a favorite subject for political scientists to examine. We have to remember, however, that Japan is neither the only nor the first non-Western society to undergo an examination using the theory of pluralism.

Before we proceed to a detailed discussion about Japan, it will be helpful to look briefly at how the former Soviet Union, another major non-Western society, was examined during the 1960s and 1970s. An interesting development in pluralism was its application to the field of Soviet studies in the mid-1960s. Some Sovietologists regarded pluralism in the Soviet Union as being beyond the original concept as applied to the field of American politics. Therefore, it became necessary to qualify the original concept, and numerous defined models of "pluralism" in the field of Soviet studies developed.

In his study of the Soviet "ministerial-party-scientific complexes," Jerry Hough (1977: 9–11) suggests the notion of institutional pluralism. He stresses the diversity of Soviet society and "a diffusion of real political power." In one discussion, Hough (1972: 25–45) makes a clear distinction between the Soviet and the American models: in the Soviet model of institutional pluralism, those who want to give input into the policymaking process have to work within existing institutions, whereas the American notion of pluralism allows citizens to organize new interest groups outside existing institutions, to advance their own interests.

Other defined concepts of pluralism in the field of Soviet studies include bureaucratic pluralism, limited pluralism, quasi-pluralism, and a pluralism of elites. All these models have tried to differentiate themselves from the American model of pluralism by saying, "The USSR is not a truly pluralistic system" (D. Hammer 1974: 223–224). At the same time, attention has been paid to group activities in Soviet society. Despite some dissatisfaction with the above-mentioned concepts (W. Odom 1976: 566), many of these arguments have strengthened the field of comparative politics.

Since the 1970s, the notion of pluralism has been frequently applied to the study of Japanese politics. As early as 1972, for example, Haruhiro Fukui (1972: 327) examined the making of economic policy in postwar Japan. He called this process "a form of limited pluralism in the process of authoritative policymaking." Fukui's seemingly contradictory terms, *limited pluralism* and *authoritative policymaking*, may well indicate the transitional process of Japanese politics in the late 1960s and early 1970s. The term *limited pluralism* continued to be used in the 1980s. J.A.A. Stockwin (1988: 11), for example, argues that, "Although pluralist models of Japanese political decision making appeared well suited to the diversifying trends of the early and middle 1970s, a more up-to-date perspective suggests that progress towards pluralism has been rather limited in its scope." Nevertheless, the characteristics of this "limited pluralism" need further examination.

According to Haruhiro Fukui (1977), studies on Japanese politics and policy-making can be divided into two categories: the elitist perspective and the pluralist model. The elitist perspective is based on the concept of a tripartite power elite composed of leaders of the ruling LDP, the government bureaucracy, and organized business. According to this perspective, these three major groups comprise a regular and effective alliance and control decision-making on major policy issues. Nobutaka Ike's (1972) notion of "patron-client democracy," for example, reflected this elitist concept.[4] This school of thought was later developed by Chalmers Johnson as "bureaucracy leads politics" in *MITI and the Japanese Miracle* (1982).

The second school of thought has emphasized the pluralistic nature of Japanese politics. According to Daniel Okimoto (1988: 308), pluralists contend that the exercise of political power varies with the issues, and no single group or elite coalition controls outcomes across all policy issues. Pluralism is built into democratic systems by the dispersion of political resources over a wide range of political actors. Policymaking thus features conflict and open competition among interest groups.

Instead of viewing Japan as "Japan, Inc."[5] or as having a "soft authoritarian system,"[6] most recent researchers on Japanese politics argue that, for the last two decades or so, the roles of politicians and mass participation have become more and more prominent. Increasing numbers of scholars have argued that Japan has entered a pluralistic stage in its politics and policymaking process (Inoguchi 1983; Muramatsu and Krauss 1985; Pempel 1987; and Zhao 1989).

There is evidence to support this argument. Takashi Inoguchi (1983), for example, advocates a model of "bureaucratic and mass inclusionary pluralism." He states that the monopolistic role of the bureaucracy in the policymaking process has been broken, while the roles of politicians and mass participation in Japan have become increasingly prominent. Ellis Krauss and Michio Muramatsu (1988) demonstrated a "patterned pluralism" model. They justify the characterization by proposing that (1) there is a dominant party perennially in power; (2) there is an ideological cleavage between that party with its interest group allies and the opposition parties with their own interest group allies; and (3) the bureaucracy remains the pivotal point of the policymaking process, with coalitions forming around the particular ministry in a specific policymaking area. There are also other models of Japanese pluralism, such as "channeled pluralism" (S. Satō and T. Matsuzaki 1986).

The difference between the elitist perspective and the pluralist notion is obvious. While recognizing that both schools have advantages and disadvantages and that both "are inadequate to explain a specific policymaking case," we may also conclude that "the pluralist approach suggests what to look for and the elitist model suggests perhaps what not to look for" (T. Lowi 1964: 685–686).

The concept of informal mechanisms can be regarded as one of the efforts to advance the pluralist approach by which to examine Japanese politics and policymaking. The notion of informal mechanisms differs in fundamental ways from the elitist approach by insisting on the pluralistic nature of Japanese politics. Pluralist models such as "bureaucratic and mass inclusionary pluralism" and "patterned pluralism" are useful in providing a precise picture of structural changes in Japan's political life for the last two or three decades.

The focus of informal mechanisms is different, however: while based on a similar assumption that Japanese politics has entered a pluralist stage, it concentrates on mechanisms of policy formation and political influence in Japanese politics and the policymaking process. It looks not only at formal political institutions such as political parties and governmental bureaucracy, but also at the social and cultural environments such as social groups and networks. Furthermore, it does not attempt to cover the entire Japanese political system. Rather, it emphasizes one important aspect of Japan's political life—its informality.

This first level of analysis—social environment—is conducted in Part II (Chapters 2 and 3) through a case study on Japan's protectionism of raw silk importation concentrating on Sino-Japanese trade relations. The following sections first discuss the evolution of trade relations between Japan and China as a background introduction, and then enter discussions of the controversies that surrounded the Japanese protectionist policy.

BACKGROUND OF JAPAN'S CHINA POLICY
AND SINO-JAPANESE TRADE

How to deal with China has traditionally been a major concern in Japan, in both foreign relations and domestic politics. As Haruhiro Fukui (1970: 227) states, "in the history of Japan's foreign relations, no issue has received such attention from her leaders and people as the relations with her vast continental neighbor, China." The China issue "continually faced and resolved throughout the history of Japanese thought, presents itself in radically different guise in different ages" (D. Pollack 1988: 228). Japan has always attached great importance to its China policy. There is a historical basis for this attention. Warren Tsuneishi (1966: 199) explains,

> From pre-historic until relatively recent times, *the outside world to the Japanese meant China*. China was the source of all the great civilizing influences: Buddhism, naturalized in the "central kingdom" after its Indian beginnings; Confucianism, which molded the Japanese character; the Chinese styles of writing, art, and architecture; and law and the social and political institutions of the successive dynasties. [emphasis added]

Indeed, the historical ties between China and Japan are strong. Japan, like Korea and Vietnam, evolved from the Sinic civilization and was profoundly affected by Chinese culture. Even though Japan never came under Chinese political control, as Korea and Vietnam did, it borrowed extensively from Chinese culture (A. Barnett 1977: 89). Since the thirteenth century, geographic proximity that enabled exchange of personnel and trade and the absence of a Chinese military threat to Japan strengthened these ties. After World War II, Beijing repatriated 30,000 Japanese between 1953 and 1955 and returned about a thousand "war criminals" in 1956. On many occasions since the end of the war, the Japanese have expressed their deep regret for their nation's war behavior (D. Mendel 1961: 216–220).

Because of these historical and traditional links, China has always been an emotional and sometimes controversial issue in Japanese society. The China issue, as Peter Duus (1989: xii) pointed out, was important to Japan's domestic politics. This was the case at the beginning of the century, when Sun Yat-sen and his associates carried out revolutionary activities in both China and Japan. From the 1920s until 1945, the China issue was a major consideration in Japanese foreign policy. After World War II, although the United States had become Japan's main ally and Japan followed U.S. policy on containment of China in the Cold War period, relations with China remained an important issue in Japan. This was particularly true in the early 1970s when Japan and China finally reached rapprochement and began a new era of bilateral relations.

Internationally, Japan's China policy was also controversial. As Warren Cohen (1989: 57) pointed out, "China was unquestionably an issue in Japan-American relations." On the one hand, Sino-Japanese rapprochement was likely to improve Japan's overall bargaining position with the United States, since the prospect of too close a coalition between Asia's two most important and powerful nations was not likely to be welcomed in Washington (P. Mueller and D. Ross 1975: 122). On the other hand, Japan was still under tight constraint in terms of its foreign policy—the first priority of Japan's foreign policy was to maintain a good relationship with the United States, which until the early 1970s was anticommunist and anti-Beijing. The initial move by Richard Nixon and Henry

Kissinger to open up China in 1972, the changing mood in the international community (notably in the United Nations), and Beijing's new outlook toward the outside world were crucial external conditions prompting Japan to make a major switch in its China policy. Furthermore, as many observers of international relations have recognized, Sino-Japanese relations "will assume increasing importance in Asia as both the U.S. presence and Soviet ambitions in the region fade in the post–Cold War era."[7]

Bilateral trade between Japan and China was not important until the late nineteenth century when both countries began to strive for modernization. It became increasingly important to both countries during the pre–World War II period. It reached a peak during the 1930s and the early part of the 1940s, when Japan pursued a policy of military invasion against China by exploiting natural resources and pushing for industrial programs in northeast China (Manchuria). Japan was also active in expanding its substantial economic and commercial activities in other parts of China. China was Japan's largest export market and the third largest import supplier (after the United States and Korea).

During this period, Japanese industry relied heavily on raw materials from China. From 1934 to 1936, for example, China supplied 34 percent of Japan's imports of iron ore, 38.6 percent of its salt, 68.4 percent of its coal, 71.3 percent of its soybeans, and 100 percent of its tung oil. The importance of China to Japanese foreign trade can be demonstrated by the proportion of Japan's trade with China in Japan's total foreign trade: from 1930 to 1939, for example, trade with China accounted for 21 percent of Japan's total exports and 12.4 percent of its total imports (G. Jan 1969: 900).

In the immediate postwar period after 1945, Sino-Japanese trade decreased substantially. This was due primarily to the civil war in China between the Chinese Communist Party (CCP) and the Kuomintang (KMT), and the surrender of Japan's diplomatic autonomy to the Supreme Commander for the Allied Powers (SCAP). Under American occupation, Japan was strictly controlled politically and economically, and was not in a position to have an independent economic policy toward China. However, this situation did not prevent Japan from conducting trade with China through nonofficial and private channels. Even before the establishment of the People's Republic in 1949, there were negotiations between the Chinese Communist Party and Japan for possible restoration of bilateral trade (R. Jain 1981: 26–27). Such trade was started in 1950 and was channeled mainly through Hong Kong. The total volume of trade for this initial year reached about $59 million for Japan's exports of machinery and imports of soybeans, salt, peat, and rice (Japan-China Economic Association 1975c: 24).

This effort was quickly curtailed by the outbreak of the Korean War in June 1950. The United States imposed a strict embargo on the shipment of goods to China. This restriction caused a sharp decline in Sino-Japanese trade in terms of the variety of commodity exchanges and its total value.

From the early 1950s to 1971 (the year prior to normalization of relations between the two countries), Sino-Japanese trade was conducted through three channels: nonofficial trade agreements, friendship trade, and memorandum trade. An explanation of each channel follows.

There were four nonofficial trade agreements. The first such arrangement was a barter trade agreement, signed on June 1, 1952, by three members of the Japanese Diet, Tomi Kōra, Kei Hoashi, and Kisuke Miyakoshi, who visited China as private citizens. Nan Hanchen, chairman of the China Council for Promotion of International Trade, signed on behalf of the Chinese. Three more private trade agreements were signed in October 1953, May 1955, and March 1958. The first three agreements were only partially carried out in practice, fulfilling 5.1 percent, 38.8 percent, and 75.1 percent of the agreements, respectively.

The last agreement was never carried out as a result of the Nagasaki flag incident of May 1958, when two Japanese youths pulled down a Chinese flag at a stamp show in a Nagasaki department store. This incident occurred around the same time as Prime Minister Nobusuke Kishi's official trip to Taiwan where he encouraged Chiang Kai-shek to achieve his goal of retaking the Mainland (Ogata 1977: 180). These actions led the Chinese leaders to believe that the Kishi government was hostile toward China and that the flag incident was a Tokyo–Taipei "plot." In order to "maintain the dignity of an independent sovereign state and to protect its rights," the Chinese government said that it had no choice but to suspend trade relations with Japan.[8] A nonofficial fishery agreement, signed in April 1955, was also suspended in 1958 because of the Nagasaki flag incident.

During the 1950s the cold war dominated the international environment, and the United States became displeased about increased nonofficial bilateral trade between Japan and China. Taipei also repeatedly expressed dissatisfaction over the Sino-Japanese trade relationship. Therefore, under pressure from the United States and Taiwan, the Japanese government pursued a *seikei bunri* policy, meaning to separate trade and economic issues from political issues.

In August 1958 Zhou Enlai reacted to this practice with his "three political principles," which stated that Japan should not: (1) regard China as an enemy; (2) participate in any plot to create "two Chinas"; or (3) obstruct normalization of relations with China.[9] Zhou's principles later became the criteria by which the Chinese chose Japanese firms to do business with. These firms, numbering about three hundred, were designated as "friendly firms." Though relatively small in size, they became the main channels for Sino-Japanese trade at that time.

In the early 1960s the changing international environment, especially an intensifying Sino-Soviet conflict, increased mutual interest in both political and economic terms for a normalized trade relationship between China and Japan. This brought about another nonofficial bilateral trade agreement, known as the L-T Memorandum, which was concluded in November 1962. The memorandum was named using the initials of its two signatories—Liao Chengzhi, chairman of the China-Japan Friendship Association and member of the Communist party Central Committee, and Tatsunosuke Takasaki, a senior LDP Diet member and former member of the Ministry of International Trade and Industry (MITI). The significance of this agreement in Sino-Japanese trade relations was that senior ruling party leaders from both sides signed the agreement, giving it some official significance despite its nonofficial title. Some well-known LDP politicians were also deeply involved in this agreement, including Kenzō Matsumura, Yoshimi Furui, and Aiichirō Fujiyama. They all played important roles during the pre-normalization period in Sino-Japanese trade relations.

In preparation for final normalization and as part of an effort to enlarge pro-Beijing forces in Japan's business community, on April 19, 1970, Zhou Enlai added four additional conditions—the "four principles"—for Sino-Japanese trade: No trade would be allowed to (1) those who assisted Taiwan and South Korea; (2) those who invested in Taiwan and South Korea; (3) those who produced weapons for the American war of aggression against Vietnam, Laos, and Cambodia; and (4) American companies in Japan.[10] These conditions were later included in the communique issued at the conclusion of the nonofficial trade negotiations in 1971.

Table 1 shows that Sino-Japanese trade closely corresponded to the political changes in China and to relations between the two countries. Politics indeed played an important role in the evolving bilateral economic relationship.

As mentioned previously, after the outbreak of the Korean War in 1950, Sino-Japanese trade declined sharply for the next three years. The Nagasaki flag incident hurt trade even more severely. Japan's exports to China, for example, dropped from $60.5 million in 1957 to $2.7 million by 1960, and its imports from China fell from $80.5 million in 1957 to $20.7 million by 1960. The chaotic situation in China from 1967 to 1969 (the peak of the Cultural Revolution) also stifled trade development.

Because of its internal political instability, on most occasions it was China that took the initiative (to start or stop) trade relations, depending on its domestic condition at the time. The Japanese were generally passive. The nonofficial trade arrangements before normalization enabled the Japanese to act more pragmatically and therefore more flexibly. This flexibility also reflected the open, pluralistic, and competitive nature of Japan's political and economic system. As Chae-Jin Lee points out, "The fact that associations acted as representatives of private companies and nongovernmental organizations also made it easier than it otherwise would be for the Japanese to accept China's tough political demands" (1984: 11–12).

Normalization was achieved in the fall of 1972 when Japan expressed its willingness to accept China's three conditions concerning Japan's relationship with Taiwan: recognition of the People's Republic as the sole legal government of China; acceptance of Taiwan as an inalienable part of the territory of the People's Republic; and abrogation of Japan's peace treaty with the Taipei government (for details, see Part III).

Rapprochement was a strong stimulus to bilateral trade, and the Japan-China Economic Association was established in November 1972 to formally take over

Table 1
Sino-Japanese Trade 1949–71 (in millions of U.S. dollars)

Year	Japanese Exports	Japanese Imports	Total
1949	3.1	21.8	24.9
1950	19.6	39.3	58.9
1951	5.8	21.6	27.4
1952	0.6	14.9	15.5
1953	4.5	29.7	34.2
1954	19.1	40.8	59.9
1955	28.5	80.8	109.3
1956	67.3	83.6	150.9
1957	60.5	80.5	141.0
1958	50.6	54.4	105.0
1959	3.6	18.9	22.5
1960	2.7	20.7	23.4
1961	16.6	30.9	47.5
1962	38.5	46.0	84.5
1963	62.4	74.6	137.0
1964	152.7	157.8	310.5
1965	245.0	224.7	469.7
1966	313.2	306.2	621.4
1967	288.3	269.4	557.7
1968	325.4	224.2	549.6
1969	390.8	234.5	625.3
1970	568.9	253.8	822.7
1971	578.2	323.2	901.4

Source: Japan-China Economic Association.

the responsibilities of the L-T Memorandum trade office. This in turn led to a brisk exchange of economic and trade delegations. Two-way trade increased almost twofold from $1.1 billion in 1972 to $2.0 billion by 1973. The rapid increase in bilateral trade after rapprochement is shown in Table 2.

Normalized relations immediately opened the door for governmental economic agreements, which replaced previous nonofficial agreements. These agreements and the dates of initiation are as follows:

- Trade Agreement, January 5, 1974
- Aviation Agreement, April 20, 1974
- Maritime Transport Agreement, November 13, 1974
- Fisheries Agreement, August 15, 1975
- Long Term Trade Agreement, February 16, 1978
- Governmental Loan Agreement, April 25, 1980

These agreements established a firm basis for further development of economic relations between the two countries. Sino-Japanese negotiations for the first

Table 2
Sino-Japanese Trade 1972–90 (in millions of U.S. dollars)

Year	Japan's Exports	Japan's Imports	Total
1972	609	491	1,100
1973	1,040	974	2,014
1974	1,985	1,305	3,289
1975	2,259	1,531	3,790
1976	1,663	1,371	3,034
1977	1,939	1,547	3,486
1978	3,049	2,030	5,079
1979	3,699	2,955	6,654
1980	5,078	4,323	9,402
1981	5,096	5,292	10,387
1982	3,511	5,352	8,863
1983	4,912	5,087	9,999
1984	7,216	5,957	13,173
1985	12,477	6,488	18,965
1986	9,856	5,652	15,508
1987	8,250	7,401	15,651
1988	9,476	9,859	19,335
1989	8,516	11,146	19,662
1990	6,130	12,020	18,150

Source: Compiled from Japan-China Economic Association publications, Keizai Koho Center, *Japan 1991: An International Comparison* (Tokyo, 1991), (quoted from Roger Bowen 1992), and Robert Delfs, "Sense or Sensibility: Historical Mistrust Hampers Marriage of Capital and Cheap Labor," *Far Eastern Economic Review*, April 25, 1991, pp. 52-55.

four economic agreements (trade, aviation, maritime transport, and fisheries) are discussed in detail as a case study in Part IV.

Economic exchange between Japan and China has expanded into many new fields, beyond purely bilateral trade, to include joint ventures, direct investments, and cooperative projects. In the middle of the 1980s, however, the trade imbalance had become a major issue in Sino-Japanese relations. China reached a record deficit of $6 billion in 1985 in its trade with Japan. This deficit cast a considerable shadow over the economic relationship, and the Chinese appealed to the Japanese to further open Japan's markets to Chinese commodities.

One such case in point is Japan's protectionism toward raw silk imports from China. Through the specifics of this case study we can examine participation by various interest groups in the formation of Japan's China policy.

THE PROTECTIONIST POLICY OF
RAW SILK IMPORTATION

At the end of 1985, the director of the Japan division of China's Ministry of Foreign Trade and Economic Relations published a highly critical article urging Japan "to eliminate man-made obstacles, and to provide favorable conditions for increasing the import of Chinese commodities." He used Japanese imports of raw silk, silk piece goods, rice straw and its products as examples to demonstrate that "Chinese commodities are restricted in Japan."[11]

In general, public attention to Japan's protectionism and trade barriers focuses on its policy toward the United States and Western Europe, and not on Japan's policy toward its Asian neighbors and Third World countries. Therefore, China's protests gave rise to considerable interest in the restrictions that Chinese commodities faced and in the reasons behind Japan's decision to set up such restrictions. One may also ask the following questions: Why were the Japanese able to maintain protectionist measures in the 1970s and 1980s despite increased external pressure? How did these restrictions affect various social forces in Japanese society? This case study attempts to answer these questions and thereby seeks to explore the influence of various social groups on Japan's political life.

Traditionally, both China and Japan have been major raw silk-producing countries. For many years, their combined output accounted for more than 70 percent of the world's total volume of raw silk. However, since the 1970s Japan's raw silk production has continually declined, while China's production has increased. Since raw silk is made from the silkworm cocoon, let us first look at the production of cocoons in both countries (see Table 3).

China surpassed Japan's silkworm cocoon production in 1970 and raw silk production in 1977. Since then China has become the number one raw silk producer in the world (Japan-China Economic Association 1986: 128). By 1983 China's raw silk made up 57 percent of the world production, three times that of Japanese production (Yano 1986: 321). In 1988 China's total silk production of 440,000 tons accounted for 60 percent of the world's total output (Wen 1990: 25).

Japan has held the leading position in the consumption of raw silk for many years. In the mid-1970s, Japan's domestic consumption of raw silk accounted for 64 percent of the world's total production; more than half was used for traditional Japanese clothing such as the kimono (Japan-China Economic Association 1976: 157). Even after its domestic consumption declined during the 1970s, Japan remained far ahead of other raw silk-consuming countries in the 1980s, in both total and per capita consumption. In 1983, for example, Japan's total raw silk consumption was three times that of China, whereas production was only one third that of China's (see Table 4).

Traditionally, Japan had been a raw silk-exporting country. However, beginning in 1962, Japan began to import raw silk, and by 1974 it stopped exporting raw silk completely (Bureau of Silkworm and Horticulture of the MAFF 1986). Traditional support alone was not enough to protect its raw silk industry; government policies were also important.

As early as 1951, the Japanese government established a public corporation, the Corporation on the Stabilization of Raw Silk and Sugar Prices (CSRSSP; *Sanshi-Satō-rui Kakaku Antei Jigyō-dan*) under the jurisdiction of the Ministry of Agriculture, Forestry, and Fisheries (MAFF), and issued a protectionist statute

Table 3
Production of Silkworm Cocoon of China and Japan, 1949–85 (1,000 tons)

Year	China	Japan
1949	31	62
1950	34	80
1951	47	93
1952	82	103
1953	59	93
1954	65	100
1955	67	114
1956	72	108
1957	68	119
1958	74	117
1959	70	111
1960	62	111
1961	37	115
1962	37	109
1963	41	111
1964	52	112
1965	66	106
1966	78	105
1967	85	114
1968	105	121
1969	113	114
1970	122	112
1971	123	108
1972	136	105
1973	146	108
1974	163	102
1975	153	91
1976	163	88
1977	168	79
1978	173	78
1979	213	81
1980	250	73
1981	252	65
1982	271	63
1983	268	61
1984	306	50
1985	336	47

Sources: *Zhongguo Tongji Nenjian*, (Year-book of Statistics of China), Beijing: Zhongguo Tongji Chubanshe, 1986; and Bureau of Silkworm and Horticulture, the MAFF, *Saikin-no sanshi gyo-o meguru joho* (Recent Situation of Silkworm and Raw Silk Industry), Tokyo, 1986.

entitled Statute on the Stabilization of Raw Silk Prices. The Statute provided detailed regulations on both domestic and foreign raw silk (discussed later in this chapter), which in fact prohibited the importation of foreign raw silk.[12] This was due to a surplus in production of raw silk over domestic consumption during that time period, which continued until the early 1960s.

In 1962 the Japanese government abandoned its protectionist law on raw silk and moved toward adoption of a free trade policy. This change of policy was effected for two reasons. First, domestic demands on raw silk increased without a corresponding production increase, thereby gradually surpassing domestic production and necessitating the importation of raw silk from abroad. Second,

Table 4
Raw Silk Consumption of Major Countries, 1983

Country	Total Consumption (ton)	Per Capita (gram)
Japan	18,936	159
China	6,438	6
U.S.	6,030	26
USSR	4,836	18
India	4,578	6
Italy	2,436	43
Thailand	960	19
W. Germany	876	14
France	588	11
N. Korea	504	26
Turkey	342	7
Iran	336	8

Source: Ichiro Yano, ed., *Nihon kokusei zue*, p. 321.

it was also necessary for the Japanese to convey an image as a supporter of free trade policy in the international community, owing to demands from Japan's export-oriented economy.

Even before World War II, Japan emphasized international trade. In 1960 Prime Minister Hayato Ikeda developed this tradition by initiating an export-oriented economic growth plan called the Income-Doubling Plan. As Takafusa Nakamura argues, "the fact that Japan's exports were highly elastic with respect to world trade means that the Japanese economy was sensitive to the world business cycle" (1981: 59), making the Japanese economy extremely dependent on the world economic situation. A worldwide move toward trade liberalization began in the mid-1950s. Western Europe, having recovered from World War II, pressed for greater dismantling of import restrictions. As an exporter of industrial goods, Japan also faced increasing demands for trade liberalization, and under these circumstances, the Japanese government decided in principle to carry out a policy of liberalizing trade (Nakamura 1981: 81). This policy led to the abolishment of restrictions on raw silk imports.

Japan began importing raw silk from China in 1962, with a shipment of about 8 tons. By 1971 shipments had reached 2,830 tons, and in 1972, the year Sino-Japanese diplomatic relations were normalized, the figure increased sharply to a record 6,190 tons (see Table 5). Trade in raw silk surpassed soybeans and became the largest single item imported from China. The total value for raw silk accounted for almost a quarter of all imports from China (Japan-China Economic Association 1975b: 13). In 1973 the amount of Chinese raw silk exported to Japan remained at a comparable level.

Japan's free trade policy did not last long, however. In August 1974 the Japanese government reissued the 1951 Statute on the Stabilization of Raw Silk Prices with a few minor changes. It was renamed the Statute on Centralized

Table 5
Chinese Raw Silk Exported to Japan, 1969–86

Year	Amount (ton)
1969	1,260
1970	1,350
1971	2,830
1972	6,190
1973	5,760
1974	2,620
1975	1,480
1976	1,500
1977	2,170
1978	3,220
1979	2,530
1980	2,080
1981	650
1982	1,670
1983	2,180
1984	1,590
1985	2,250
1986	2,045

Source: Japan-China Economic Association.

Control of Raw Silk Importation (*Kiito no ichigenka unyū-hō*) and will be referred to hereafter as the Statute on Centralized Control. The second chapter of the statute focused on the stabilization of raw silk prices. Section One was concerned with domestic raw silk, and Section Two targeted foreign raw silk. The sixth provision of Article Twelve stated that "any raw silk imported from abroad must obtain prior approval from the CSRSSP (the Corporation on the Stabilization of Raw Silk and Sugar Prices), or the minister of the MAFF." Furthermore, it gave detailed restrictions on the price and set up quotas on imported raw silk.[13] Through such regulations, the Japanese government placed strict control on the quantity and price of imported raw silk.

The CSRSSP annually negotiates with foreign countries to set up quotas for buying raw silk. It buys and stores raw silk, and then releases it into the domestic market according to changes in demand. By using this method, the high price of raw silk in the Japanese domestic market can be maintained, and the interests of silkworm farmers can be protected.

During the same year (1974) the statute passed in the Diet, the quantity of raw silk imported from China fell by more than one half. Since then, except for one or two years, the amount of raw silk imported from China has remained at a level of around 2,000 tons a year. Chinese raw silk exported to Japan has never returned to the 1972–73 level (see Table 5).

Over the years, China has increased its exports of oil, coal, agricultural products, and textile goods to Japan, while its exports of raw silk have declined proportionately. In 1972 raw silk accounted for about one fourth of China's exports; in 1974 it fell to 4.1 percent, in 1975 to 2.9 percent, and by 1985 to only 0.8 percent of total exports (Japan-China Economic Association 1986: 236). In addition, with the ongoing economic reforms in China, the Chinese silkworm farmers have also turned to more profitable cash crops. The expanding silk processing industry in China has also stimulated domestic demand, thereby reducing the amount of Chinese raw silk exported to the international market.[14]

Nevertheless, the raw silk trade is still important to China's economic development and foreign trade. In 1989, for example, there were about 20 million Chinese silkworm raisers and 885 silk enterprises employing 670,000 people. The silk industry grew at an average annual rate of 10.7 percent over the forty-year period from 1949 to 1989. China's silk export, which represents 20 percent of the nation's total textile exports, earned $1.3 billion in 1988; the export of raw filature (reeled) silk reached 10,000 tons in the same year.[15]

Even though the raw silk trade today may no longer be as important as before to bilateral economic relations between China and Japan, the Japanese government's protectionist policy on raw silk is quite significant. It may be viewed as being representative of an effort to continue its protectionist policy at that time (the 1970s). The analysis that follows reveals that the Statute on Centralized Control has involved several important social forces in Japanese politics, namely, the agricultural interest groups, the ruling Liberal Democratic Party, and the central bureaucracy.

FARMERS AS A SOCIAL GROUP

Farmers have been important in Japanese society. They have had influential electoral power since 1947 when the first national election was held. The boundaries of the electorates were drawn up in accordance with the population distribution at that time, when more than half (54 percent) of the population lived in rural areas and engaged in agricultural activities. When the agricultural population declined following the rural to urban migration that accompanied rapid economic growth in the mid-1950s, there was no corresponding adjustment in electoral boundaries to reduce the farmers' voting power. One reason for this was the mutually supportive relationship between farmers and the conservative ruling party. Robert Scalapino and Junnosuke Masumi (1962: 88–90) point out that the social bases of the governing Liberal Democratic Party came mainly from organized business and agricultural areas. Business provides money and the agricultural areas provide the votes. The farmers' electoral support for the LDP has been consistent and predictable, and there has been a strong, vocal, pro-farmer lobby within the ruling party. In turn, the LDP has been reluctant to readjust the electoral boundaries.

According to Gerald Curtis (1988: 236–237), over the years the LDP has considerably enlarged its base of support by representing the interests of the new urban middle class, but the farmers' electoral support of the LDP has remained important. For example, the LDP failed to gain majority seats in the

Table 6
Changes of Japan's Silkworm Farmers (SF), 1944–85

Year	Number of SF households (1,000)	Percentage of all farmers (%)	Total area in mulberry fields (1,000 ha)	Raw silk production (ton)
1944	1,139	20.4	302	9,242
1950	835	13.5	175	10,620
1955	809	13.4	187	17,868
1960	646	10.7	166	18,046
1965	514	9.2	164	19,106
1970	399	7.5	163	20,515
1975	248	5.0	151	20,169
1980	166	3.6	121	16,155
1985	100	2.2	97	9,561

Source: Bureau of Silkworm and Horticulture, the MAFF.

1989 Upper House election (the first time in its history). One reason for this failure was the farmers' resentment of the LDP's liberalized agricultural trade policies of the late 1980s (Baerwald 1989: 835–836).

The farmers have a strong organization, the Association of Agriculture Co-operatives, called Nōgyō Kyōdō Kumiai, or *Nōkyō*. Virtually all farmers belong to this close-knit nationwide organization. Membership numbered eight million in the early 1980s, making *Nōkyō* the largest voluntary organization in Japan. In addition, *Nōkyō* has served as an electoral force in its own right by actively participating in election campaigns (Aurelia George 1986: 95–97).

The farmers also have "psychological power," which can be attributed to the traditional importance attached to agriculture. Older Japanese in particular believe that Japan should maintain its self-reliance in food production as a vital contribution to national security. As the nation's self-sufficiency rate in food has declined, many people argue it is a matter of "urgent necessity to support existing genuine farm families" (Fukutake 1981: 52).

Farmers have conducted intensive campaigns against liberalization of agricultural trade by not only lobbying politicians and bureaucrats, but also by generating public support. For example, *Nōkyō* has mounted a series of successful campaigns to forge a "community of interests" between city consumers and rural producers, playing on fears of the presence of food additives and agricultural chemicals in imported foods. As a result, farmers received support from a broad range of social circles including consumer organizations, such as the Housewives' Association with its four million members (George 1986: 106–107). This community support added more strength to the farmers' social network aimed at protecting agricultural interests.

Now, let us turn specifically to silkworm farmers in Japan. Since the end of World War II, the number of silkworm farmers and the proportion of silkworm farming households to all farmers have steadily declined along with the total acreage of mulberry fields. From Table 6, we can see the that raw silk production,

Table 7
Differences in Raw Silk Prices Between Japan and the International Market,
1976–85

Year	Japanese Production (Yokohama market) (yen/kg)	International Market (Lyons market) (yen/kg)
1976	12,437	7,355
1977	13,164	7,368
1978	14,758	6,178
1979	14,825	8,092
1980	14,642	8,944
1981	14,241	7,620
1982	14,861	7,900
1983	13,911	7,529
1984	13,474	7,380
1985	12,365	7,090

Source: Bureau of Silkworm and Horticulture, the MAFF.

owing to the application of advanced technology and machinery, increased during the 1950s and the 1960s, and then started to decline in the early 1970s.

For the thirty-year period from 1955 to 1985, the number of silkworm farming households decreased from 809,000 to 100,000. The proportion of silkworm farmers to total farmers fell from 13.4 percent to 2.2 percent, indicating that the decreasing rate of silkworm farming was much greater than that of farming as a whole. The total area in mulberry fields dropped from 187,000 ha (hectare) to 97,000 ha. Raw silk production increased from 17,368 tons to 20,515 tons, because of improvements in mechanized production, but then fell rapidly to 9,561 tons. Each of these categories decreased by anywhere from 45 percent to 88 percent. During this period, 709,000 silkworm farming households, accounting for 88 percent of the total, switched to industry or changed to the production of other crops.[16]

One of the most important reasons for this decline was the continuous and rapid growth of the Japanese economy, which had begun in the early 1960s. This rapid economic growth caused a great number of farmers to switch to industrial and service trades. The broad application of advanced technology and equipment also promoted this trend. This alone, however, does not explain why the number of silkworm farmers decreased more rapidly than the number of farmers as a whole. Japan's domestic consumption of raw silk has to be taken into account.

Beginning in 1960, the economy's high growth brought about an upsurge in consumption. The demand for traditional Japanese style clothing such as the kimono increased steadily and finally reached a historic peak in 1972. This trend did not last long. In the middle of the 1970s, the demand for silk began to fall rapidly because (1) Japan's economic growth began to slow down following the "oil shock"; (2) the Japanese lifestyle became westernized, that is, the kimono was gradually phased out as common daily apparel; (3) both the absolute number and the percentage of young females decreased in terms of total population since the "baby boom" generation of the postwar period entered its middle years; and (4) the kimono's price rose rapidly as a result of the trend toward higher standards and variety.[17]

Furthermore, the cost of raw silk in Japan increased considerably as the standard of living and production costs increased. Therefore, Japanese raw silk became much more expensive than foreign raw silk, especially Chinese raw silk. The difference in price sometimes amounted to twice the amount (see Table 7).

These factors made Japanese raw silk lose its competitive edge in the international market. Japan's silkworm farmers were hard hit by the cheaper imported raw silk. The free trade policy of 1962 further exacerbated the silkworm farmers' plight, and Japan's silkworm and raw silk production declined rapidly.

A large number of silkworm farmers began switching to industrial jobs or to other crops such as rice. A few silkworm farmers (100,000 households in 1985), however, remained concentrated in the mountain areas. Most of those who stayed on were older farmers, since it was difficult for them to switch to other types of work. This group's livelihood became an urgent issue. Although there were only 100,000 silkworm farm households, they constituted an interest group capable of generating political influence through their social connections.

GROUPS REPRESENTING OPPOSING INTERESTS

Interest groups can influence policymakers in two interrelated ways: "by obtaining access (to policymakers) and by influencing decisions" (Ornstein and Elder 1978: 82). The influence of silkworm farmers was no exception. They organized themselves to work for their own interests by appealing directly to society and by drawing public attention to "Japan's declining agriculture." Furthermore, they frequently put pressure on the LDP and government agencies. Farmers used various techniques to do this: they presented their positions forcefully at the LDP committee hearings and in the Upper and Lower House agriculture-related standing committees; they held large rallies with prefectural assembly members and national Diet members in front of the MAFF building in Tokyo, and engaged in various mass action rituals to demonstrate the intensity of their support for raw silk farming in a highly visible manner, which attracted the attention of the press; they also requested Nōkyō to pressure the ruling Liberal Democratic Party.[18] (The special relationship between the raw silk farmers and the ruling party/bureaucracy apparatus is discussed in detail in the next chapter.)

In response to pressure by the farmers, the Statute on Centralized Control came into being. After implementation of the statute, raw silk prices went up and were maintained at a stable level. This helped increase the income of the silkworm farmers. These benefits lasted only a few years however. Since the

Table 8
Income of Silkworm Farmers, 1965–85

Year	Daily Income of Per SF Family (yen)	Raw Silk Price (yen/kg)
1965	723	685
1970	1,729	1,172
1975	2,607	1,667
1980	3,072	2,172
1983	1,972	2,058
1984	1,530	2,009
1985	1,244	1,836

Source: Bureau of Silkworm and Horticulture, MAFF, *Saikin-no sanshigyo-o.*

beginning of the 1980s, the income of silkworm farmers has rapidly declined due to the further decline of raw silk prices. From 1980 to 1985, for instance, daily income per silkworm farming family fell 60 percent (see Table 8).

It is believed that without the Statute on Centralized Control, the silkworm industry would have disappeared entirely.[19] This situation made the statute all the more important for the survival of silkworm farmers. Therefore, farmers have maintained pressure to keep the statute alive, while opposing interest groups have worked hard either to block or cancel the statute. These groups were composed of the raw silk import trading companies and kimono manufacturers—mostly small and medium-sized enterprises.[20]

The implementation of the statute sharply reduced raw silk imports from abroad, directly affecting the raw silk trading companies. Meanwhile, it raised raw silk prices on the domestic market, which in turn raised the cost for silk, silk piece goods, and the kimono. This, then, further reduced the domestic demand for raw silk and its products, and caused a number of manufacturers to go bankrupt (Japan-China Economic Association 1980: 177). The number of raw silk manufacturers has correspondingly declined since the implementation of the Statute on Centralized Control. From 1975 to 1985, 249 raw silk manufacturers (out of 429) went out of business, accounting for about 60 percent of the total (see Table 9).

These manufacturers were concentrated in the big cities, mainly in the Kansai area (the western part of Japan, such as Kyoto). About 30,000 workers in the raw silk industry were affected.[21] They became a strong voice against the protectionist policy on raw silk and were joined by the small and medium-sized manufacturers and trading businesses.

The Statute on Centralized Control attracted two social groups representing different interests. Both groups voiced their demands to the public and put considerable pressure on political leaders and government agencies. The energetic lobbying activities by interest groups and the availability of various

Table 9
Decline of the Raw Silk Industry, 1975–85

Year	Number of Manufacturers	Raw Silk Production (1,000 bushel)
1975	429	336
1976	390	298
1977	350	268
1978	341	266
1979	318	266
1980	304	269
1981	271	247
1982	250	217
1983	231	208
1984	195	180
1985	180	160

Source: Bureau of Silkworm and Horticulture, MAFF, *Saikin-no sanshi gyo-o.*

channels for policy input are important factors in a pluralistic political system.

This chapter has introduced the notion of pluralism and social network, provided a detailed background of Sino-Japanese trade relations and Japan's protectionist policy over raw silk importation from China, and illustrated how various interest groups represented different interests. But several important questions have not yet been answered: How have interest groups, such as organized farmers, influenced political leaders and the governmental bureaucracy? Under what circumstances and through what channels will interest groups and the party-government apparatus have greater impact on one another? What specific role will social networks and groups play in Japan's policymaking process? The next chapter answers these questions, and also provides specific examples on the strategies and tactics used by opposing interest groups and the reactions from the LDP and the bureaucrats.

NOTES

1. See, for example, E. Ben-Ari, B. Moeran, and J. Valentine, ed., *Unwrapping Japan* (1990).

2. See also Reiko Atsumi, "Tsukiai, Obligatory Personal Relationships of Japanese White-Collar Company Employees," *Human Organization* 38, no. 1 (1979): 63–70.

3. One of the best studies of the school on pluralism in this debate is Nelson W. Polsby's *Community Power and Political Theory* (1980). For the school of stratification, see G. William Domhoff's *Who Rules America Now?* (1983).

4. Ike (1972: 16–20) agrees with the notion of "essentially an elitist type," and argues that in Japan voters tend to trade their ballots for anticipated benefits that are particular in character—questions of ideology are relatively unimportant.

5. The "Japan, Inc." argument was first raised by Eugene Kaplan (1972: 14) in a U.S. Department of Commerce publication.

6. This school of thought is represented by Chalmers Johnson (1985: 64). He argues that "since 1947, despite its adoption of a formally democratic constitution and the subsequent development of a genuinely open political culture, Japan seems to have retained many 'soft authoritarian' features in its governmental institutions: an extremely strong and comparatively unsupervised state administration, single-party rule for more than three decades, and a set of economic priorities that seems unattainable under true political pluralism during such a long period."

7. *Far Eastern Economic Review*, August 23, 1990, p. 32.

8. Commentator, "Why Was Sino-Japanese Trade Interrupted?" *Renmin Ribao*, May 20, 1958.

9. *Peking Review*, September 14, 1960, pp. 25–26.

10. *Nihon keizai shimbun*, April 16, 1970.

11. See Wei Xiaorong, "Kuoda duiri chukou shi dangwu zhiji [To expand export to Japan in the most urgent matter]," *Guoji Maoyi* [International trade], November 1985, p. 17.

12. See the CSRSSP, *Sanshi satō rui kakaku antei jigyō dan hō kankei hōki binran* (Guide book of related statutes on the stabilization of raw silk and sugar prices) (1986).

13. See CSRSSP, *Kankei hōki binran*, pp. 14–19.

14. *The Korea Times*, August 23, 1988.

15. For a detailed account, see Wen Tianshen, "Silk Country," *China Today* 39, no. 1 (January 1990): 24–26.

16. See Bureau of Silkworm and Horticulture, the MAFF, *Saikin-no sanshi gyō-o meguru jōhō*.

17. Interview with Toshiro Eda, deputy director of the Silkworm Division, MAFF, July 4, 1986, Tokyo. Eda, as an expert on the silkworm, had worked for MAFF for twenty-one years. He was extremely knowledgeable of matters relating to the silkworm.

18. Interviews with Kihei Aoki, an official of CSRSSP, who had worked with the Silkworm Division of MAFF for seven years before his transfer to the CSRSSP, June 12, 1986, Tokyo.

19. Interview with Hiroshi Sugiura, June 27, 1986, Tokyo. Sugiura, a retired MITI official, was working as a lawyer for the Japan-China Economic Association at the time of the interview.

20. Interview with Kōichi Yamaura, July 3, 1986, Tokyo. Yamaura used to be director of the North Asia Division of MITI.

21. Interview with Toshiro Eda, deputy director of the Silkworm Division of MAFF, July 4, 1986, Tokyo.

3

Social Groups and Pluralistic Operations

This chapter continues to examine the social environment as it relates to Japan's policymaking process. Special attention is given to the following questions: How do social groups influence political leaders and the central bureaucracy? How do social networks contribute to the political interaction in the decision-making process?

SOCIAL GROUPS AND JAPAN'S PLURALISTIC POLITICS

The level of political community that a society achieves, as Samuel Huntington (1968: 8–9) points out, reflects the relationship between its political institutions and social forces. Huntington defines a social force as "an ethnic, religious, territorial, economic, or status group"; "kinship, racial, and religious groupings are supplemented by occupational, class, and skill groupings." In order to make their voices heard in the policymaking process, different social forces tend to organize themselves into various interest groups to put pressure on both political leaders and the governmental bureaucracy.

In a democratic and pluralistic society, Robert Dahl (1956: 150) states, "decisions are made by endless bargaining." Social groups are important components in this process. Based on this assumption, social scientists have developed group theory and widely applied it to the policymaking process as an analytical framework. Group theory is closely connected to the study of pluralism. In the field of political science, a person who believes in social groups must also believe in pluralism. Advocates of pluralism argue that there is no single source of authority in a pluralistic society, and that there are always various social groups that have a legitimate right to exist and be independent outside the power of the state (Nicholls 1975: 36–54).

The political function of social groups and network cannot be fully developed without an appropriate social environment—a system of political pluralization. (This point is discussed further in the concluding chapter.) Thus, it is necessary to provide a brief introduction to historical backgrounds in order to gain insight into the evolution of the process of Japan's political development. Since the focus of this book is not on Japanese history and I am not a historian, the review will be brief.

Japan was one of the first non-Western countries to borrow the modern political and economic institutions that had emerged in Europe after the sixteenth century.[1] Despite its quick adoption of Western influence, the Japanese political system remained essentially authoritarian until the end of World War II. Modern Japan went through several major political changes, such as the Meiji Restoration and the 1889 constitution, the Popular Rights Movement, the Taishō Democracy Movement, the rise of militarism, and its defeat at the end of World War II.[2] Nevertheless, it was not until the American occupation of 1945–52 that Japan experienced a radical shift toward democracy. U.S. occupation and the resulting 1947 constitution altered the course of Japan's modern history. Japan's democratization is a combination of external force (the American occupation) and internal political development.

The American occupation and the 1947 constitution played a decisive role in guiding the Japanese in a more democratic and pluralistic direction. The defeat of Japan in World War II provided a rare opportunity for one nation to reform another. The Supreme Commander for the Allied Powers (SCAP) had far more authority in 1945 than the Meiji government had in 1868. This enabled SCAP to impose even more rapid political and social changes (P. Duus 1976: 239). Two of the most important achievements of the American occupation were the new constitution and its related reforms.[3]

Although an external force played an important role in pushing Japan's political development in a more democratic direction, we cannot regard the Japanese people as being totally passive or reluctant to carry out these reforms. Without the cooperation of internal forces, no change implemented by outside forces can last long.

Some continuities in Japanese politics become evident when we compare the prewar and postwar periods. One important continuity is that since the Meiji Restoration Japan has maintained the tradition of a strong government bureaucracy. The Statute on National Examination for Government Bureaucracy of 1947 maintained the basic spirit of the previous system of examinations for the senior civil service. This system guaranteed that the best personnel resources flowed into the government bureaucracy year after year (S. Satō 1984). Another continuity is the weak position of the united labor movement. Instead of independent unions, "enterprise unions" (organized in individual enterprises) emerged in Japan. This weakness is largely due to the tightening of governmental control over union organizations and the public sector (T. Pempel 1982: 308), as well as the failure of the leftist unions to gain a broad support from workers.

On the other hand, we have to recognize fundamental changes between the prewar and postwar periods. It is clear that the 1947 constitution laid a foundation for "the transition from imperial to popular sovereignty" (D. Henderson 1968: xv) and has provided basic structures to guarantee the responsibility of elected politicians to voters and political rights such as freedom of expression, speech, and assembly. In this sense, the 1947 constitution has opened a new era for Japan's postwar political development.[4]

Another change occurred in the structure of the conservative coalition in Japanese society. During the prewar period, there were four key social groups: the government bureaucracy, organized business, the rural landlords, and the armed forces. The postwar land reform and the disbanding of the military rendered two of the prewar forces—rural landlords and the armed forces—virtually powerless politically. The postwar conservative coalition is made up of organized business, the government bureaucracy, and farmers. The representative of this coalition is the ruling Liberal Democratic Party. This basic structure has laid a foundation for social groups and network (in this case, the farmers) to operate and to play their political functions.

To understand structural changes in Japanese politics, it is necessary to examine the process of the changing relationship between the bureaucracy and the LDP. As Kenneth Pyle (1989: 47) has suggested, since the late 1970s "many knowledgeable observers have called attention to the weakening bureaucratic leadership structure and the concurrent increase in the power of the party politicians." According to Takashi Inoguchi (1983: 178–191), this process can be divided into four periods. The first period lasted from 1945 to 1955—the period of occupation and economic recovery. During this period, the Japanese government was under the guidance and protection of the occupation authority. The central government, together with SCAP, took main responsibility for carrying out political and economic reforms and for promoting economic development. This situation made it inevitable for the government bureaucracy to play a leading role in Japanese society, since interest groups were still weak and disorganized, and political parties, conservative and liberal alike, were in a process of recovery, reorganization, and realignment.

The second period lasted from 1955 to 1964. This was the first half of Japan's speedy economic development. Most political parties began to develop their own power, but economic development was guided by the government bureaucracy, resulting in the bureaucracy's continuing political dominance.

The latter half of Japan's fast economic development (1964–73) was the third period of the changing relationship between the bureaucracy and the LDP. During these years, the bureaucracy experienced several serious policy failures, such as the 1965–66 economic recession and the oil crisis of the early 1970s. The LDP started gradually to expand its influence owing to its longtime rule, becoming an equal force to the bureaucracy in terms of influence over the policymaking process. Other interest groups also had become increasingly active, especially by the beginning of the 1970s.

The last period of change began in 1973 and continues to the present. This is a period of lower level economic growth. Economic activities and policies have become much more complicated, which has led the government bureaucracy to reduce its control over economic life. The new trend of economic liberalization reduced the role of government and increased the position of various interest groups. The rising power of the LDP and its Diet members began in the early 1970s and marked the maturing of career politicians and the continuing growth of the ruling party.

The whole process illustrates the gradual breakup of bureaucratic dominance and the corresponding increase of the LDP's influence. The weakening of the bureaucracy is evident in the frequent intervention by the LDP members even in internal bureaucratic personnel affairs. The four-stage evolution of the relationship shows how and why Japan has entered a pluralistic stage of political development.

In their discussion on the relationship between state and society, John Hall and G. Ikenberry (1989: 13) contend that state intervention in society may eventually lead to "the creation of new and entrenched pressure groups." The school of pluralism not only advocates the legitimate and autonomous status of social groups, but also believes that social groups can play important functions in state-society relations and the decision-making process. Under a pluralistic political system, the coercive nature of state authority, vis-à-vis individual freedom, may be buffered by the voluntary nature of social groups, creating a social environment that would be conducive to maximum development of individual creativity (Lindsay 1943: 245). In this sense, social groups can produce a cushioning effect between state authority and individual freedom. On the other hand, they can also create obstacles to building broad consensus and achieving effective policy implementation.

THE LDP AND THE FARMERS

To understand the relationship between the ruling Liberal Democratic Party and the raw silk farmers and their interest groups in this context, we must first look at the *tsukiai* or social links between them. Robert Scalapino and Junnosuke Masumi (1962: 53) referred to the phenomenon of the LDP's single-party domination as the "one-and-one-half-party system." The ruling LDP is one party; opposition parties that have never been in power since 1948 can be regarded as only "one-half-party." Sustained political support to the conservative ruling coalition from a broad range of social forces is one of many reasons for this phenomenon of one-party domination. One source of such support came from the influential electoral power of Japanese farmers.

In the 1960s and the early 1970s, the LDP encountered a strong challenge from opposition parties in most urban areas and, as a result, lost a number of Diet seats. However, they managed to maintain or even strengthen their superior

Table 10

Number and Percentage of Seats Held by LDP House of Representatives
Elections (according to type of constituency)

Year	Seats & share	Metro-politan	Urban	Semi-urban	Semi-rural	Rural*
1976	LDP seats	40	44	75	60	30
	LDP (%)	29.0	51.2	55.6	60.4	58.8
1979	LDP seats	38	43	75	59	33
	LDP (%)	27.6	50.0	55.6	58.4	64.7
1980	LDP seats	48	47	85	65	39
	LDP (%)	34.8	54.7	61.5	64.4	76.5
1986	LDP seats	53	52	86	73	36
	LDP (%)	36.8	62.7	63.7	71.6	75.0

Source: This was compiled from two accounts: Stockwin 1982: 118 (covered the 1976, 1979, and 1980 elections); and Miyagawa 1987: 211-254 (covered the 1986 election).
* In Stockwin's account, constituency classification is: urban, semi-urban, medium, semi-rural, and rural. The first three categories are different from that used by Miyagawa.

position in the rural areas (Stockwin 1982: 117). This made support from the rural areas all the more important for the LDP. In the 1980 and 1986 House of Representatives national elections (see Table 10), for example, the LDP won 75 percent or more of the total votes in the rural area seats, while winning only around 35 percent of the urban area votes.

Despite increasing rural-to-urban migration, votes from rural areas, and thus their agricultural interests, have remained vital to the LDP. Traditionally, the national gerrymander favored the rural areas. In his detailed study, T. J. Pempel (1977: 38) illustrates this point by giving concrete examples:

Even after the 1975 redistricting it was possible for a JCP candidate in the metropolitan third district of Osaka to be defeated although he received 115,000 votes, while in rural Ehime an LDP candidate who received only 37,000 could be elected. In 1980, one JCP candidate in Hokkaido's first district received 126,000 votes and lost, while in the second district of Kagawa barely over one-quarter this number was sufficient to elect an LDP candidate. In the 1977 upper house election, 187,000 votes secured a victory in Tochigi, while 549,000 votes in Osaka was not enough.

Furthermore, the percentage of eligible voters who actually voted was much higher in rural areas. The higher voting rate reflects a higher degree of discipline and social pressure (Scalapino and Masumi 1962: 109). Farmers are one of the social groups that "are more involved in networks than people in other occupational categories" (J. Watanuki 1991: 71). This obviously worked for LDP interests, since rural voters are more "faithful" to the LDP than urban voters. This tradition can often bring landslide victories to the LDP in the rural constituencies. In the 1986 summer national election, for example, the LDP took all the seats in fifteen rural prefectures. These areas were called *dokusen ku* (all-LDP areas).[5]

Although the total population of farmers declined, the trend of migration from the countryside to cities slowed beginning in the mid-1970s (Yano 1986: 70–71). There has even been a small return of people to their home towns from the big cities. Instead of moving to big cities, more and more farmers became part-time farmers devoting part of their time to local manufacturing.[6] This new trend stabilized the seats in rural areas.

More importantly, many high-ranking LDP officials were from rural areas, linking the LDP with the interests of such areas. In addition, despite the decline of the agricultural sectors, traditional attachment to the rural areas still remained in the minds of many people, especially among the elderly. Since elders often enjoy higher social status in Japan, they more or less maintain certain political influence in the Japanese society. As an official of the LDP headquarters put it, "We need the votes from the grandfathers."[7]

In return for loyal rural support, the LDP always paid careful attention to the farmers' interests. Every year, for instance, the government fixed the price of imported rice and extended subsidies for agricultural activities. The issue of protectionist rice policy became much more controversial in the 1980s and even the 1990s. With increasing pressure from the United States and European Economic Community (EEC) countries, Japan was forced to make adjustments in its rice importation policy. In 1992, for example, general elections were held in Japan (the Upper House of the Parliament) and in the United States. The LDP was described as facing "a nightmare choice" in its rice policy between alienating its rural supporters that would damage Prime Minister Kiichi Miyazawa's political future and further antagonizing the United States, where Japanese protectionism had already emerged as a powerful and divisive issue in this American presidential election year. But whenever it is faced with domestic difficulties that would jeopardize its own political base, the LDP is likely to toughen its position on rice imports.[8] In short, the LDP has been able to provide farmers with financial incentives. The driving force behind the LDP's supportive policies toward farmers was the special connections (*tsukiai*) between the two groups, which generated a strong sense of mutual obligation—a foundation for obtaining votes.

Common interests between the LDP and silkworm farmers lay in a home constituency connection. Japan's silkworm production was concentrated in the Kantō (near Tokyo), Tohoku (northeast of Japan), and Kyushu (south Japan) areas. The silkworm cocoons of the top ten prefectures accounted for more than 80 percent of the total production. Gunma and Fukushima, the top two prefectures, produced 45 percent of the entire silkworm cocoon production in 1985.[9] Two powerful presidents of the LDP and prime ministers—Yasuhiro Nakasone (1982–87) and Takeo Fukuda (1976–78)—came from Gunma Prefecture. And the biggest group of LDP politicians within the influential Agriculture and Forestry

Division under the LDP's Policy Affairs Research Council (PARC) came from Fukushima Prefecture (Inoguchi 1985: 40–41). These home constituency ties led to a strong connection between silkworm farmers and leading political figures and institutions within the ruling party.

All senior politicians who came from the rural areas depended heavily on rural votes to remain in office. Local branches of *Nōkyō* (the agricultural cooperatives) functioned as a rural, grass-roots electoral base for the LDP and as the principal organizational intermediary linking the ruling conservative coalition to their rural voting base (T. Tanaka 1971: 424). With this special connection, the Gunma and Fukushima branches of *Nōkyō* (a large proportion of which was comprised of raw silk farmers) were particularly active in campaigning for Nakasone, Fukuda, and other top politicians, while at the same time working hard to represent the interests of silkworm farmers through LDP decision-making organs. After ensuring their positions through successful elections, LDP politicians would then make "policy arrangements" to protect the vital interests of silkworm farmers.[10] The special connection and the feeling of *giri* between the two, therefore, generated significant mutual benefits and enabled a small group such as raw silk farmers to have direct links to the highest levels of Japanese politics.

A direct benefit of such "policy arrangements" can be seen in the case of silkworm production in Gunma and Fukushima. The general trend of a gradual decline in Japan's silkworm and raw silk industry did not affect these two prefectures. On the contrary, Gunma and Fukushima were the only exceptions when all other silkworm prefectures experienced a decrease or plateau in production levels. For example, from 1975 (shortly after the Statute on Centralized Control went into effect) to 1985, Gunma's production rose from 24.3 percent to 27.9 percent, and Fukushima's went up from 12.2 percent to 16.8 percent, in terms of shares of the country's total production of silk cocoons (see Table 11).

The total share of Gunma and Fukushima production rose from 37 percent to 45 percent, making them the largest silkworm bases in Japan. Thus, these two prefectures became the principal beneficiaries of the new law. Apparently, the farmers in these areas took full advantage of being both major silkworm bases and the home constituencies of top politicians. Wu Xuewen, a longtime Japan watcher in China, noticed that senior LDP politicians (often including prime ministers) who were elected from rural areas would constantly examine agricultural policies, making sure that their sphere of social network was well protected.[11]

The decision-making organs of the LDP also provide important examples of political structure and social environment. Because of the LDP's majority position, a bill cannot be passed in the Diet without approval from the LDP. It is believed, therefore, that the LDP's policymaking organs are more important than committees of the Diet. The most important organ is LDP's Policy Affairs Research Council (PARC). PARC's chairman is one of the four highest officials in the party (the other three being president, secretary general, and chairman of

Table 11
Ranks of Prefectures According to Shares of Silkworm Cocoon
Production

	1975		1985	
Rank	Prefecture	Share (%)	Prefecture	Share (%)
1	Gunma	24.3	Gunma	27.9
2	Fukushima	12.2	Fukushima	16.8
3	Saitama	10.2	Saitama	8.6
4	Yamanashi	9.7	Yamanashi	6.3
5	Nagano	9.4	Ibaraki	6.1
6	Ibaraki	5.1	Nagano	5.8
7	Yamagata	3.3	Tochigi	3.4
8	Kumamoto	3.0	Yamagata	2.7
9	Kagoshima	2.6	Kagoshima	2.2
10	Tochigi	2.2	Kumamoto	2.1

Source: Bureau of Silkworm and Horticulture, MAFF.

the Executive Council), and the Council is subdivided into seventeen divisions that connect to the respective ministries and to correlating standing committees in the Diet. In addition, PARC has a large number (about 80) of less formal investigative and special committees. An executive committee of PARC collects recommendations from all divisions and sends them to the LDP's Executive Council.

PARC is important because it has also produced some powerful political figures. These politicians are called *zoku* Diet members, which can roughly be translated as "tribe members" or "family members." In the policymaking process, PARC and its policy divisions are influential, as are the policy-oriented subcommittees. Those members who are able to attain responsible positions, such as chairman or vice chairman, or those who can manage to stay in a certain committee for more than ten years, combine political influence with broad knowledge of the fields in which they specialize. Because of their expertise in specific fields, they are identified as *zoku*. All *zoku* are LDP Diet members, including both ex-bureaucrats and career politicians, although the number of career politicians is larger.

The *zoku*'s specialized fields include the agriculture and forestry *zoku*, construction *zoku*, commercial and industry *zoku*, foreign affairs *zoku*, culture and education *zoku*, financial *zoku*, transportation *zoku*, and so on. The agriculture, construction, and commercial groups are the most desirable and the largest. The three groups are called *gosanke* (the top three families) (Inoguchi 1985: 43). The *gosanke* is popular in part because of their ability to influence government policies that will provide certain benefits to the Diet members' constituencies. In return, *gosanke* members normally enjoy possessing strong *kōenkai* (a local supportive organization specifically working for an individual Diet member's election campaign) in their constituencies, securing their chances to be reelected.

Although there are different patterns, normally a *zoku* member will have progressed in his career through one or more of the following stages for a particular field: parliamentary vice-minister (a political appointee position within the government), PARC division chairman or vice-chairman, Diet standing committee chairman, and, occasionally, minister or director-general. This process usually requires ten or more years of service as a politician.

During the period of service in one or more specific policy areas, a *zoku* member becomes familiar with governmental affairs and the bureaucrats who handle such matters, and thereby acquires enormous influence over the central bureaucracy. In other words, the *zoku*'s experience enables them to become leaders in certain areas of public policy, and to effectively nurture personal ties with followers in their own constituencies and within governmental agencies, thereby creating an influential and powerful social environment for themselves. This network demonstrates that the leader-follower pattern can apply not only to party factions, but also to *zoku* politics.

Zoku politics worked well with the issue of raw silk importation. PARC set up the Special Committee on the Silk and Silk Yarn Industries with Takashi Satō, an agriculture *zoku*, as chairman. A graduate of Tokyo Agriculture University, he first served as an agricultural expert in the government agencies for seventeen years. Later, Satō became a LDP Diet member working in various agriculture-related positions, such as parliament vice-minister of MAFF (Yu and Hua 1984: 147). Among five vice-chairmen of the Committee, four came from the silkworm areas, having close ties with the silkworm farmers' interest groups. Yoshirō Mori was the only non-silkworm vice-chairman and openly opposed the Statute on Centralized Control. However, his opinion never carried weight with the Committee.[12]

This discussion of *zoku* politics is a good example of social network in action since the *zoku* members had special relations with silkworm farmers and their activities often took place behind-the-scenes. Although there are formal LDP organizations such as PARC and its divisions and committees (for example, the Agriculture and Forestry Division, known as *nōrin.bukai*), the real decisions on agriculture policies, including the raw silk protectionist policy, are made by a small group of agriculture *zoku*. For example, in 1987 within the agriculture community including MAFF and *Nōkyō*, this *zoku* group was known informally as the agriculture policy of eleven (*nōsei jūichininshū*). As Aurelia George (1988: 26) points out, this group of agriculture *zoku*

represent[s] the LDP's inner party Cabinet on agricultural matters. They act as a direct channel for MAFF proposals into the party and engage in extensive behind-the-scenes negotiations with all major participants in the agricultural policy process. They are the prime movers in molding the party consensus on agricultural policy, working hard to obtain agreement amongst members of agricultural committees before they actually sit.

It is not difficult, therefore, to see that the combination of farmers' interest groups and the agriculture *zoku* was a powerful element in the ruling party's policymaking apparatus. The combination enabled the smooth passage of the Statute on Centralized Control within the LDP.[13]

COUNTERACTIONS BY SMALL- AND MEDIUM-SIZED BUSINESSES

Small- and medium-sized businesses and labor unions have a strong voice in the public and private sectors. The lobbying activities of these businesses concerning raw silk were no less vigorous than those of their agricultural counterparts. Their main strategy was to appeal directly to the ruling LDP/bureaucracy apparatus by sending letters opposing raw silk protectionism. As early as 1976, the Association for Importing Chinese Raw Silk and Silk Yarn sent a letter to MAFF Minister Shintarō Abe, MITI Minister Toshio Kōmoto, and MOFA Minister Kiichi Miyazawa. The letter argued that the Statute on Centralized Control violated the spirit of the 1974 Sino-Japanese trade agreement, which required that both sides provide a "favorable trading environment." The small-medium business interest groups demanded that the statute be abolished (Japan-China Economic Association 1977: 184–185).

In 1980 three trading organizations—Japan Raw Silk Import Company, the Japan Fiber Import Company, and the Japan Association for Promoting International Trade—wrote a strong letter to the four leaders of the LDP: President (and Prime Minister) Masayoshi Ōhira, Secretary-General Yoshio Sakurauchi, General Council Chairman Zenkō Suzuki, and PARC Chairman Shintarō Abe. The letter argued that the statute "has violated the principle of free trade," and would provoke bad reactions both domestically and internationally. The letter demanded that the statute be removed (Japan-China Economic Association 1981: 387).

The small-medium businesses and affiliated labor unions further argued that protectionist policies such as the Statute on Centralized Control caused damage to society as a whole, despite protection of certain sectors such as the farming community. They criticized protectionism as only increasing the farmers' dependence on the government, adding to governmental expenditures. The CSRSSP buys both domestic and foreign raw silk, stores it, and then sells the silk according to demand. In this way they can maintain relatively high raw silk prices to protect silkworm farmers. On the other hand, the storage cost for the government is rather high and causes severe deficits (see Table 12).

To solve this deficit problem, the Japanese government has combined the raw silk business and the sugar business into one organization. Since Japan has traditionally imported sugar from abroad, the need for protection of domestically produced sugar is much less than that of raw silk. The government does not need to buy and store domestic sugar at high prices; therefore, the sugar business is

Table 12
Raw Silk Storage and Finance of the CSRSSP, 1975–85

Year	Storage (1,000 bushel)			Gain and Loss (100 million yen)
	Imported	Domestic	Total	
1975	18	16	34	6
1976	37	0	37	8
1977	45	11	56	11
1978	52	0	52	56
1979	77	14	91	14
1980	108	41	149	0
1981	94	52	146	-39
1982	92	58	150	-57
1983	84	92	176	-95
1984	56	115	171	-165
1985	45	107	152	-208

Source: Bureau of Silkworm and Horticulture, MAFF,
Saikin-no sanshi gyo-o meguru joho.

always profitable. To keep a balanced budget, the government links raw silk trade and the more profitable sugar trade by putting the two into one corporation. This "clever" linkage, however, only helped the CSRSSP for a short period. From Table 12, we can see that in the first several years after the statute went into effect, the CSRSSP could finance itself and even earn a small profit. But since the beginning of the 1980s, the CSRSSP has lost substantial amounts of money even with the combination of raw silk and sugar. In 1985 the deficit reached 47.5 billion yen (about $240 million).

Small-medium businesses and labor unions also argued that Japanese agricultural goods, including raw silk, had gradually lost their competitiveness in the international market. In some cases local raw silk prices reached a point twice as high as the international market price. How could Japanese silkworm farmers compete with farmers of other countries, they asked.

They also pointed out that the high price of raw silk made silk, silk goods, and kimonos more expensive in Japan, which hurt the interest of importers, manufacturers, and consumers, and ultimately decreased the domestic demand for raw silk. This development became a vicious cycle. An ex-MITI official sharply criticized this policy as "no different from committing suicide."[14]

Their final argument was that as an export-oriented economic superpower, Japan badly needed a free trade policy. However, such a policy was being damaged by Japan's own protectionist policies. It was believed that if protectionism were to spread, Japan would probably be hurt most (J. Woronoff 1986: 89). With all these arguments, the interest groups concluded that Japan should abolish protectionism of agricultural goods.[15]

The argument had a great impact on some key branches in the governmental bureaucracy, such as the Ministry of International Trade and Industry (MITI).

In 1979, for example, a vice-minister of MITI published an article suggesting that the remaining silkworm farmers should switch to other activities, so that the statute could be abolished. This article drew a storm of protests from silkworm farmers and the LDP.[16]

Although the small-medium businesses and the labor unions actively lobbied the ruling LDP and the government bureaucracy, their social network at that time was mainly with the opposition parties. The opposition parties' mainstream opposed the statute in the Diet,[17] but their minority position made it impossible to block its passage.

When we compare the actions of the silkworm farmer groups vis-à-vis the small-medium business groups, we can see that in Japan it is not only important for interest groups to have the right channels to express their demands, but they must also have the right social network, or *tsukiai*, through which to do so.

MAFF, MITI, AND MOFA

Japan has traditionally had a strong governmental bureaucracy, despite the chaos that followed World War II. Its superior position in providing information and expertise to top politicians and the public strengthened the bureaucracy's power. Furthermore, the bureaucracy was aided by the practice of *amakudari* (literally "descent from heaven"), which enabled retired bureaucrats to move to the private sector or public corporations and hold responsible and prestigious positions as second careers (Kishimoto 1988: 87). This enabled bureaucrats to cultivate intimate relations and establish a close-knit social network with leaders of industries and big businesses. As a result, the bureaucracy enjoyed the benefits of being independent, capable, powerful, and well connected in society.

During the period of rapid economic growth between the 1960s and the mid-1970s, the Japanese bureaucracy played a prominent role in policymaking. Middle- and high-level bureaucrats of MITI and the EPA (Economic Planning Agency) made strategic plans for all industrial development. Some Japan specialists believe that, in Japanese politics, the bureaucracy makes most of the decisions, initiates virtually all legislation, and controls the national budget.[18] According to this school of thought, the bureaucracy has a dominant role in Japan's policymaking process.

Michio Muramatsu holds an opposite view and examines this issue from another angle. He surveyed politicians and bureaucrats in the early 1980s, asking them which force in Japan was the most influential in terms of the policymaking process. He received the following results: Among high-level bureaucrats (vice-ministers and bureau directors), 47 percent said politicians and 46 percent said the bureaucracy. In the middle-level bureaucracy (section chiefs), 45 percent said politicians, while 40 percent said the bureaucracy. Among the LDP Diet members, 68 percent agreed that politicians were in charge, while 30 percent chose the bureaucracy. Among opposition parties Diet members, 43 percent said politicians, and 41 percent answered the bureaucracy. Others (around 10 percent) chose either big business, the news media, or interest groups as the most influential in policymaking (M. Muramatsu 1981: 27). This survey shows that most people regarded politicians and the bureaucracy as the most influential political forces in Japan. All groups, however, put more emphasis on politicians. This was especially true among LDP members.

In his *Gendai seiji* [Contemporary politics], Junnosuke Masumi (1985: 409) argues that beginning in the late 1960s, the influence of the LDP began to increase. The longer a political party holds the ruling position, the deeper its social network grows, enhancing the party's political influence in the decision-making process. In the 1980s more and more people were saying that "the central government was the LDP's headquarters."

There were interdepartmental disputes among bureaucrats on the raw silk issue. Three ministries were involved in the Statute on Centralized Control: MAFF, MITI, and MOFA. MAFF strongly favored the statute and was eager to put it into effect. MITI and MOFA were opposed to it.[19]

To understand the involvement of various ministries, first we have to look at the different jurisdictions among the governmental agencies. There are four stages of production for silk and its goods: from silkworm cocoon to raw silk to silk and finally to silk garments. The first two stages (silkworm cocoon and raw silk—agricultural products) are under the jurisdiction of MAFF, and the latter two (silk and silk garments—industrial products) are MITI's responsibilities. Since the actual social consequence of the statute, unintended perhaps, protected raw silk farmers while damaging the interests of the small-medium businesses, it provided protection to the first two but threatened the latter two.[20] MITI was not happy with the statute because of the law's impact on products that came under its jurisdiction.

Because the interests of various ministries were different, the spheres of social connection were different. MAFF had closer ties with farmers, whereas MITI represented the interests of commerce and industry. The two ministries could not achieve a consensus on a statute that benefited both farmers and small-medium businesses. MOFA was concerned primarily with reactions from abroad and did not want to damage Japan's image as a supporter of free trade in the international community. Furthermore, because MOFA did not want to see a trade issue (such as raw silk importation) evolve into a political issue that could hurt Sino-Japanese relations, it went along with MITI.[21]

With encouragement from MOFA, MITI proposed its own proposals to respond to pressures from small-medium businesses and to counter MAFF's protectionist policy. These proposals were to block efforts to stop the import of raw silk from abroad and to keep the free trade policy alive. At the same time, MITI prepared an alternative proposal: if MAFF insisted on imposing a protectionist policy on raw silk importation, then the government agencies should take over the responsibility of controlling the raw silk industry. In other words, MITI was willing to make a compromise by allowing some protectionist measures such as a quota system to maintain raw silk imports at a stable level, which would prevent protectionism from going to an extreme. MITI officials regarded this alternative proposal as "the second best."[22]

As the internal disputes between the ministries intensified, maneuvering on policy by the ruling party and its *zoku* took on a greater role. The LDP's two policymaking organs—the Division of Agriculture and Forestry and the Special Committee on the Silk and Silk Yarn Industries—as well as the agriculture *zoku* exercised their power on MAFF bureaucrats.

When the statute was in the process of deliberation within the bureaucracy, the LDP's agriculture *zoku* launched an all-out campaign to lobby bureaucrats by utilizing the special network cultivated over the years between the LDP and MAFF. The agriculture *zoku* lobbied through face-to-face formal discussion; informal discussions over lunches and dinners; and frequent telephone calls.

In general, the LDP *zoku*'s influence on MAFF was so extensive that it often affected personnel matters, including promotions of certain MAFF officials to key positions. Through such special relations, the agriculture *zoku* developed a network of followers within the MAFF bureaucracy. The leader-follower nature of these relations was such that one would hear MAFF officials referring to opinions from the LDP as "instructions."[23]

Tadao Kuraishi, then MAFF's minister and an agriculture *zoku* who came from a prefecture with silkworm farming, supported the statute. As a result, the LDP's Division of Agriculture and Forestry pushed for complete cessation of the importation of raw silk. The LDP's demand enhanced MAFF's protectionist position. By using the LDP's blessing as a bargaining chip, MAFF forced MITI and MOFA to agree to passage of the statute.

On the one hand, passage and implementation of the statute represented a victory for the LDP agriculture *zoku* and MAFF, since it established strict controls over raw silk importation. On the other hand, the statute did not stop the importation of raw silk completely as the agriculture *zoku* had originally demanded, and it was also the "second best" choice for MITI. Therefore, the statute was a compromise between the three ministries, which allowed the importation of raw silk but put this practice under strict governmental control. In negotiations with foreign governments on the issue of raw silk, all three ministries sent their representatives with the Japanese delegation.[24]

INTERNATIONAL PRESSURE

The silkworm farmers' problems of livelihood due to competition from abroad, the decrease in domestic demand, the overstocking of raw silk in government storage, and, more importantly, the mutual obligation between the ruling party and the raw silk farmers (which resulted in the LDP agriculture *zoku*'s vigorous lobbying of MAFF bureaucrats) are all behind Japan's protectionist policy for raw silk. (It is also true that many countries engage in protectionism of agricultural goods.) These factors make it difficult for the Japanese government, at least for the near future, to abandon the Statute on Centralized Control.

Table 13
Shares of Raw Silk from China and South Korea in Japan, 1969–86

Year	China's Share (%)	S. Korea's Share (%)
1969	42.5	39.4
1970	34.1	48.5
1971	47.8	35.0
1972	61.2	27.9
1973	67.0	21.8
1974	44.2	39.5
1975	60.7	27.3
1976	69.7	16.8
1977	64.7	27.0
1978	64.0	31.7
1979	69.6	24.4
1980	69.8	18.7
1981	70.6	0.06
1982	72.9	10.9
1983	76.5	17.5
1984	82.4	2.2
1985	86.7	0
1986	86.4	0

Source: Japan-China Economic Association.

The first session in the negotiations on raw silk between China and Japan, under the new Statute on Centralized Control, was held in January 1976. Despite China's strong request that the statute be abolished, the Japanese government insisted on keeping raw silk under strict control.[25] From then on, the two sides held negotiations every year to set up quotas for raw silk imported from China. This quota system effectively put China's raw silk at a lower quantity level (compared to the previous years) in the Japan market.

In general, the Japanese government consistently refused to give up its stand on protectionism of raw silk in any of the negotiations. However, to smooth relations with foreign countries, the Japanese government showed a willingness to compromise through symbolic changes. For example, in 1974, the year in which the statute was issued, China's raw silk share in the Japanese market fell from 67.0 percent to 44.2 percent, while South Korea's raw silk share increased from 21.8 percent to 39.5 percent. The Chinese protested the "unequal treatment." The next year, China's share recovered to 60.7 percent, while South Korea's fell back to 27.3 percent (see Table 13).[26]

This concession was more likely a goodwill gesture. In 1981, for example, Chinese raw silk exported to Japan fell sharply (by 69 percent) from the previous year's (1980) 2,080 tons to 650 tons (see Table 5). At the Sino-Japanese Cabinet Conference of December 1981, Zheng Tuobin, the Chinese foreign trade minister, urged Japanese MITI Minister Shintarō Abe to "restore and expand the importation of China's raw silk" (Japan-China Economic Association 1982: 399–400). To placate China's concerns, and in particular, to show special favor to the

Chinese foreign trade minister (with the expectation of a reciprocal favor from China in the future), Abe promised to increase China's raw silk importation quota. The next year's (1982) exports of Chinese raw silk to Japan increased by 1.6 times.

Overall, the development of China's raw silk trade in the Japanese market was rather successful in terms of overall share. In the 1960s and 1970s China's main rival in the raw silk market was South Korea. The two countries' raw silk accounted for 80 to 90 percent of the entire Japanese market (see Table 13).

China's raw silk was more competitive than South Korea's in both price and quality (Japan-China Economic Association 1979: 272–273), and beginning in the 1980s, China's share increased further. South Korea's market share continued to fall until it was totally out of Japan's raw silk market by 1985. In 1985 China's share was up to 86.7 percent, with Brazil second (12.4 percent) and North Korea third (0.9 percent) (Japan-China Economic Association 1986: 237).

The decline in South Korea's market share was due to a pattern similar to Japan's: an increase in domestic demand for silk goods, a decline of raw silk production due to industrialization and urbanization which sharply reduced the rural population, and competition from China.[27] Furthermore, raw silk as a trade item long ago became insignificant in the Korean-Japanese trade; therefore, much less importance was placed on it as compared to trade between China and Japan.[28] In fact, South Korea began importing raw silk from China in the mid-1980s owing to the shortage of raw silk in its domestic market. In 1988, for example, Chinese raw silk accounted for 60 percent of the total demand of South Korea's silk industry.[29] South Korea has gradually become an important buyer of Chinese raw silk. For example, during the first three months of 1988, out of 943 tons of Chinese raw silk transshipped through Hong Kong, South Korea received 588 tons, West Germany 35 tons, Italy 28 tons, the United States 24 tons, Singapore 15 tons, Japan 13 tons (most of the Japanese importation of Chinese raw silk is through a direct trade route instead of via Hong Kong), and Taiwan 5 tons.[30]

The decrease in the absolute quantity of Chinese raw silk in Japan was due mainly to the sharp drop in its domestic demand. In 1985 China already had a share of 86.7 percent of the imported raw silk market in Japan and, therefore, did not have much room to expand. After the record deficit in bilateral trade with Japan in 1985, China began to control its imports from Japan while promoting exports to Japan. As a result of this effort, Sino-Japanese trade became healthier, and in 1988 China turned deficit to surplus in its trade with Japan (see Table 2). In 1990 China was one of the few Asian countries enjoying a healthy trade surplus ($5.9 billion) with Japan, and this trend continued in 1991.[31]

It would benefit foreign countries to better understand the internal dynamics of Japanese politics, in particular the networks among various social forces. This will enable them to negotiate more effectively with Japan in resolving trade issues. This is because most protectionist policies are closely connected to internal political maneuvering that heavily involves social network activities among interest groups, the governmental bureaucrats, and the ruling LDP.

MECHANISMS OF POLITICAL INFLUENCE

We have just examined Japan's protectionist policy of raw silk importation. Two major elements were involved in its policymaking process. The first was historical legacy. As former Minister of Foreign Affairs Saburō Ōkita points out, Japan has a long tradition of exporting raw silk. During the 1920s, for example, raw silk exportation accounted for as much as 40 percent of the total value of exports, which created a lasting emotional attachment to the issue of raw silk among the Japanese.[32] The second element was a sense of national security. Although Japan long ago became a highly industrialized country, many Japanese still regarded agriculture and its products as crucial to national security. They also attached pride to the kimono as the national costume, so Japan must have its own raw silk production and industry to meet the demand for making the kimono.[33]

These two arguments are reasonable, but they do not explain the political maneuvering by social forces in the policymaking process. We must look for yet another ingredient that shapes policies, and that is the phenomenon of social network in Japanese society. The issue of raw silk protectionism, as Saburō Ōkita points out, "is not in the field of foreign policy, but in the scope of domestic politics."[34]

Different interests were involved in the policymaking process for the statute on raw silk importation. The silkworm farmers needed protection to survive the decline in silkworm agriculture and raw silk production. The small-medium businesses and the labor unions worked hard to abolish the protectionist policy so that their businesses could survive. The ruling Liberal Democrat Party and its agriculture *zoku* supported protectionist measures to please their constituents from the rural areas in order to maintain their power and expand their influence. The government bureaucracy (MAFF, MITI, and MOFA) had differing interests and opinions as regards raw silk protection, but nevertheless worked out a compromise as a second best choice. The statute was indeed a pluralistic political operation, and the social networks played an impressive role.

The basic functions of social networks are to effectively get the message across, to coordinate various power centers, and to achieve a relatively balanced representation among the main players. On the issue of the statute, both sides—silkworm farmers and small-medium businesses—had forceful lobbying activities and policy input within the LDP and the central bureaucracy. The result in favor of the farmers only reflected the imbalance of different social connections. The imbalance between these two groups lay, not necessarily in absolute numbers of people, but more importantly, in political influence. The silkworm farmers with the ruling party connections were in a much stronger position than their counterparts—the small and medium-sized businesses—which were represented mainly by opposition parties.[35]

It is no secret that the LDP's sensitivity to agricultural policies is due largely to the party's dependence on the organized farmers—through the Association of Agricultural Cooperative—for electoral support. Following the guidelines of the ruling party, MAFF is responsible for a large amount of subsidies to farmers, which constitute more than 14 percent of the total of all governmental subsidies to local government and private enterprises (Hirose 1981: 93–107).

There are drawbacks to this intertwining of social networks: an imbalance in political influence results from the special relationship the farmers have with the ruling apparatus. It may protect the interests of certain groups (such as raw silk farmers) at the expense of other groups (such as the raw silk industry and import companies). Furthermore, it may also cause corruption under the name of social networks. It is believed that the social causes of what Chalmers Johnson (1986) called Japan's structural corruption are due largely to the basic political structure, but these complicated social networks also bear some responsibility.

Many scholars have recently begun to pay close attention to the LDP's decision-making organs such as PARC and its powerful *zoku*, and to their relationships to corresponding ministries (Inoguchi 1985; Satō and Matsuzaki 1986; and Zhao 1988). Research in this area has shown that the influence which PARC's Agriculture Division and the agriculture *zoku* have over MAFF has been tremendous: a leader-follower relationship between *zoku* and key bureaucrats has been strong, according to these studies.

Within the LDP organizations, there is also a division of labor. The raw silk policy, for example, is under the jurisdiction of PARC's *nōrin bukai* (the Division of Agriculture and Forestry). Although other divisions are involved in the issue and may have different opinions, they normally do not intervene in another division's jurisdiction. The Division of Foreign Affairs, for example, despite its disagreement with the Statute on Centralized Control, showed an "understanding" toward the statute owing to considerations of maintaining good social relations within the LDP.[36] We can find similar examples of cooperation among various governmental agencies that have often been in conflicting positions, but have always managed to reach a compromise.

When I interviewed a veteran official of silkworm affairs in MAFF, he drew a linear diagram to illustrate the process with regard to making of agriculture policies:

FARMERS ——— LDP ————— MAFF ————— NEW POLICIES
     (pressure)   (instructions)   (deliberation)

Farmers put pressure on the LDP; the LDP and its agriculture *zoku* give instructions to MAFF; the bureaucrats in MAFF go through internal deliberation within and outside of the ministry (mainly with MITI and MOFA) and initiate new policies.[37] At each link, special social relations are involved: the sense of mutual obligation between farmers and key LDP decision-makers; the leader-follower relationship between the agriculture *zoku* and their local constituencies as well as between the *zoku* and specific MAFF bureaucrats. These relationships present a picture of intertwined social connections in the policymaking process.

This network further explains the internal mechanism of Japan's "mutually controlled tripod machine,"[38] a longstanding school of thought on Japanese politics which asserts that big business and interest groups pressure the LDP; the ruling party has the ability to control the direction of the government; and the governmental bureaucracy has power to guide business. Yet, Japanese society has entered a more pluralistic stage, with more complicated and intertwined interests and social groups. We can see an increased interdependence and integration among various social forces. It becomes clear that no single social group controls society. Every force is expected to follow the rules, and an important rule in the game is *tsukiai* representing social activities and network.

NOTES

1. For detailed discussion, see Peter Duus, *Feudalism in Japan* (1969).

2. For detailed accounts, see Mikiso Hane, *Modern Japan* (1986); Edwin Reischauer, *The Japanese Today* (1988); Peter Duus, *The Rise of Modern Japan* (1976); and R.H.P. Mason and J. G. Caiger, *A History of Japan* (1972).

3. The new constitution contains eleven chapters and 103 articles. (For the full document of the constitution, see Theodore McNelly [1972], *Politics and Government in Japan*, pp. 261–270.) Its main aim was Japan's political democratization and demilitarization. Under this principle, many drastic reforms were undertaken. The position of the emperor was changed—he became a mere symbol of the state with no political power. The constitution established a bicameral Diet as the highest organ of national authority, with a Lower House (the House of Representatives) and an Upper House (the House of Counsellors). The members of both Houses were to be popularly elected. The principle of a collective cabinet responsible to the Diet was also instituted. The constitution specifically gave executive powers to the cabinet. Freedom of speech and other fundamental rights were guaranteed. Japan's armed forces were disarmed and then disbanded. War criminals were arrested, tried, and punished. Militarists and war leaders were purged for a time from public office and educational positions. The Privy Council and the peerage were abolished. The police system was decentralized. The rights of women to vote and hold public office were guaranteed. Organized labor and left-wing political parties were granted freedom of expression, and their activities were encouraged. Some of the most noteworthy economic and social reforms were land reform and the dissolution of the *zaibatsu*—family-oriented, large, monopolized business groups. Educational reform was also undertaken. Japan was to be demilitarized institutionally and ideologically. All these reforms were to ensure that sovereignty was vested in the people.

4. This democratic foundation has changed Japan's political structure in many ways. The first significant change in Japanese politics is the broad acceptance of popular sovereignty. In postwar Japan, elections and political parties have become the essential vehicles to political power. Under the new constitution, a parliamentary cabinet system was established. The National Diet, a bicameral system composed only of publicly elected members, became "the highest organ of state power" (Article 41 of Constitution of Japan of 1947) which replaced the emperor. The importance of the National Diet has been

addressed by T. J. Pempel (1982: 16) as a place where there is "the freedom of debate, the increased role of political parties, the tightness of the parliamentary calendar, the relative autonomy of parliamentary committees, the media coverage given to parliamentary activities"; all these have combined to make the Diet a "major institutional locus of conflict between the government and opposition parties." The cabinet is responsible to the national Diet. The prime minister must be selected from among the Diet members. The majority of the cabinet must also be Diet members. The authority of the prime minister vis-à-vis his cabinet members has increased considerably.

5. Interview with Tomomitsu Iwakura, a staff member of the Agriculture Division of the LDP's PARC, August 11, 1986, Tokyo.

6. Learned from a one-week research trip to the farming areas of Nagano Prefecture, August 1986.

7. Interview with Tomomitsu Iwakura, August 11, 1986, Tokyo.

8. Robert Delfs, "Question of Survival: LDP Toughens Its Line on Rice Imports," *Far Eastern Economic Review*, March 12, 1992, p. 11; and Robert Delfs, "Rural Retreat: Miyazawa's Position Eroded by Another Poll Loss," *Far Eastern Economic Review*, March 19, 1992, p. 11.

9. See Bureau of Silkworm and Horticulture, the MAFF, *Saikin-no Sanshi gyō ho.*

10. Interview with Hiroshi Sugiura, a retired MITI official, June 27, 1986, Tokyo.

11. Interview with Wu Xuewen, July 15, 1986, Fukuoka. Wu is one of a few Japan-hands in China. He received his education in Japan when he was young and served as correspondent of China's Xinhua News Agency in Tokyo in the 1960s and 1970s.

12. Interview with Toshiro Eda, deputy director of the Silkworm Division of MAFF, July 4, 1986, Tokyo.

13. Interview with Yoshio Isogaya, director of Corporation of Raw Silk Importation of Japan, May 27, 1986, Tokyo.

14. Interview with Hiroshi Sugiura, June 27, 1986, Tokyo.

15. Interviews with Michihiko Kunihiro, general director of the Bureau of Foreign Economic Relations of MFA, June 4, 1986; Tokyo; and Kōichi Yamaura, former director of North Asia Division of MITI, July 3, 1986, Tokyo.

16. Interview with Lin Liande, October 28, 1986, Beijing. Lin, former director of Japan Division, deputy general director of Bureau of District Policy of the Chinese Ministry of Foreign Trade (1972–82), and former commercial counsellor of the Embassy of the PRC in Tokyo, is now retired.

17. Interviews with Haruo Okada, a veteran Diet member of the Japanese Socialist party since 1946, February 27, 1986, Tokyo. Okada served as vice-president of the Diet during the late 1970s and the early 1980s.

18. This typical argument is presented in Johnson's book, *MITI and the Japanese Miracle* (1982). He examines the history of MITI's fifty years of development and set up the school of thought that "bureaucracy leads politics." See p. 20.

19. Interview with Kōichi Yamaura, former director of the North Asia Division of MITI, July 3, 1986, Tokyo.

20. Ibid.

21. Interview with Michihiko Kunihiro, June 4, 1986, Tokyo. Kunihiro was director of the China Division of MOFA during the period 1973–74.

22. Interview with Kōichi Yamaura, July 3, 1986, Tokyo.

23. Interview with Kihei Aoki, deputy director of the Silkworm Division of MAFF, June 12, 1986, Tokyo.

24. Interview with Junji Matsui, general director of the Bureau of Investigation and Statistics of MITI, June 11, 1986, Tokyo. Matsui served as commercial counsellor in the Japanese Embassy in Beijing during the mid-1970s.

25. Interview with Lin Liande, October 28, 1986, Beijing.

26. Ibid.

27. Interview with Dr. Ki Dong Lee, director of the Institute of Industry and Economic Policy of Korea, August 23, 1988, Seoul.

28. Interview with Tae Yong Shin, researcher at the Institute of Industry and Economic Policy of Korea, August 23, 1988, Seoul.

29. Interview with Sung-Jin Koo, manager of the International Affairs Department, the Korea Chamber of Commerce and Industry, August 26, 1988, Seoul.

30. *The Korea Times*, August 23, 1988.

31. Louise do Rosario, "Winning Both Ways: Japan's Trade Surplus with Asia Is Growing," *Far Eastern Economic Review*, August 1, 1991, p. 57; and Anthony Rowley, "A Bigger Stick: Bush's Japan Visit Offers Little for Asia," *Far Eastern Economic Review*, January 23, 1992, pp. 45–46.

32. Interview with Saburō Ōkita, chairman of the Institute for Domestic and International Policy Studies, July 4, 1986, Tokyo.

33. Interview with Tomomitsu Iwakura, August 11, 1986, Tokyo.

34. Interview with Saburō Ōkita, July 4, 1986, Tokyo.

35. Interview with Toshiro Eda, July 4, 1986, Tokyo.

36. Interview with Yukio Nakamaru, staff member of the LDP Division of Foreign Affairs, August 28, 1986, Tokyo.

37. Interview with Toshiro Eda, July 4, 1986, Tokyo.

38. Interview with Yaeji Watanabe, former president of the Japan-China Economic Association and a retired high-ranking MITI official, June 27, 1986, Tokyo.

PART III

Political Institution and Organizational Theory
Case Study: Sino-Japanese Rapprochement

4

Informal Political Actors and Organizations[1]

In the Japanese kabuki theater, there are players who act as informal actors called *kuromaku* (meaning "black veils"). They set the stage and assist the formal actors in full view of the audience, but they are not acknowledged as part of the performance because of their black dress. They can be seen on the stage, but the audience is supposed to ignore their presence. Richard Samuels (1982: 127–146) used this analogy to refer to behind-the-scenes figures in Japanese politics who are really in charge. In this study, I will use this behind-the-scenes concept[2] to include not only individual actors but also organizations, whose activities are normally invisible to the public. I define the *kuromaku* concept neutrally without the somewhat negative sense it may have in the Japanese language (e.g., a *yakuza*, or a mafia head). In this book, the concept of *kuromaku* indicates informal political actors and organizations that do not necessarily have formal (or official) status, but who often use behind-the-scenes channels to get things done. These figures may include both "big fish" and "small fry," that is, someone who is in control of others or someone who is being used by others.

In their study of the U.S.-Japan conflict over textile issues, I. M. Destler, Haruhiro Fukui, and Hideo Satō (1979: 122, 183–184, 197) paid special attention to a phenomenon called back-channel negotiation, where both sides (the Japanese in particular) made extensive use of behind-the-scenes channels to solve difficult political issues. These back channels were used to counter information leaks and to "strengthen national leaders' capacity to manage the politics of the issue by controlling what information became available to the public—and to different parts of the two governments" (327–328). The motivations are similar when the Japanese conduct these informal practices—the back channels and *kuromaku* activities.

It is easy to find a real *kuromaku* in kabuki theater, but it would be difficult to identify and understand *kuromaku* activities that are part of the process of

Japanese foreign policy. An understanding of Japanese policymaking requires thorough investigation and research of informal political actors and organizations, and a detailed knowledge of Japan's political institutions, as well as Japanese society.

For a better understanding of informal mechanisms in Japanese politics and its influence on foreign policymaking, Part II focused on the political system and social environment through application of notions of pluralism and social network. Part III (Chapters 4 and 5) will examine Japan's "informal mechanisms" from the second level of analysis—the institutional level—by applying organizational theory.

Japan's decision to normalize relations with China has been studied in great detail by several Japan specialists (see note 1 of this chapter). This author does not disagree with the main arguments of these scholars that Japan's decision was not only a natural consequence of the changing international environment (U.S. policy in particular), but also the result of much political maneuvering within various sectors of the Japanese society (H. Fukui 1970 and 1977; S. Ogata 1977 and 1988; and C. Lee 1976). Rather, Part III attempts to provide new interpretations of this well-known case by focusing on the informal aspects of policymaking in Japan, which has not been treated systemically in previous studies.

ORGANIZATIONAL THEORIES AND POLICYMAKING

Important parts of organizational theories include the internal structures of the organizations, the relationship between the leaders and the people, and the issue of legitimate authority. These structures and relations can be established either through legality and formality, or through informality and tradition. Studies on formal and informal organizations have received wide attention in the field of organizational theories. A significant part of the informal mechanisms concept grows out of this notion of formality and informality.

Max Weber (1968: 46–47) identified three types of legitimate authority in his analysis of charisma and institution building: rational, traditional, and charismatic. The first describes "the legally established impersonal order," which extends to leaders exercising the authority of office under it only by virtue of the formal legality of their commands, and only within the scope of authority of the office they hold. The second type of legitimate authority emphasizes "personal loyalty within the area of accustomed obligations," which requires impersonal order as a base. The third type refers to "the charismatically qualified leader as one who is obeyed by virtue of personal trust in him and his revelation, his heroism or his exemplary qualities." The function of these classifications of legitimate authority, according to Weber, is to promote systematic analysis of organizational and institutional structures. To examine organizations and political institutions using Weber's approach is to view "rational" legitimate rule as formal organizations, and "traditional" and "charismatic" rule as informal organizations.

In the case of Japan, informal organizations are often based on a second type of authority—personal loyalty within the area of accustomed obligations.

According to Nicos Mouzelis (1967: 59–61), a formal organization consists of rules that define the tasks and responsibilities of each participant, as well as the formal mechanisms that could permit the integration of these tasks. Such rules constitute the formal structure of the organization, whereas rules and mechanisms of informal organizations appear to be more flexible and more difficult to identify. "This formal-informal conflict," Mouzelis claims, "gives to the organization a dynamic, ever-changing aspect." This chapter examines activities and interactions among formal and informal organizations in Japan's political life with regard to the 1972 Sino-Japanese rapprochement. The study of Japan's political institutions by using formal-informal organizational theories will shed new light on the idea of the "dynamic, ever-changing aspect" of organizations, and will provide a deeper understanding of Japanese politics and foreign policymaking.

Chester Barnard (1938: 73) defined a formal organization as "a system of consciously coordinated activities or forces of two or more persons." F. J. Roethlisberger and W. J. Dickson (1941), and Wilbert E. Moore (1946) emphasized the importance of informal structures within various types of organizations. Philip Selznick (1961: 22) claimed that "in large organizations, deviations from the formal system tend to become institutionalized, so that 'unwritten laws' and informal associations are established." He further elaborated that "The informal pattern (such as cliques) arise spontaneously, are based on personal relationships, and are usually directed to the control of some specific situation." The LDP's internal factions have followed this formal-informal pattern in their development.

There are many informal organizations in Japanese political life. Bradley Richardson and Scott Flanagan (1984: 100) define informal organizations as "interpersonal networks of friendship and mutual ideological agreement, and as other relationships or groups which come to exist within parties and which are not called for by the party's formal organizational plans." They conclude that, "in Japan, informal relationships and groups are so important in party organizations that it is at times possible to see them as more important than the parties' formal structures." John Campbell's argument (1984: 305) further enhances Richardson and Flanagan's observation. He took the ruling Liberal Democratic Party and its policy issues as an example, contending that open polarization of LDP's informal groups seems to occur often with regard to foreign policy. It makes this study, a closer examination of Japanese foreign policy toward China, more necessary.

Many political actors and organizations were involved in the 1972 Sino-Japanese rapprochement. This study does not explore this process in every detail. Instead, emphasis is placed on those elements that are closely connected with formal and informal political actors and organizations, including LDP politicians, the bureaucracy, leaders of organized business, Diet members of opposition parties, intellectuals, and the news media. With time, interviews with Japanese politicians and government officials, and data related to the rapprochement process have become more accessible, compared to the period of normalization in the early 1970s when behind-the-scenes negotiations were considered highly confidential and sensitive. In addition to the internal actors, the changing international environment and China's strategies toward Japan will also be taken into consideration.

BACKGROUND AND THE INTERNATIONAL ENVIRONMENT

The Japanese move toward normalizing relations with China was not as dramatic or shocking as the changes in U.S. foreign policy toward China in the period of 1971–72, known as Nixon-Kissinger diplomacy. Instead, the 1972 rapprochement between China and Japan is viewed as an evolution of the pro-normalization movement that had existed for over twenty years prior to 1972.[3] Yet, the Sino-Japanese rapprochement initiated a new direction for Japanese foreign policy, as veteran Socialist Diet member Haruo Okada pointed out.[4] Seiichi Tagawa, a senior politician and a pro-Beijing LDP Diet member during the process of rapprochement, indicated that significant differences existed before and after the 1972 rapprochement with regard to Japan's China policy.[5]

In Japan, the decision to normalize relations with China was both highly political and controversial. It attracted attention from virtually all circles of Japanese society. The China issue became a topic of national debate. The Japanese were concerned about China mainly for three reasons: (1) Chinese culture greatly influenced Japanese culture; the traditional relationship between the two countries needed to be restored after Japan's invasion of China during the Sino-Japanese conflict beginning in the early 1930s and ending in 1945. (2) China was a huge, untouched market, and Japan should not be left behind by the United States and Western European countries. (3) Maintenance of good Japanese-American relations was in Japan's national interests; therefore, any move toward rapprochement with China required consultation with the U.S. government.[6]

Japan's historic decision to establish formal diplomatic relations with the People's Republic of China in the fall of 1972 was heavily influenced, if not determined, by the changing international environment. This environment included the global strategic structure of the United States, the Soviet Union, and China, and regional changes in the East Asian and Pacific areas. Several external factors significantly influenced Japan's decision: China's changing attitude toward the outside world in the beginning of the 1970s; the dramatic change in the United States' China policy marked by the "Nixon Shock"; the question of China's legal seat in the United Nations; and the development of new structures in world politics and East Asia.[7]

China's domestic political development and its changing status in the world community was an important factor for Japan's normalization decision. China's Cultural Revolution beginning in 1966 brought disaster to China in both domestic politics and foreign policy. In the late 1960s and the beginning of the 1970s, China was in a very different position: it was encircled by hostile powers and neighbors from virtually all directions. In the north, China was fighting against the Soviet Union in a series of border clashes. In the south, the Chinese People's Liberation Army was committed to support North Vietnam's war against the United States. In the west, the border dispute between China and India, which precipitated the 1962 China-India War, remained unsettled. In the east, there was a U.S.-supported South Korea, and an old rival, the Taiwan regime, headed by the Nationalist Party (KMT), which was defended by the Seventh Fleet of the United States. In the northeast, there was what Chinese officials called revived militarism in Japan.

The concern over the revival of Japanese militarism was expressed by Chinese Premier Zhou Enlai when he visited North Korea in the spring of 1970. The Zhou Enlai-Kim Il-song Joint Communique claimed, "Japanese militarism has revived and has become a dangerous force of aggression in Asia. . . . The Japanese militarists are directly serving U.S. imperialism in its war of aggression against Vietnam, actively taking part in the U.S. imperialist new scheme of war in Korea, and widely attempting to include the Chinese sacred territory of Taiwan in their sphere of influence."[8]

At this time, China's international policy, under the leadership of a group of ultra-leftists, advocated a strategy of promoting world revolution. The leftist leaders, such as Defense Minister Lin Biao and Mao's wife Jiang Qing, believed that China was the center of the world revolution.[9] According to them, all other communist or socialist countries and parties were not as revolutionary as China and its Communist party. During the 1960s, China had few friends in the world: only Albania, North Vietnam, and a few countries in Africa were considered friends. As a result of this isolation in the international community, China lost its diplomatic flexibility in world affairs.

Domestically, China was then at the peak of the Cultural Revolution (1966–69)—the most chaotic period since the establishment of the People's Republic in 1949. A stagnant economy put China further behind the dynamic East Asian NIEs (newly industrialized economies). The Lin Biao incident in the fall of 1971, in which Lin attempted a military coup d'état and defection to the Soviet Union, disillusioned many Chinese with the goal of world revolution. In contrast to Jiang Qing and her leftist supporters, a group of pragmatic leaders represented by Premier Zhou Enlai were trying hard to pull China away from the Cultural Revolution. These events led Mao Zedong and Zhou Enlai to seek open relations with the Western bloc powers, especially the United States and Japan.

China's efforts were successful. The United States made a dramatic change in its policy toward China (with consideration of its own interests). In 1971 Henry Kissinger, U.S. national security adviser to the president, visited China and subsequently made an announcement that President Richard Nixon would visit Beijing in 1972. This news had a tremendous impact on leaders of major countries in the world and significantly altered the balance of international relations. Japanese leaders were among those most affected by this change in U.S. policy.

At the time Nixon made his televised announcement at San Clemente on the evening of July 15, 1971 (the morning of July 16, Tokyo time) that he would visit China before May 1972, Japan's Prime Minister Eisaku Satō was presiding over a cabinet meeting. Ironically, the cabinet was discussing a draft of Satō's speech reconfirming Japan's cooperation with Taiwan and South Korea prepared for the sixty-sixth session of the Diet. The cabinet members were debating whether to include a general statement with regard to the improvement of Japanese relations with neighboring countries, including China. The shocking news of Sino-American rapprochement was delivered to the cabinet meeting room shortly before Nixon's speech (Furukawa 1981: 333; and Ijiri 1987: 75–76). This incident was called the "Nixon Shock" because few Japanese could believe the United States would reconcile with "Red China" ahead of Japan without prior consultation. Virtually every politician in Japan remembered this shocking incident.[10]

With the impact of the Nixon Shock and China's persistent lobbying, in the fall of 1971 Beijing acquired legal seats in the United Nations General Assembly and Security Council. Taipei representatives were expelled from the organization, despite strong opposition from the United States and Japan. Many countries, following the U.N. accord and the changing international situation, decided to switch their positions from formal ties with Taiwan to establishing diplomatic relations with the People's Republic. This development had a great impact on Western bloc countries in terms of their China policy. By the end of 1971, Canada and Italy, for example, established formal diplomatic relations with Beijing and cut off official ties with Taipei.

Now came the question of whether Japan's China policy needed a change. As early as 1958, Zhou Enlai announced guiding principles for future Sino-Japanese relations, known as "the three political principles"[11] (see Chapter 2). With regard to Sino-Japanese normalization of relations, Beijing further elaborated that Japan must acknowledge that there was only one China and that the PRC was the sole legal government representing the Chinese people; that Taiwan Province was an inalienable part of the territory of the PRC; and that the Japan-Taiwan peace treaty was illegal and invalid and must be abrogated. These principles became the focus of controversy. The Japanese were divided on whether or not to accept them.

Other developments regarding China also caused concern in Japan. The Zhou-Nixon Shanghai Communique of 1972, issued during Nixon's highly publicized visit to China, indicated the emergence of the U.S.-USSR-China strategic triangle in global politics and highlighted the multipolarity of international relations. In East Asia, the four-power structure became clear: China, Japan, the Soviet Union, and the United States. These regional and global changes prompted Japanese leaders to reconsider Japan's China policy.

China's own changing international outlook, the United States' shift in its policy toward China, the changing status of the PRC and Taiwan in the United

Nations, and the emergence of a multipolar structure were four major international factors that greatly contributed to Japan's decision to normalize relations with the PRC. However, external elements alone are not enough to explain Japanese foreign policy and its policymaking process. We must also examine the internal factors of Japanese politics.

THE RULING PARTY: "STUDY GROUPS" AND FACTIONS

Between 1948 and 1955, two conservative parties, the Liberal Party and the Democratic Party, took turns as the ruling party in Japan. In 1955 these two parties merged into the Liberal Democratic Party which has ever since remained in power. Thus, since 1948 no single outside-conservative-coalition opposition party, such as the Socialist Party, the Democratic Socialist Party, the Clean Government Party (Kōmeitō), or the Communist Party, has ever been strong enough to challenge the ruling position of the mainstream conservative coalition. Although the LDP lost its majority position in the Upper House election of summer 1989 (the LDP still maintains a majority in the more powerful Lower House), internal disputes among opposition parties have so far prevented them from uniting together as a coalition to replace the LDP's ruling position.

The LDP's formal organizations and top official posts include the party's president, vice-president, secretary-general, the General Council, and the party's policy deliberation organ—the Policy Affairs Research Council (PARC). Under PARC, there are seventeen divisions corresponding to the major ministries of the central government and approximately eighty research commissions and special committees on a wide range of subjects.[12]

Students of Japanese politics have correctly paid close attention to the formal LDP organizations, which normally play a critical role in major policy-oriented decisions. It was the informal LDP organizations, however, that played a distinctive and impressive function during deliberation within the party for normalizing relations with Beijing.

The process of normalizing relations with China took place under two different leaderships in Japanese politics—the Satō period and the Tanaka period. Eisaku Satō was president of the LDP and prime minister from November 1964 to July 1972. Kakuei Tanaka was Satō's successor, and his tenure ran from July 1972 to December 1974.

Satō's priority in foreign policy during his seven and a half year rule was to maintain a good relationship with the United States. The top item on the agenda was the return of Okinawa from the U.S. to Japanese administration (Fukui 1977: 63). Nevertheless, Satō was aware of the changing international situation and did not ignore the China issue entirely. But Satō's efforts to open Beijing's door were severely constrained by internal and external factors, and ran into some serious problems with the Chinese.

From the Chinese perspective, two actions taken by the Satō administration became major obstacles to normalization. The first obstacle was the Satō-Nixon Joint Communique of November 1969, which included a so-called Taiwan clause. In the Communique, the Japanese prime minister claimed that "the maintenance of peace and security in the Taiwan area is also a most important factor for the security of Japan."[13] This meant that the Japanese would consider a threat to Taiwan from outside forces as a threat to Japan's security. The Joint Communique stated that Japan would allow U.S. armed forces to be stationed in Japan (in Okinawa, for example) to defend Taiwan under such circumstances. The Beijing government regarded this clause as Japanese intervention in China's domestic affairs. Chinese leaders believed that the Satō-Nixon talks brought military collaboration between the "American imperialists" and the "Japanese reactionaries" to a new stage. The *Renmin Ribao* (People's Daily) further criticized Japan and the United States for "intensifying their military collaboration and hatching a new war plot."[14]

The second obstacle was the issue of the PRC's representation in the United Nations. Frustrated by previous failures, Beijing blamed the United States for leading the "reactionary forces" that prevented China's entry into the United Nations. Japan was a faithful follower of the anti-PRC policy by the United States. As the international situation was changing during the United Nations' 1969, 1970, and 1971 General Assemblies, the battles between pro-Beijing and pro-Taipei forces over the issue of China's representation in the United Nations became fierce.

During this period, the United States changed its stance from "there is one China and Taiwan represents the whole of China" to a "one China, one Taiwan" known as the two-China policy. The United States urged the Satō government to co-sponsor two American-drafted resolutions. One resolution defined the U.N. expulsion of Taiwan as an important question (known as a "reverse important question"), so that expulsion would require two thirds of the total General Assembly vote. The other resolution, permitting PRC permanent membership on the Security Council, while at the same time allowing Taiwan to maintain its seat in the General Assembly, was known as the dual representation resolution.[15]

Heated debates took place within the top political circles in Japan on whether Japan should co-sponsor the two resolutions. Opposition to the co-sponsorship came not only from the opposition parties, but also from within the LDP itself. A significant proportion of LDP Diet members felt that Japan should change its China policy, and therefore should not co-sponsor the two resolutions. In a joint session of the LDP Executive Council and the Foreign Affairs Research Council, ten of seventeen members who expressed their positions at the meeting supported co-sponsoring the resolutions, while seven opposed. Many top LDP politicians expressed an unwillingness to approve the co-sponsorship, because the issue had already created rifts and they were afraid that further dispute might lead to a split in the LDP. The issue was so sensitive that the Council finally chose "not to decide" the matter, and the decision was turned over to the prime minister. Satō had to take full responsibility for whatever decision he might make (Tanaka 1985: 229–231).

On September 22, 1971, Satō announced his decision for Japan to co-sponsor the two resolutions with the United States, making Japan "the only major state" to do so (F. Langdon 1973: 177). Despite the efforts of the United States and Japan to save Taiwan's seat, one month later the "reverse important issue" resolution was defeated at the General Assembly by a vote of fifty-nine to fifty-five with seventeen absentees. The U.N. defeat was a heavy blow to Satō, and placed him in a vulnerable position both within and outside of his party (C. Lee 1976: 103).

Both opposition parties and pro-Beijing LDP groups strongly protested Satō's decision. After the defeat of the two resolutions at the United Nations, opposition parties made alliances to introduce a no-confidence motion in the Diet against Satō and his foreign minister Takeo Fukuda. Pro-Beijing LDP members also took strong actions by dramatizing their protest against the government's anti-PRC stance. Twelve Liberal Democrats known as the LDP's twelve samurai, led by veteran LDP member Aiichirō Fujiyama, showed their support to the opposition parties' no-confidence motion by not attending the vote so that they did not have to follow the party line (Park 1975: 566). This unusual method of symbolic absence expressed their unmistakable protest against the Satō administration's China policy.

Japan's political advances toward rapprochement with the PRC suffered as a result of Satō's decision. The Chinese government decided that the Satō administration was "a double accomplice of U.S. imperialism," and China would not open normalization talks as long as Satō was at the helm of the Japanese government.[16] In other words, under Satō's leadership, any overtures toward Beijing through the LDP's formal organizations would not be accepted. As a result, informal organizations and channels became more important.

Within the LDP, there were pro-Beijing forces and pro-Taipei forces that were not necessarily bound to formal organizations such as councils, divisions, and committees, nor to any one of the LDP's factions. The pro-Taipei forces included four groups. The first was the Asian Problems Study Group (hereafter the Asian Group). It was formed in December 1964 to examine the government's China policy. This interfactional group was known by its conservative members, such as Okinori Kaya, Nobusuke Kishi, Mitsujirō Ishii, and Naka Funada (Fukui 1970: 251–254). The second group formed that same year was the Asian Parliamentary Union, an anticommunist organization sponsored by the Asian Group. The third was Nikka Kyōryoku Iinkai (Japan-Taiwan Cooperation Committee) which was established in 1957; it later joined the Asian Group. The fourth group was the Sōshinkai (the Plain-Heart Association). It consisted of right-wing members of the LDP (Fukui 1970: 223–226, 253–254). These groups had a sizable overlapping membership and were known as the Taiwan lobby. Their leader was Nobusuke Kishi, a former prime minister and a senior statesman. For a long time the Taiwan lobby maintained a majority within PARC and was supported by the ruling party's mainstream. The Asian Group's study sessions were usually held once every two weeks. Satō's pro-Taiwan stand was significantly influenced by these groups.

The pro-Beijing informal intraparty groups started their activities in 1960 by organizing themselves into the China Problem Study Group and Study Group for the Improvement of Japan-China Relations. Several months later in the same year, these two groups merged into a single group named the Japan-China Problem Study Group. The mainstream LDP leaders (normally factional leaders who occupied top positions within the party) were apparently not happy with these informal activities, insisting that debate on the China issue "should take place within the official Investigation Committee on Foreign Affairs." The senior leaders put pressure on the pro-Beijing forces to end their activities (Fukui 1970: 250).

But the pro-Beijing groups resumed their activities four years later by establishing the Afro-Asian Problems Study Group (hereafter the Afro-Asian Group) in January 1965. It originally had 104 members, most of them from nonmainstream factions. The members of the Afro-Asian Group, though neither socialist nor communist, put great emphasis on promoting normalization of relations with the PRC. There were two groups within the Afro-Asian Group. The first was led by Kenzō Matsumura, who was the founding father (along with China's Liao Chengzhi) of the pro-normalization Sino-Japanese trade organization known as Memorandum Trade (see Chapter 4). The second was headed by former Prime Minister Tanzan Ishibashi, who was prominent in promoting trade relations with China known as "friendship trade" and was president of the Japan Council for the Promotion of International Trade (JCPIT). After these elder leaders retired, the leadership was taken over by younger Diet members. The first group was led by Yoshimi Furui and Seiichi Tagawa, and the second by Tokuma Utsunomiya, vice-president of JCPIT.[17]

None of these pro-Taipei or pro-Beijing groups such as the Asian Group or the Afro-Asian Group belonged to formal organizations or factions within the LDP. Rather, their members were from cross-sections of the party, accounting for about half of the total LDP members. The other members remained more or less uncommitted in their attitudes toward the China issue. This "neutral group" included such senior leaders as Ichirō Kōno, Hayato Ikeda, Eisaku Satō, Masayoshi Ōhira, Hirohide Ishida, and Etsusaburō Shiina. All the activities of the informal groups were "outside the official organ and, therefore, beyond the party leaders' direct control" (Fukui 1970: 254–260).

The most well-known informal organizations in the LDP are its factions (Hrebenar 1986: 27), which are called "parties within a party" (Thayer 1969: 305). Although these factions are known for a mixture of personal bonds and mutual benefit rather than for ideology or common policy positions, they often freely express their opinions on certain policy issues (Satō and Matsuzaki 1986: 52–77).

During the last year of the Satō administration in 1972, leaders of all major LDP factions cast their eyes on the position of party president/prime minister. The China issue became one of the "hot topics" for all contenders. Chiefs of powerful factions such as Kakuei Tanaka, Masayoshi Ōhira, Aiichirō Fujiyama, Takeo Miki, and Yasuhiro Nakasone became dissatisfied with Satō's pro-Taiwan orientation. They openly called for speeding up the process of normalization with China (Langdon 1978: 403–415).

Kakuei Tanaka and Takeo Fukuda were the two front runners for the premiership. Although both were close to Satō, they were rivals. Fukuda tried to show that he was able to handle the China issue by giving a statement before a Diet Foreign Affairs Committee meeting, that the Japanese government would support the PRC's three political principles for normalizing relations. One the other hand, Fukuda maintained close connections with the pro-Taiwan force, which made him somewhat ambiguous as to the directions of his China policy.

By contrast, Tanaka's positive posture toward rapprochement with Beijing was more straightforward. In June 1972 Tanaka stated that to achieve normalization of relations with the PRC Japan should "apologize from our hearts, first of all, for having caused trouble on the Chinese continent during World War II." On another occasion, Tanaka put forth this action of apology as "the precondition for rapprochement with China."[18]

During the last stage of the campaign for the premiership, every candidate made clear his determination to pursue a solution to the China issue. Besides the front runners Tanaka and Fukuda, two other leading candidates, Masayoshi Ōhira and Takeo Miki, also made strong postures toward rapprochement. Both Ōhira and Miki claimed that it was time for a new Japanese prime minister to visit China.

After a series of political maneuvers, Tanaka successfully made an alliance with Ōhira and Miki. At the three-faction meeting concluding the alliance that would effectively prevent Fukuda from winning, the three leaders reached a consensus on a new China policy: "Normalization of Japan-China relations is now the demand of the entire nation. We will enter into negotiations [with Beijing] with a view to concluding a peace treaty with the People's Republic of China through contacts between the two governments."[19] Tanaka won a clear victory over Fukuda by a vote of 282 to 190 on July 5, 1972, at the LDP's presidential election (Fukui 1977: 71). The door was opened for negotiations with Beijing.

The new China policy was formed neither by the governmental bureaucracy nor by the LDP's formal organizations. Rather, it was informally decided through a coalition of three faction leaders, Tanaka, Ōhira, and Miki. "Election politics" played a major role in this coalition. While Ōhira and Miki promoted normalization because of their beliefs as well as out of a need for political maneuver, Tanaka was concerned about the China issue only as it related to a strong popular demand and thus to his election campaign. Tanaka decided to join in a coalition to politically "maintain face" for Miki and Ōhira who made pledges of a new China policy, and at the same time bolster his chance for winning the election. In doing so, Tanaka came out as the leader in normalizing relations with China.

With a clear victory at hand, Tanaka started to mobilize both formal and informal organizations within the LDP to work on normalization issues. Other than PARC's formally established seventeen policy divisions, there were also a large number of ad hoc, issue-oriented special committees. With regard to the issue of normalization, for example, there was a special committee under PARC called the Subcommittee on the China Problem. These less formal special committees became the main battlefield of interparty debates and had a decisive influence over the party's policy.

A week after Tanaka's inauguration as prime minister, the LDP decided to upgrade the Subcommittee on the China Problem and changed its name to the Council for the Normalization of Japan-China Diplomatic Relations. The new council would be directly responsible to Party President Tanaka, bypassing regular policymaking organs, that is, the PARC and the Executive Council. On July 24, 1972, when its first meeting was held, the Normalization Council had a membership of 249 LDP Diet members. At this meeting, Zentarō Kosaka, chairman of the Council, announced that by September 10 the Council would work out a consensus in support of the party and the government's rapprochement policy with China.[20] After this "deadline," the LDP party leaders could have a free hand in forming a new China policy, although the pro-Taiwan groups might still oppose the pro-normalization movement. The council's decision clearly gave the Tanaka pro-normalization campaign the green light.

Three characteristics can be attributed to the internal maneuvers of the LDP during this period. First, informal organizations like internal factions and study groups were very active in the policymaking process. Once the coalition of the Tanaka-Ōhira-Miki factions came to power, its new China policy became the mainstream policy of the party. Second, these coalitions and groups were often issue-oriented and temporarily organized together. Both the Asian Group and the Afro-Asian Group were deeply involved in the China issue. One seldom heard of their activities after the Japan-China rapprochement. Third, these informal organizations provided forums for interparty deliberation over controversial issues. As Jōji Watanuki points out, these forums allowed opposing interests within the LDP an opportunity to freely express views prior to making formal party decisions (1977: 20).

THE BUREAUCRACY: OFFICIAL AND UNOFFICIAL STANCES

Generally speaking, both the initiation and the implementation of foreign policy are under the jurisdiction of the Ministry of Foreign Affairs (MOFA). However, when a major controversial issue such as the normalization of relations with China arises, the role of the Foreign Ministry bureaucrats is marginal. As an official from the Asian Affairs Bureau of MOFA stated, the China policy "will be decided by the cabinet, not by the Foreign Ministry."[21] This statement should be explained.

The bureaucracy, as Haruhiro Fukui argues, "is constitutionally subordinate to the Diet. In theory, and to a large extent in practice, bureaucrats are subordinate to politicians, both individually and collectively."[22] MOFA is particularly weak in terms of domestic political power. According to Yukio Nakamaru, a staff member of the LDP's Foreign Affairs Division, it is common practice for high-ranking MOFA bureaucrats, normally at the level of bureau chiefs, to come to LDP Headquarters once or twice a week to "report" on the ministry's foreign policy deliberation process. In highly sensitive cases, this kind of party-government consultation is more frequent, sometimes as often as several times a day, through face-to-face discussions or telephone conversations.[23]

Because of the complex nature of foreign policy, which frequently involves both international and domestic factors, political leaders often use information and advice from sources other than MOFA and disregard recommendations from officials of that ministry. In addition, the role of Foreign Ministry bureaucrats is constrained by the political nature of foreign policy. Many important foreign policy decisions are made primarily by political leaders, namely, the LDP's top leaders and its PARC. MOFA bureaucrats made decisions mainly on routine and noncontroversial issues. The position of MOFA was also often weakened by the bitter interministry dispute over jurisdiction and policy issues with other ministries, notably the Ministry of International Trade and Industry (MITI).

In any bureaucratic setting, we can often see differences between official and unofficial stances. Official stances follow formal rules and procedures, whereas unofficial stances are often seen in informal activities and channels. These two different stances are not necessarily always in conflict; actually, they can sometimes complement one another. In other words, unofficial stances may be used as either a leeway for convenience or as a trial run for future changes.

During the Satō period, Foreign Ministry bureaucrats carefully maintained the official line set by political leaders with regard to the China policy. They left the debate on the issue to the LDP and followed its lead. In the 1969 edition of the Foreign Affairs Blue Book, the statement on the China issue says: "Japan will maintain friendly relations with the Republic of China," and "Peace and security in the Taiwan area will be an important factor for the security of Japan" (Ijiri 1987: 134; MOFA 1970: 65–66).

At the beginning of 1970, Satō made some positive remarks about China after the U.S.-China Warsaw talks (the only open channel between the two countries at that time) were restored. MOFA officials began steps to approach Chinese diplomats abroad. When government leaders returned to their original position, after Taipei made a strong protest, MOFA stopped actions immediately and labeled those approaches "unintended and accidental."[24] These actions demonstrate that MOFA bureaucrats strictly followed the official line of the government leaders and were not able to bypass the official position.

MOFA also used a "wait-and-see" policy to follow official lines. When the international environment changes to a more favorable position of accepting China into the United Nations in the fall of 1970, many MOFA officials believed it was necessary to reexamine China policy. However, MOFA decided to wait until after the U.N. vote and after Japan's political leaders had set a clear direction on China policy.

Unofficial stances were often expressed in heated internal debates among Foreign Ministry bureaucrats. Internal debates were mainly at the bureau level. Major MOFA bureaus that were involved in the China question were the Asian Affairs Bureau, the United Nations Bureau, the American Affairs Bureau, the Economic Affairs Bureau, and the Treaties Bureau. At the early stage, most of these bureaus were not enthusiastic about normalizing relations with the PRC. They either felt Japan's first priority was maintaining good relations with the United States, and therefore it was essential to follow the American direction (the United Nations Bureau and the American Affairs Bureau); or they assumed that the Japan-China trade was not as prosperous as many businessmen expected (the Economic Affairs Bureau) and that it was inappropriate to cut off official relations with Taiwan (the Treaties Bureau), and therefore rapprochement was not a priority. A few MOFA leaders were well aware of the potential Sino-Japanese rivalry for regional leadership, and therefore were reluctant to promote better relations. Former Foreign Minister Etsusaburō Shiina, for example, said in 1965, "competition [with China] for Asia has already begun."[25]

The opposite position, which represented an unofficial view, was held by the Asian Affairs Bureau (AAB). The AAB strongly advocated a new China policy that would give up a position of two Chinas on the basis that there was no country that could maintain embassies in both Beijing and Taipei. With a belief that China would soon be accepted into the United Nations, the AAB also urged that Japan not co-sponsor with the United States the "important issue resolution."[26] In addition, there was a general recognition within Japan that a new "independent" foreign policy was needed (D. Hellmann 1974: 168) and that it was not necessary for Japan to follow every step the United States would take. However, this pro-normalization view was held by a minority in MOFA and was considered an impractical stance at that time.

Among the government bureaucrats, the Ministry of International Trade and Industry (MITI) was the strongest challenger to MOFA's official stance. One dispute between the two ministries was over whether Export-Import Bank loans should be granted to finance plant exports to the PRC. MOFA insisted that Japan should not grant such loans used for PRC-related trade, because this was not in line with Japan's official policy of maintaining good relations with Taiwan.

In contrast, MITI was strongly in favor of granting such loans. According to the director of the Japanese External Trade Organization (JETRO) Yoshihei Hara, MITI's concern was that China's markets would be penetrated by other countries, especially Western European countries (West Germany and France, for example), if Japan did not act quickly. MITI officials, under instructions from then Minister Kiichi Miyazawa, had in fact already examined a series of projects for loans on trade with China from the Export-Import Bank.[27]

A politically oriented MOFA was more conservative than the economically oriented MITI and Ministry of Finance (MOF). After the Nixon Shock, MOFA had few deliberations on a new concrete China policy, because the prime minister and top politicians had not changed their positions on this issue. MITI and MOF acted differently, however. Both ministries made positive moves in favor of improving relations with China. In July 1971 Tanaka, then minister of MITI, approved a plan for Export-Import Bank and commercial bank loans to be extended to PRC-related trade on a case-by-case basis. In addition, MITI officials signaled leaders of the business community to encourage politicians to normalize relations with China as soon as possible.[28] Around the same time, MOF moved one step closer to relaxation of trade barriers with China by announcing a reduction of the tariff rate on Chinese imports to the General Agreement on Tariffs and Trade (GATT) standard.[29] Despite pressures from these ministries, Foreign Ministry bureaucrats continued to stress that "everything is meaningless unless Prime Minister Satō comes to a decision on the government's basic policy line."[30]

The official and unofficial actions of the government bureaucracy can also be seen as a combination of rigidity and flexibility in MOFA's behavior. Even though MOFA had a reputation of being politically conservative, on some occasions it appeared more flexible than other ministries. In the 1950s and 1960s, for example, MOFA was at odds with the Ministry of Justice (MOJ). The disputes between the two ministries centered on whether Japan should allow visits of Chinese delegations, headed by such important communist leaders as Peng Zhen (politburo member) and Liu Ningyi (central committee secretary), to attend either international conferences or Japanese Communist party conventions in Japan. On these issues, MOFA bureaucrats often presented more flexible views than their MOJ counterparts.[31]

The official China policy was partly due to Japan's gratitude to Chiang Kai-shek for his postwar statement and policy that China would not seek revenge against Japanese soldiers but would treat them with mercy. Therefore, Japan should keep "international faith" with the Chiang-led Taipei government. Because of this consideration, MOFA bureaucrats made every effort to save Taipei's seat in the United Nations. MOFA bureaucrats were relieved after the reverse important question resolution was defeated in the U.N. General Assembly vote on October 25, 1971, because they no longer felt obligated to Taipei and promptly began efforts to promote relations with the PRC. For instance, Administrative Vice Foreign Minister Shinsaku Hogen, a main advocate of Japan's co-sponsorship of the reverse important issue resolution, became one of the most powerful promoters of Japan-China normalization after China joined the United Nations and Prime Minister Tanaka took office.

One of Tanaka's first acts as prime minister was to inform Hogen that he was determined to support Japan-China rapprochement. This clear message gave

MOFA the go-ahead to prepare a drastic change of direction in its China policy. Soon after, the Asian Affairs Bureau, a vanguard of pro-normalization forces in MOFA, established a cooperative relationship with the new leadership of Tanaka and Ōhira (who became foreign minister) in terms of China policy, and began working against the LDP's pro-Taiwan forces. Other bureaus, such as the Treaties Bureau, then began to favor this new direction. The AAB's minority position gradually evolved to a majority position, and its previously unofficial stance became official policy.

Finally, MOFA established a task force, the Council for China Policy, made up of fifteen members, including Vice Foreign Minister Shinsaku Hogen and other high-ranking officials. The four key individuals within the Council were Asian Affairs Bureau Director Kenzō Yoshida, Treaties Bureau Director Masuo Takashima, China Division Head Hiroshi Hashimoto, and Treaties Division Head Shōichi Kuriyama. On August 15, 1971, the task force worked out its basic position on Taiwan and submitted it to the LDP's Normalization Council. This position included two points: (1) no country could maintain diplomatic relations with both the PRC and the Taiwan government at the same time; and (2) normalization of diplomatic relations between Japan and China did not mean the automatic termination of the Japan-Taiwan Peace Treaty. The first point reflected MOFA's readiness to take any action necessary to set up formal diplomatic relations with the PRC, including termination of its diplomatic relations with Taipei. The second point indicated that Foreign Ministry bureaucrats were more concerned with the legalistic aspects of the China issue than with international and domestic political implications.[32]

Eleven months later, Foreign Minister Ōhira openly rejected the second point of the MOFA bureaucrats by making it clear that when diplomatic relations with the People's Republic of China were established, the peace treaty with Taiwan would automatically cease to be valid.[33] This moved Japan one step closer to normalization.

"DUCK DIPLOMACY"

The actions of those who work behind-the-scenes in informal diplomatic negotiations, or what is termed *kuromaku* here, have also been called informal channels as a research topic.[34] Informal political actors and organizations indeed played a large part in the process of Japan-China rapprochement.

Japan's informal diplomacy toward China can be traced back to as early as the 1950s. According to Heishirō Ogawa, Japan's first ambassador to Beijing, in the early 1950s Japan's official position was to prohibit its citizens from visiting "Red China." The Ministry of Foreign Affairs was extremely unhappy with the illegal visit to China by three opposition party Diet members in 1952. Nevertheless, MOFA gradually relaxed its rules and developed a policy known as *seikei bunri* (differentiation of economic from political activities), which was initially put forward by Ogawa himself. Under *seikei bunri*, any Japanese, except governmental officials, could go to to China without having to obtain a permit from MOFA.[35] This practice greatly facilitated nonpolitical contact, especially in the economic arena such as with the Memorandum Trade Agreements of the 1960s (see Chapter 2).[36]

Under the Satō administration, little progress was made toward normalizing relations with China. Nevertheless, it would be wrong to say that Satō did nothing to explore possibilities for a new China policy. For a better understanding of the Japanese foreign policymaking process, we should examine Satō's informal diplomacy, or *ahiru gaikō* (duck diplomacy). The analogy of a duck was used because just as a duck may appear to look calm above water, it busily uses its feet under water (Iwanaga 1985: 174; and C. Lee 1976: 106).

Satō and other top leaders under his administration seriously considered sending messages to the Beijing government regarding normalization negotiations by using duck diplomacy. It is still an open question as to how many people were involved and what kind of actions actually took place, but we can now name at least five *ahiru* in Satō's duck diplomacy. They were LDP Secretary General Shigeru Hori, Tokyo Governor Ryōkichi Minobe, Japanese Consul General in Hong Kong Akira Okada, the Japan-China Memorandum Trade Office Director Yaeji Watanabe, and pro-Beijing LDP Diet member Seiichi Tagawa (Ijiri 1987: 107; Tagawa 1972: 24–25).

After the Nixon Shock and the entry of the PRC into the United Nations, LDP's Secretary General Shigeru Hori was eager to find informal channels of communication with China to prepare for normalization negotiations. He first contacted pro-Beijing Diet member Seiichi Tagawa and asked him to communicate with Beijing. After receiving oral assurance of a one-China position from Hori, Tagawa wrote to Wang Guoquan, vice-chairman of the China-Japan Friendship Association, informing him of Hori's strong desire to visit China. In early October 1971, Tagawa talked about Hori's intention in a telephone conversation with a Chinese official working at the China-Japan Memorandum Trade Tokyo office. The Chinese official quickly received approval from China to contact Hori. Through Tagawa's arrangements, the trade official and a Chinese journalist held a two-and-a-half-hour secret meeting with Hori (Tagawa 1983: 128–136).

In December 1971, Tagawa and Yaeji Watanabe visited Beijing with a memorandum trade delegation and tried to clarify Japan's position to his Chinese counterparts, including Wang Guoquan, on a wide range of topics, such as the Taiwan issue and the territorial dispute over the islands of Diaoyu (or "Senkaku" as named by the Japanese) (Tagawa 1973: 303–334).

At almost the same time, the Satō administration opened up another channel. Hori asked Tokyo Governor Minobe of the Japan Socialist Party, who was about to visit Beijing in mid-October, to carry his personal letter to Zhou Enlai. This "personal letter" was the result of consultations with both Satō and Ōhira. On the one hand, the letter claimed that "The People's Republic of China is a government representing China," and stated that Hori hoped to visit Beijing in preparation for normalization. On the other hand, it indicated that Taiwan was a "territory of Chinese people." The ambiguity of the letter was not to Zhou Enlai's liking. Zhou criticized the letter as a deception, because of the phrase "territory of Chinese people," which might be construed as supportive of a Taiwan independence movement, instead of "territory of China."[37] The Chinese leaders were also unhappy about Satō's decision to co-sponsor, with the United States, the pro-Taiwan resolution at the United Nations. Zhou Enlai rejected the Satō-Hori overture and said China would not consider governmental negotiations "as long as Satō was the leader of the Japanese government." Therefore, Hori failed to make a breakthrough.[38] After the Hori letter incident was publicized, the Foreign Ministry bureaucrats were upset and embarrassed for not being informed of the Satō-Hori move. They requested a clarification of the China policy from leading politicians.

The case of Akira Okada, the consul general in Hong Kong, was a different story. Okada was a "dissident" within the Foreign Ministry in terms of China policy. He was one of the few who very early on predicted the possibility of a Sino-American rapprochement when the majority opinion within MOFA was that "it is impossible that the Americans would go over our heads in opening talks with the Chinese." Even after the Nixon Shock, MOFA bureaucrats maintained the majority position. On September 1, 1971, at the Asia-Pacific region Ambassadorial Conference, MOFA bureaucrats reached a "unified view" that it would be premature to take an active approach toward normalization talks with the PRC. Okada, representing the minority view at the conference, said he would like to openly oppose (which was unusually bold within the Japanese bureaucratic world) this "unified view," and hoped that his opinion on China policy would be communicated to the government leaders (Ijiri 1987: 148–149 and Okada 1983: 147).

Okada's dissident opinion was referred to LDP's Secretary General Hori by a *Sankei Shimbun* reporter. Hori quickly arranged to meet Okada for two hours to hear Okada's proposals regarding the China policy. Then Hori made arrangements for Okada to meet Prime Minister Satō. On September 11, at the prime minister's office, Satō listened to Okada's views and then disclosed his own position that "Taiwan is a province of China," and Japan would not block China's entry to the United Nations. Satō also made it clear that he would send the foreign minister or the secretary general to visit China. However, Satō expressed reservations about immediately breaking ties with Taiwan. Satō gave Okada a special assignment to visit Beijing to communicate the prime minister's message to the Chinese. Satō also asked Okada to keep his assignment secret, even from Foreign Ministry colleagues, and to report directly to him or Secretary General Hori (Ijiri 1987: 149–150 and Okada 1983: 150–151).

Since Okada had previously lived in both Hong Kong and Beijing, he had many Chinese friends, including high-ranking officials. Through these connections, Okada did pass Satō's message on to Chinese leaders including Premier Zhou Enlai and top Japan-hand Liao Chengzhi who was a member of the Party

Central Committee and the Chinese cabinet. Nevertheless, like the Hori letter, Okada's duck diplomacy did not bring results, simply because of the previous "unfriendly actions" by the Satō government, such as its pro-Taiwan position in the United Nations. Again, Foreign Ministry bureaucrats were kept unaware of this behind-the-scenes action. After the failure of Satō's duck diplomacy, further overtures toward normalization had to wait until the next administration.

Although Satō's duck diplomacy was not successful, it had significant implications: Informal actors and channels were important in both Japanese thinking and Japanese behavior, especially when facing issues that were controversial. New directions could be explored while maintaining official and formal policies on the surface. At the same time, numerous channels for different opinions were made available within and outside of the ruling party/bureaucracy apparatus as indicated by the case of Okada.

BEIJING'S STRATEGY

Informal political actors and organizations are so important in Japan that they should not be ignored. At the same time, since they are informal, it is important to identify their background and real intent. The important thing is "to learn, to know, and to play the game." And China played it well.

At various stages the PRC leaders, particularly Premier Zhou Enlai, skillfully used a strategy of insisting on certain principles, such as the three principles for normalization and the four conditions for trade,[39] to enlarge Japan's pro-Beijing forces. This effort to create a China bandwagon phenomenon was known as people's diplomacy, which applied pressure to Japan through the cooperation of the Japanese people. The strategy was especially effective with opposition parties and the business community. Besides these tactics, China had more direct ways by which to influence Japanese politics. As A. Doak Barnett (1977: 126) suggested, although the Japanese had had no direct impact on politics within China since 1949, the Chinese involved themselves "deeply in Japanese domestic politics."

Before 1971 China constantly criticized the "revival of Japanese militarism." After the 1969 Satō-Nixon Joint Communique, Zhou Enlai accused the Satō government of attempting to step up militarism and realize its old dream of a "Greater East Asia Co-prosperity Sphere."[40] In April 1971, Zhou visited Pyongyang and issued the China-North Korea Joint Statement, which claimed that Japanese militarism was already revived.

In the prevailing international situation marked by competition and hostility between the United States and the Soviet Union, however, Mao Zedong developed the idea that Japan and West Europe should be regarded as an intermediate zone between the revolutionary forces and the two reactionary superpowers. It became necessary for China to cultivate friendly relations with these countries. The need for economic development was also a catalyst for China to seek closer relations with Japan. After Nixon's visit, vigorous criticism of Japanese militarism in the Chinese press gradually diminished and then completely disappeared after Tanaka had become prime minister. A new campaign calling for Sino-Japanese friendship and normalization of relations was launched. Chinese leaders believed that the political transition from Satō to Tanaka presented the best opportunity for China to conduct direct contacts with the Japanese government.

Allen Whiting (1989: 193–196) pointed out that positive and negative images of Japan and the Japanese coexisted in official Chinese statements and media at that time. Since the state controlled virtually all the propaganda tools (newspapers, books, films, and other media) in China, Japan's image in China could be manipulated by the Chinese government corresponding to the normalization steps between the two countries.

China's campaign for friendship encompassed three routes. The first route used Zhou's conditions for selecting "friendly firms" and promoting economic rapprochement prior to political rapprochement. The second route carried out propaganda in the Chinese news media and worked hard at gaining support from the Japanese news media. According to Seiichi Tagawa, an agreement to an exchange of reporters between the two countries was concluded in the negotiation on memorandum trade in 1968, based on the understanding that China's three political principles would be a guideline. Unless a Japanese newspaper signed a pledge to abide by the three principles, Japan could not dispatch a correspondent to China. Japanese reporters who violated these principles were either expelled from China (*Mainichi, Sankei, Yomiuri*, and *Nishi Nippon* dailies), denied reentry into China (NHK, Japan Broadcasting Corporation), or arrested on charges of espionage activities (*Nihon Keizai*). These strict rules in Beijing and intense competition among the Japanese newspapers subsequently forced the Japanese press to practice self-restraint in editing and writing articles on the China issue (Miyoshi and Etō 1972).

The third route sent China's informal envoys, who were China's diplomatic Japan-hands (but without official status when visiting Japan), to go to Japan on various crucial occasions. These were the so-called first Wang whirlwind, second Wang whirlwind, and Sun whirlwind, each of which created an enormous impact on the process of rapprochement.

The first Wang whirlwind referred to the visit of Wang Xiaoyun in March-April 1971. Wang visited Japan as deputy head of the Chinese ping-pong team at the thirty-first World Table Tennis Championship in Nagoya without using his official position as deputy secretary-general of the China-Japan Friendship Association and director of the Chinese People's Association for Friendship with Foreign Countries. Wang's one-month visit proved fruitful. He held a series of meetings with the LDP's anti-Satō leaders such as Takeo Miki, and with leaders of opposition parties (the JSP Chairman Tomomi Narita in Tokyo and the Kōmeitō [CGP] Chairman Yoshikatsu Takeiri in Fukuoka). The highlight of his visit was a meeting held in Tokyo with the business organization leaders from Keizai Dōyūkai, Keidanren, and Nikkeiren. It was the first time business community leaders met with a high-ranking Chinese official. After the meeting, Dōyūkai President Kazutaka Kikawada told the press that "improvement of Japan-China relations is a national issue in the 1970s."[41]

Four months later, Wang Guoquan made a followup visit known as the second Wang whirlwind on the occasion of the funeral of Kenzō Matsumura, a longtime pro-Beijing LDP leader and active promoter of Japan-China trade. Wang was vice-president of the China-Japan Friendship Association and a veteran Chinese diplomat. During his one-week stay, he contacted various political and economic leaders. The impact of this visit was particularly notable among business leaders. Some previously pro-Taiwan leaders, such as the chairman of the Board of the Shin Nihon Seitetsu (Japan's largest steel company) Shigeo Nagano, came to announce acceptance of Zhou's four conditions and called for improvement in Japan-China relations. These meetings were in opposition to the official stance of the Japanese government at the time. Prime Minister Satō was reportedly angry about the quick switch in attitude among *zaikai* (the business community) leaders, many of whom had close relations with him (Ogata 1977: 195).

During the 1971–72 period, China made several important conciliatory overtures toward Japan in order to accelerate the normalization process. In May 1972 Zhou Enlai received an opposition party delegation from Japan and announced that China was willing to waive its claim of war reparations against Japan estimated at $50 billion; that the Japan-U.S. Security Treaty and the Satō-Nixon Joint Communique of 1969 would no longer be regarded as an obstacle for normalization between the two countries; and that a peace treaty between China and Japan (which China had long proposed as a replacement of the Japan-Taiwan peace treaty) would not be insisted on. These announcements showed the flexibility of the Chinese leaders and encouraged the new Tanaka-Ōhira leadership to make a decisive move toward normalization.

The Sun whirlwind refers to the visit of a Chinese delegation led by Sun Pinghua in August 1972. Sun's official position was deputy secretary-general of the China-Japan Friendship Association, but during his visit to Japan he was head of the Shanghai Dance Drama Troupe. After the Tanaka administration was inaugurated in July 1972, both Japan and China speeded up the process for rapprochement. Sun's visit stimulated greater "China fever" among the Japanese. Many important political and business leaders wanted to confer with the Chinese officials. Most important was an official invitation which Sun conveyed to Foreign Minister Ōhira from Foreign Minister Ji Pengfei stating that "Premier Zhou Enlai welcomes and invites Prime Minister Kakuei Tanaka to visit China."[42] Tanaka warmly received Sun and the Chinese dancers and accepted Zhou's invitation.

Thus, this historic invitation from China's premier to Japan's prime minister was the result of a series of informal maneuvers between the two countries, conveyed through an informal channel. As a master of informal practice, Japan fully understood the official implications behind the unofficial status of the Chinese dance group.

NOTES

1. The 1972 Sino-Japanese rapprochement, as a well-known diplomatic event, has been one of the most thoroughly researched cases conducted by a number of scholars. In addition to my own research and interviews in Japan, this chapter has also depended on the published books or articles of Haruhiro Fukui (1970 and 1977), Sadako Ogata (1977 and 1988), and Chae-Jin Lee (1976) in terms of original materials. In addition, it benefited particularly from Hidenori Ijiri's dissertation (University of California at Berkeley, 1987) entitled "The Politics of Japan's Decision to Normalize Relations with China, 1969–72." A number of original sources in this case study are quoted from the works of Ijiri as well as Fukui, Ogata, and Lee. While acknowledging the valuable help from the above-mentioned works, I nevertheless bear all responsibility for conclusions based on this and other case studies.

2. The Japanese dictionary lists two explanations for *kuromaku*: (1) A black veil that is used in Japanese traditional play, such as *kabuki* or *ningyo jōruri*, for the purpose of hiding behind the scenes; and (2) people who have real influence or power but never show their movement in public (for example, *kuromaku* in politics). See Kyosuke Kindaichi, ed., *Shin meikai kokugo jiten* [New Japanese Dictionary], 2nd ed. (Tokyo: Sanseido, 1974). Also Hidetoshi Kenbo, ed., *Sanseidō kokugo jiten* [Sanseido Japanese Dictionary], 3rd ed. (Tokyo: Sanseido, 1982).

3. When I conducted interviews in Japan, I heard this argument many times from scholars, bureaucrats, and politicians alike. Among those expressing this view were Heishirō Ogawa, the first Japanese ambassador to Beijing (interviewed on February 13, 1986); Shinkichi Etō, then professor of Chinese politics and international relations at Aoyama University (February 6, 1986); and Ichirō Watanabe, a Kōmeitō Diet member (May 29, 1986).

4. Interview with Haruo Okada, February 27, 1986, Tokyo.

5. Interview with Seiichi Tagawa, March 7, 1986, Tokyo.

6. Interview with Mikio Katō, associate managing director of the International House of Japan, April 17, 1986, Tokyo.

7. For detailed accounts, see C. Lee (1976: 83–106) and H. Ijiri (1987: 298–302).

8. See *Peking Review*, April 10, 1970, p. 5; see also C. Lee (1976: 165).

9. See, for example, Lin Biao's *Renmin Zhanzheng Shengli Wansui* [Long live the victory of people's war] (1965).

10. Interview with Seiichi Tagawa, March 7, 1986, Tokyo.

11. *Peking Review*, September 14, 1960, pp. 25–26; also see Fukui (1970: 231).

12. For detailed accounts on LDP's internal structure and organizations, see Satō and Matsuzaki (1986: 184–189), and Murakawa (1989: 34–42).

13. *Department of State Bulletin*, December 15, 1969, pp. 555–558.

14. Editorial, *Renmin Ribao*, November 28, 1969; also see *Peking Review*, November 28, 1969, pp. 28, 30.

15. For detailed accounts, see C. Lee (1976: 101–104).

16. *Renmin Ribao*, September 26, 1971.

17. For more detailed accounts of the pro-Beijing and pro-Taipei forces, see Lee (1976), Fukui (1970), and Ijiri (1987).

18. *Asahi shimbun*, June 25, 1972; and Ijiri (1987: 129).

19. *Asahi shimbun*, July 3, 1972.

20. *Asahi shimbun*, July 24, 1972; also see Fukui (1977: 74–75) and Ijiri (1987: 216–221).

21. Interview with Michihiko Kunihiro, June 4, 1986, Tokyo. Kunihiro served as director of MOFA's China Division from 1973 to 1974, and was assistant vice minister of MOFA at the time of interview.

22. See Haruhiro Fukui, "Policy-Making in the Japanese Foreign Ministry," in *The Foreign Policy of Modern Japan*, ed. by Robert Scalapino (Berkeley: University of California Press, 1977), p. 4.

23. Interview with Yukio Nakamaru, August 28, 1986, Tokyo.

24. *Asahi shimbun*, January 31, 1970.

25. *New York Times*, August 25, 1965. Also see Tsou, Najita, and Otake (1978: 404–405).

26. Interview with Michihiko Kunihiro, June 4, 1986, Tokyo.

27. Interview with Toshio Ōishi, March 6, 1986, Tokyo. Ōishi was deputy director of MITI's Trade Policy Bureau (1973–75); he was president of the Japan Overseas Development Corporation at the time of interview.

28. Interview with Yaeji Watanabe, June 27, 1986, Tokyo. After his retirement as MITI's assistant deputy minister in 1966, Watanabe became director of the Japan-China Memorandum Trade Office. Later, he served as president of the Japan-China Economic Association.

29. *Asahi shimbun*, July 30, 1971.

30. Interview with Michihiko Kunihiro, June 4, 1986, Tokyo.

31. Ibid.

32. For detailed accounts, see Fukui (1977: 84–90) and Ijiri (1987: 257–265).

33. *Japan Times*, July 17, 1972.

34. See a study entitled "Informal Channels in Japanese Diplomacy," in the Japan Association of International Relations, ed., *International Relations* (1983).

35. Interview with Heishirō Ogawa, March 8, 1986, Tokyo.

36. For detailed accounts of the Memorandum Trade Agreements, see Chapter 4.

37. *Asahi shimbun*, November 11, 1971; and Ijiri (1987: 108).

38. For further details, see C. Lee (1976: 106–107) and Ijiri (1987: 102–108).

39. The four conditions for Sino-Japanese trade were raised by Zhou Enlai in April 1970.

40. *Peking Review*, December 15, 1969, p. 11.

41. *Asahi shimbun*, August 25, 1971; also see C. Lee (1976: 171–172).

42. *Peking Review*, August 18, 1972, p. 3; also see C. Lee (1976: 177).

5

The Catalytic and Valve Functions

This chapter examines the *kuromaku* phenomenon and informal political actors and organizations in the policymaking process in Japan. Chapter 4 paid close attention to the bureaucracy/ruling party apparatus and international environment. Now let us look at the nonofficial groups of Japanese society, namely, the business community, the opposition parties, the intellectuals, and the news media. Again, the emphasis is on informal organizations and channels, but with special attention to their catalytic and valve functions. These functions can be understood in two ways: on the one hand, informal political organizations facilitate the policymaking process; on the other hand, they serve as a safety valve, preventing a situation from going in extreme directions.

THE BUSINESS COMMUNITY'S FREEDOM OF ACTION

Japan's business community has a tradition of maintaining a cooperative relationship with the government. The government bureaucracy has been able to perform a function of administrative guidance to influence the industry and business community, thereby fulfilling its "developmental state strategy" (Chalmers Johnson 1982). In most circumstances administrative guidance, rather than political directions, is used in economic development. In particular, when the central bureaucracy is in a state of confusion and uncertainty and is split within itself (such as in the case of the China policy prior to normalization), the business community enjoys a greater degree of "freedom of action" in its international activities. Such actions are usually economic-oriented, but sometimes they may serve as a catalyst for political decisions. We can clearly see this catalytic role of the business community in the normalization process.

There are three different groups within the Japanese business community. In her article "The Business Community and Japanese Foreign Policy," Sadako Ogata (1977: 175–176) distinguishes the three groups: *zaikai* (the leaders of major economic organizations), *gyōkai* (the industrial groups), and *kigyō* (the individual corporations). *Zaikai* are regarded as representative of big business interests including top economic organizations, such as Keidanren (the Japanese Federation of Economic Organizations); Nihon Shōkō Kaigisho or Nisshō (the Japanese Chamber of Commerce and Industry); Keizai Dōyukai (the Japanese Committee for Economic Development); and Nikkeiren (the Japanese Federation of Business Managers). *Gyōkai* literally means "industrial world" and represents specific industrial interests, which range from manufacturing to finance and commerce and from small to large-sized industries. Steel, electricity, and banking, for example, are considered among the most powerful *gyōkai* in the business society. A *gyōkai*'s function is to coordinate competitive interests among individual *kigyō*, or corporations, within their respective spheres.

Now let us examine how the Japanese business community contributed to the normalization process. As noted earlier, in April 1970 Zhou Enlai stipulated four conditions for Sino-Japanese trade. The Taiwan issue was the core consideration behind these conditions. China made it clear that it would not have trade relations with those Japanese firms that did business with Taiwan. This move could be regarded as part of an effort by the Chinese leaders to gain support from Japanese business circles and thus pave the road to rapprochement. Each Japanese company was now forced to make a choice in its business dealings: Beijing or Taipei. Given the consideration of China's huge untouched market and the economic interests involved, we can see a gradual change in the Japanese business community toward accepting Zhou's four conditions.

Gyōkai and *kigyō* were the first to respond to the four conditions, especially those businesses that already had considerable trade relations with the PRC. In 1970 steel was the top export item to the PRC with 41.8 percent of total exports, followed by chemical fertilizer which accounted for 20.8 percent. Next came the machinery industry with 12.4 percent and the textile industry with 4.5 percent of total exports, For example, Sumitomo Kagaku, one of the biggest producers of chemical fertilizer with more than half of its annual production exported to China, was criticized as a firm "supporting Taiwan and South Korea," prompting Beijing to cut off trade ties. Sumitomo Kagaku quickly announced acceptance of Zhou's conditions, and trade relations with China were restored. This induced other major chemical fertilizer companies to follow suit.[1] By doing so, the Japanese companies were able to maintain their near monopoly share of the China chemical fertilizer market.

By contrast, *zaikai* leaders and some big trading companies, such as Mitsui Bussan, Mitsubishi Shōji, Itochu, and Marubeni, which either had deep roots in Taiwan or maintained close relations with Prime Minister Satō, were much slower to join the China bandwagon. The slowness of the Satō administration and the hesitation of MOFA in formulating a China policy led to freedom of action by the business community, given the lack of clear official guidelines. During this period, big business as a group was by no means united (Fukui 1977: 93). Therefore, any firm had a free choice in whether to side with Beijing or with Taipei.

The individual *kigyō* with vested interests in the China market took the initiative to accept the four conditions. These decisions were made as a result of profit-making calculations, and were largely in line with the people-to-people diplomacy advocated by the Beijing government. Their economically oriented actions produced significant political influence. This influence became clearer after the *zaikai* leaders took action.

The first step was taken by Keizai Dōyūkai, one of the four biggest business organizations, and indicated the position of mainstream businessmen. In the spring of 1971, its president Kazutaka Kikawada announced that "the improvement of Sino-Japanese relations is a national goal [for Japan] in the 1970s." In July, Yoshihiro Inayama, president of Shin Nihon Seitetsu (Japan's biggest steel company), announced that the company would not participate in either the Japan-Taiwan Cooperation Committee or the Japan-South Korea Cooperation Committee meetings scheduled in late July. Soon after, Japan Air Lines (JAL) made a similar decision.

In September 1971 a large business mission from the Osaka-Kobe area (Kansai—a western part of Japan) visited Beijing. It was headed by Isamu Saeki, president of the Osaka Chamber of Commerce and Industry, and included virtually every business leader in the Kansai area. In a meeting with Zhou Enlai, Saeki confirmed his organization's pro-PRC stance and one-China policy. Zhou praised the Kansai business leaders and sharply criticized the Satō administration, saying that rapprochement was possible only "after Satō's resignation." In November a large-scale Tokyo business leaders' mission made a similar trip to Beijing. The interests of the top four business organizations were well represented. This mission was headed by Takeo Shōji, former president of Keizai Dōyūkai, and included President Kazutaka Kikawada of Dōyūkai, President Shigeo Nagano of Nisshō, Director General Hiroki Imasato of Nikkeiren, and Vice-President Yoshizane Iwasa of Keidanren. Upon return from Beijing, the mission stated that Japan should begin to normalize its relations with the PRC (Japan-China Economic Association 1975c: 163–169). Shortly thereafter, the three leading *zaikai* organizations, Keidanren, Nisshō, and Dōyūkai, decided to set up their own research groups on the China problem.

On June 14, 1972, Mitsubishi Shōji and Mitsui Bussan finally announced that they would accept the four conditions. The leaders of these giant companies felt they could no longer wait for formal normalization, believing that the Japanese government was moving too slowly in this direction. Their action marked a conclusion of the business community's two-year move toward acceptance of Zhou's four conditions.

Two other business missions visited Beijing prior to Tanaka's official visit in 1972. The first one was by the Mitsubishi group led by Wataru Tajitsu, chairman of the board of the Mitsubishi Bank, Chūjirō Fujino, president of Mitsubishi Shōji (trading company), and Shigekazu Koga, president of Mitsubishi Jūkōgyō (heavy industry). Before his departure to Beijing, Koga proudly claimed that "Any corporate leader who waits for the realization of normalized relations between Japan and China, instead of visiting China before the normalization, loses all qualification for being a corporate manager" (Ijiri 1987: 279; and Yamamura and Yamamoto 1972: 228). This visit received wide attention, for Mitsubishi had strong business ties with Taiwan and had long been deeply involved in military production, thereby contributing to China's perceptions that it was one of the major foundations for "Japanese militarism."[2]

The other business group to visit Beijing at the end of August was the second *zaikai* mission, headed by Yoshihiro Inayama, president of the Shin Nihon Seitetsu. There were thirteen major business leaders in the mission, including Tatsuzō Mizukami, adviser to Mitsui Bussan; Yoshizane Iwasa, chairman of the Board of the Fuji Bank; Kenichirō Komai, chairman of the Board of Hitachi Seisakujo; and Keisuke Idemitsu, chairman of the Board of Idemitsu Kōsan. The mission reached a trade agreement with the China Council for the Promotion of International Trade whereby (1) long-term contracts would be made to provide China with a stable supply of steel and fertilizer from Japan; (2) exports of natural fiber, mineral, and marine products to Japan would be planned; (3) oil products could be used as barter for China's payment to Japan; and (4) Sino-Japanese trade should be balanced in the future. The significance of this agreement was that economic rapprochement preceded diplomatic normalization.

The go-ahead actions of the business community with regard to Japanese-Chinese relations had a major impact both directly and indirectly on the LDP leaders and the bureaucracy. After the announcement of President Nixon's visit to China, for example, Vice-President Ryōichi Kawai of Keizai Dōyūkai gave a frank suggestion to the Satō government that Japan should closely follow Nixon's lead in opening the door to China (Ijiri 1987: 191). The Foreign Ministry felt increasing pressure from business leaders who were beginning to make political demands on the bureaucracy.

Japanese corporations are well known for conducting business in informal gatherings. Similar to the informal organizations within the ruling LDP discussed earlier, the business community has its own informal groups, specifically, various social entertainments and social clubs for networking with top politicians and bureaucrats.

On December 16, 1971, Prime Minister Satō was invited as an honorary guest to participate in the twenty-fifth meeting of Keidanren's board of counselors. Chairman Kogorō Uemura, who was a personal friend of Satō and a longtime pro-Taiwan advocate, expressed his position to the prime minister that Japan should normalize its relations with China as soon as possible, inasmuch as China had already been admitted to the United Nations.[3]

Business leaders became increasingly impatient with the slow pace of the Satō administration's China policy. Many of them even advocated an early

rapprochement with the PRC at the expense of formal diplomatic relations with
Taiwan. In the spring of 1972, just before Tanaka became prime minister, top
zaikai leaders organized Getsuyō-kai (the Monday Association) to support the
future prime minister. Tanaka met with this group of business leaders every
month to discuss various issues over dinner. It was believed that the business
community was ready to approve anyone as the new prime minister who could
open the door to China.[4]

The pro-normalization movement of powerful business leaders pressed politicians to make up their minds. MITI minister Yasuhiro Nakasone went so far as
to ask Yoshihiro Inayama, who was scheduled to head the second zaikai mission
to China, to convey a clear and concrete message to their Chinese counterparts
that Japan was ready for economic cooperation with China. In particular, Japan
was interested in participating in the development of the undersea oil-fields of
Bohai. After Tanaka's inauguration, "China fever" in the business community
reached a peak. Before the Mitsubishi group left for China, its leaders paid a
visit to Tanaka. Tanaka was reportedly happy with the upcoming mission to
China, saying, "When the politically influential Mitsubishi moves, it certainly
makes things easier for us politicians" (Ijiri 1987: 279–280; and Yamamura and
Yamamoto 1972: 16).

Compared to the active involvement of top politicians and government bureaucrats, the role played by the business community in the process of Sino-Japanese
rapprochement seemed more indirect and less dramatic. But considering the
broad social base of the business community and its close ties with top political
and governmental leaders, we can discern a catalytic function and the powerful
influence it had on both politicians and bureaucrats. It was clear that a de
facto economic rapprochement between China and Japan preceded diplomatic
negotiations. In this sense, the informal actions of the business community laid
a foundation for the formal political rapprochement later.

THE OPPOSITION PARTIES' *YATŌ GAIKŌ*

Many informal political institutions from the ruling party/bureaucracy apparatus, such as the informal duck diplomacy used by the Satō administration, have
been examined. These efforts were part of Japan's informal diplomacy. However,
the ruling party and the central bureaucracy were not the only informal political
channels used during the process. Although Satō's duck diplomacy depended
heavily on the ruling party/government apparatus, Tanaka's effort to open up relations with China depended largely on yatō gaikō (opposition parties' diplomacy).

Japan has four major opposition parties: the Japan Socialist Party (JSP),
the Kōmeitō—Clean Government Party (CGP), the Democratic Socialist Party
(DSP), and the Japanese Communist Party (JCP). The opposition parties played
an important role in normalization, and it is therefore worthwhile to examine the
minor parties closely. The opposition parties had long been active in developing
relations with the PRC prior to normalization.

Table 14
Number of Japanese Diet Members Visiting China, 1955–71

Year	LDP	JSP	JCP	CGP	Others	Total
1955	29	43	2		4	78
1956	7	12	1		1	21
1957	7	27	1		1	36
1958	2	7	1		1	11
1959	7	14	2		1	24
1960	1	4	0		0	5
1961	4	8	5		1	18
1962	10	18	0		0	28
1963	6	13	1		2	22
1964	11	33	0	0	0	44
1965	5	1	0	0	0	6
1966	18	9	0	0	0	27
1967	1	3	0	0	0	4
1968	2	2	0	0	0	4
1969	3	2	0	0	0	5
1970	7	10	0	0	0	17
1971*	19	11	0	9	3	42
Total	139	217	13	9	14	392

Source: Nitchu Kankei Shiryoshu, 1945-1971 (Tokyo: Nitchu Kokko Kaifuku Sokushin Giinrenmei, 1971), pp. 637-46.
Note: *Up until October 1971.

Table 14 leads to three conclusions. First, even though the LDP commanded a much larger number in the Diet, it was not as active as the JSP in visiting China during the pre-normalization period of 1955–71. The JSP sent the largest number of its Diet members (217 out of 392) to China during this period. Second, the Japanese Communist party had been active in developing relations with China until the early 1960s when it became heavily involved in the Sino-Soviet disputes. As a result, there was a break in relations between the Chinese Communist Party and the JCP after that period. Third, in contrast, the CGP did not send any Diet member to China until 1971 when nine CGP Diet members (accounting for almost 20 percent of the total CGP Diet members) visited China, compared to 6 percent of the LDP Diet members and 12 percent of the JSP Diet members visiting China in the same year. It is not surprising then that the two largest opposition parties, the JSP and the CGP, played dynamic roles in normalization, especially during 1971 and early 1972 when the process reached final and subtle decision-making stages.

As early as 1957, the JSP made its first official visit to Beijing led by Secretary-General Inejirō Asanuma. The delegation was warmly received by Mao Zedong and Zhou Enlai. The result of this visit was a joint statement by Asanuma and Zhang Xiruo, president of the Chinese People's Institute of Foreign Affairs: Taiwan was a matter of China's internal affairs, Japan should restore diplomatic relations with China "formally and completely" as soon as possible, and the PRC's seat in the United Nations should be restored without any form of a two-China policy (C. Lee 1976: 35–36). It was the first such statement between the PRC and a Japanese political party, and, more importantly, the JSP was the first political party that explicitly accepted China's position on Taiwan.

In 1959 the JSP went even further by signing another joint statement (again by Asanuma) with Beijing, claiming that "American imperialism is the common enemy of the Japanese and the Chinese people," and "American imperialism is the common enemy of the Japanese and the Chinese people," and "American troops should be withdrawn from Japan as soon as possible" (Japan-China Economic Association 1975c: 33). This radical statement caused conflict within Japan's political circles, including JSP's more conservative faction led by Saburō Eda. The right-wing political forces in Japan vigorously opposed this second statement. A right-wing activist, for a variety of reasons, assassinated Asanuma in October 1960.

Asanuma's assassination did not stop JSP's pro-Beijing campaign. From 1965 on, the JSP had three guiding principles in foreign policy issues: normalization of relations with the PRC; unconditional reversion of Okinawa from the United States to Japan; and abolition of the Japan-U.S. Security Treaty. In February 1970 the JSP held a special meeting chaired by Party Chairman Tomomi Narita, which advocated broad mass participation in the movement for normalization with the PRC. At that time, the JSP was the only party that openly asserted the necessity of establishing formal relations with the PRC, while simultaneously cutting off official ties with Taiwan.

In August 1970 former JSP Chairman Kōzō Sasaki visited China. While in Beijing, he and the Chinese leaders discussed ways to form a broad coalition to promote a mass normalization movement in Japan. According to Sasaki, the "broad coalition" included the following six principles: (1) to support the anti-American imperialism position; (2) to oppose the revival of Japanese militarism; (3) to fight against the Japan-U.S. Security Treaty system; (4) to overthrow the reactionary Satō government and its followers; (5) to expand trade, culture, and personnel exchange with China based on principles of equality, reciprocity, and the inseparability of politics from economics; and (6) to promote true friendship and to restore diplomatic relations with the PRC (Ijiri 1987: 161).

Two months later, the JSP's fifth official mission, led by Party Chairman Narita, visited Beijing. The visit resulted in a joint statement on bilateral relations: "The movement for Sino-Japanese friendship and restoration of diplomatic relations between the two countries is a part of the Japanese people's struggle against U.S. imperialism and revival of Japanese militarism by American and Japanese reactionaries."[5] The successful visits to Beijing and the cordial relations with the Chinese helped the JSP's left-wing faction gain the upper hand over the conservative faction within the party. At the thirty-fourth party convention in December 1970, two left-wing leaders, Narita and Tanzan Ishibashi, were elected as party chairman and secretary general, respectively, defeating conservative representatives Saburō Eda and Jiichirō Matsumoto. This new leadership further paved the way for the JSP to promote relations with China.

A more direct role in the normalization process played by the JSP came in the summer of 1972, when the former Chairman, Kōzō Sasaki, visited China on July 14–20 as an informal communicator between the newly elected prime minister Kakuei Tanaka and Zhou Enlai. Before this visit, Sasaki had a meeting with Prime Minister Tanaka and Foreign Minister Ōhira. In Beijing, Sasaki gave the Chinese a detailed and frank assessment of Tanaka's China policy. He told Zhou that Tanaka and Ōhira were sincere in accepting China's condition on Taiwan. In return, Zhou stated that Tanaka's visit to Beijing would be welcomed.[6]

In addition to the informal invitation for Tanaka, Sasaki also received personal assurances from Zhou Enlai on several important issues: (1) China would be satisfied if Japan expressed a "full understanding"—short of acceptance—of the three principles (on the issue of Taiwan); (2) China would accord the same protocol to Tanaka's visit as it did to Nixon's; (3) an arrangement would be made for Tanaka's direct flight from Tokyo to Beijing; (4) China understood the LDP's internal disputes over the question of Taiwan and allowed Tanaka more time to deal with the issue of the Japan-Taiwan peace treaty; and (5) China would take a flexible position on the issue of war reparations (C. Lee 1976: 114). All these messages were passed on to Tanaka and Ōhira immediately upon Sasaki's return to Tokyo.

The CGP was the second largest opposition party during the normalization process. As early as January 1969, the CGP issued a new China policy with the following four points: (1) to recognize the PRC and restore diplomatic relations; (2) to refrain from interfering in the problems between Beijing and Taipei, regarding them as China's internal affairs; (3) to actively promote the PRC's entry into the United Nations; and (4) to promote intergovernmental trade and cultural exchanges. This was in opposition to the Satō government's official line. In June 1970 CGP Chairman Yoshikatsu Takeiri claimed that the "Japan-China normalization was the most important task for the party." To fulfill its promise, the CGP sponsored the National Council for the Normalization of Japan-China Diplomatic Relations, which was inaugurated that December. Among the 210 members of this new Council were leading politicians, university professors, and novelists.[7]

In June 1971 Takeiri announced for the first time that the CGP would call for the abrogation of the Japan-Taiwan Peace Treaty. The PRC welcomed this gesture of a one-China policy. China then invited the first CGP official mission to visit Beijing. This pro-PRC position made it possible for the CGP to play in important role in the rapprochement process. The CGP mission was led by Takeiri. During his visit, Takeiri conveyed to Premier Zhou Enlai that he expected Tanaka and Ōhira to become Japan's next leaders. Takeiri also indicated that, because he was a close friend of Tanaka, he could be influential in the quest for normalization.

In May 1972 Vice-Chairman Bunzō Ninomiya led the CGP's second official mission to China. At the end of the visit, to Ninomiya's surprise, Zhou Enlai asked him to relay an important message to would-be Prime Minister

Tanaka—an invitation to visit Beijing. Zhou promised that Tanaka's visit was not subject to any preconditions and that it was not necessary for Tanaka to accept the three conditions before the visit. Zhou also stated that the Chinese fully understood Japan's domestic situation, and he promised that China would refrain from doing anything that might embarrass Tanaka politically (Fukui 1977: 78). These messages were immediately passed on to Tanaka when Ninomiya returned to Tokyo.

The most dramatic role undertaken by CGP leaders occurred two months before Tanaka's visit. In July 1972, although it was broadly believed that Sino-Japanese rapprochement would soon be realized, no one could forecast the method or the timing. There was no preliminary discussion between China and Japan. Before his visit to Beijing, Takeiri discussed the China issue four times with Prime Minister Tanaka and Foreign Minister Ōhira. After these discussions, Takeiri made a twenty-one-point draft proposal based on his understanding of the Tanaka cabinet's negotiating position. He showed the draft to Tanaka and Ōhira, who expressed neither approval nor objection. Meanwhile, Tanaka and Ōhira expressed their willingness to visit Beijing (C. Lee 1976: 116–117; and Jiji Tsūshinsha Seijibu 1972: 27).

On July 25, five days after JSP's Sasaki returned from China, Takeiri began his second visit to Beijing that year. Takeiri presented Zhou Enlai the twenty-one-point draft, which contained some differences from the previous official Chinese stance. It did not mention, for instance, the issue of the Japan-U.S. Security Treaty (T. Ishikawa 1974: 158–159). Takeiri had a total of nine hours of discussion with Chinese leaders. At the end of the discussions, Zhou bluntly asked whether the Japanese government would move to normalization if China accepted the draft proposal. Takeiri guaranteed the proposal by taking personal responsibility. That evening he telephoned Tokyo to consult Tanaka and Ōhira, and he received positive answers.

On the third and last day of Takeiri's stay in Beijing, Zhou made a surprising move by presenting Takeiri with the first Chinese draft of a tentative Zhou-Tanaka Joint Communique. Takeiri took notes word by word through an interpreter and was amazed by the Chinese leader's flexibility. It was later labeled the "Takeiri Memo," and it was quite similar to the final communique actually signed in late September establishing formal diplomatic relations between Japan and China. The Takeiri Memo did not mention the Japan-U.S. Security Treaty and the Satō-Nixon Joint Communique, which had long been criticized by the Chinese (Tanaka 1985: 234–236). This flexibility paved the way for Japan's leaders to visit Beijing in late September, for this was an appropriate time for the Chinese. On August 4, the day after Takeiri's return to Tokyo, Tanaka received the Takeiri Memo. After two hours of reviewing the memo, the prime minister told the CGP chairman that he would go to Beijing (Ijiri 1987: 223–230; and Japan-China Economic Association 1975a: 5).

The DSP was somewhat more friendly toward Taiwan than the JSP and the CGP. The party convention of February 1970 adopted a new China policy which asked for "immediate regular ambassador-level talks between Japan and the PRC," and for promotion of "the PRC's entry into the United Nations." Meanwhile, it also called on Japan "to respect the will of the Taiwanese people and leave the matter of status of Taiwan to them." In other words, this was a one-China, one-Taiwan or two-China position. However, this position was modified quickly as the international and domestic situation changed. In October 1970 the party leadership claimed that the Taiwan issue was China's internal affair, and it urged the Satō government not to co-sponsor the pro-Taiwan resolution in the forthcoming United Nations General Assembly.

In the fall of 1971, the DSP completed its process of switching to a one-China position. Chairman Kasuga clearly stated DSP's new China policy: (1) there was only one China; (2) the Beijing government was the sole legitimate government representing China; (3) Taiwan was a territory of China; and (4) the Taiwan issue was a domestic matter for China to decide and should be settled peacefully as the Beijing government's responsibility. He also urged Satō to visit China prior to the Nixon trip (Ijiri 1987: 175). A month later, Zhou Enlai invited Kasuga to lead a DSP mission to visit China. This visit reaffirmed the similar stances of the DSP and Beijing toward the issue of Taiwan.

Relations between the JCP and the Chinese Communist Party (CCP) were broken off after a JCP mission to China in 1966 led by Secretary General Kenji Miyamoto, owing to disputes over the return of the international communist movement. After that time, the CCP labeled the JCP as one of the "four common enemies" of the Japanese and Chinese people, along with American imperialism, Soviet revisionism, and the reactionary Satō government. The JCP faced a dilemma: On the one hand, the JCP opposed "Mao Zedong clique's unwarranted interference with the JCP and Japanese democratic forces." On the other hand, the JCP supported a clear-cut one-China policy, including the PRC's entry into the United Nations, abrogating the Japan-Taiwan Treaty, and concluding a peace treaty with the PRC.[8] However, this pro-normalization position was not helpful in restoring relations between the two Communist parties.

Japan's opposition party diplomacy is often well coordinated with the ruling Liberal Democrats.[9] For example, on September 9, 1972, five weeks after the Takeiri Memo was issued, pro-Beijing LDP Diet members Yoshimi Furui and Seiichi Tagawa visited China ostensibly for the purpose of memorandum trade negotiations. With this secret cover, Furui delivered Ōhira's proposals for the Zhou-Tanaka statement to the Chinese leaders, and he conducted preliminary diplomatic negotiations with Zhou Enlai and Liao Chengzhi. Chae-Jin Lee (1976: 117–118) gave a detailed description of Furui's function as an informal actor: "Furui, who had in the long process of trade negotiations accumulated a great deal of first-hand knowledge on China's thinking and negotiating patterns, became a principal element of Ōhira's brain trust, as well as a confidential messenger in the execution of Ōhira's diplomatic strategy toward China."

In the middle of 1970, there was an increasing demand for the formation of a pro-China coalition, known as the united front, that would promote early normalization of relations with China. This united front included not only opposition parties, but sometimes also members from the ruling LDP, making it a nonpartisan, informal organization.

One of the first joint actions taken by three major opposition parties (namely, the JSP, CGP, and DSP) was for all three opposition leaders to meet Prime Minister Satō two days before his departure to the United States. They strongly urged Satō not to co-sponsor with the United States the anti-PRC resolutions in the U.N. General Assembly, but to support China's entry into the United Nations.[10]

Nonpartisan organizations also existed in the Diet which favored promoting normalization of relations with the PRC. One such organization was *Nitchū Bōeki Sokushin Giin Renmei* (the Diet Members' League for Promotion of Japan-China Trade), which was composed of the LDP and opposition parties' pro-Beijing members. In the fall of 1970 before the United Nations General Assembly, leading LDP members of the Afro-Asian Group such as Aiichirō Fujiyama, Tokuma Utsunomiya, and Seiichi Tagawa met the leaders of the opposition parties, including Susumu Kobayashi of the JSP and Tadasuke Matsumoto of the CGP. Together they established an expanded nonpartisan Diet members organization for promoting the pro-rapprochement movement, which they named *Nitchū Kokkō Kaifuku Sokushin Giin Renmei* (the Diet Members' League for Promoting Restoration of Japan-China Diplomatic Relations). The LDP's Disciplinary Committee criticized this action out of fear of disturbing the forthcoming party presidential election. However, the pro-Beijing LDP members ignored this warning, and in December 1970 ninety-five LDP Diet members joined with opposition Diet members in the inauguration of the new nonpartisan Diet members' League (Taylor 1985: 4). This was an unprecedented action in the history of the LDP.

In the beginning, the membership of the league was 379 (95 from the LDP, 154 from the JSP, 71 from the CGP, 36 from the DSP, 21 from the JCP, and 2 independents). LDP's *Aiichirō* Fujiyama became president, and LDP's Kenzō Kōno, JSP's Seiichi Katsumata, CGP's Ichirō Watanabe, and DSP's Ikko Kasuga became vice-presidents. This antimainstream or anticonservative league had a great impact on the senior leaders of the LDP and the government.

In July 1971 the Diet Members' League introduced a resolution in the Lower House calling for normalization of relations with the PRC and the recovery of China's seat in the United Nations. This time they collected signatures from 54 LDP members and 184 opposition members and independents. The total number of co-sponsors (238) fell only six votes short of a simple majority of the House of Representatives. After dissuasion by top leaders of the LDP, thirty-three LDP members "changed" their minds and withdrew their endorsement of the resolution. But twenty-one LDP members went forward to co-sponsor the resolution with opposition members. Although the resolution eventually failed to reach the floor, it represented a new pattern of cooperation between opposition members and dissident LDP members.

In April 1972 a new united front of pro-Beijing forces called *Nitchū Kokkō*

Kaifuku Sokushin Renraku Kaigi (the Council for Promoting Restoration of Japan-China Diplomatic Relations) was established. This was a coordinating organ for the nationwide pro-rapprochement forces including the Diet Members' League, the JSP, and the DSP (Ijiri 1987: 80 and 175–176). It gave the opposition camp great leverage to begin its own diplomacy, and it allowed *yatō gaikō* (opposition parties' diplomacy) to become more active. As it became increasingly clear that the top foreign policy issue would be normalization of relations with China, opposition parties competed with one another to open new channels for carrying out the rapprochement task with Beijing.

Yatō gaikō was an important channel for opening up negotiations for rapprochement. The actions of both DSP's Sasaki and CGP's Takeiri prepared the way for the visit of Japan's prime minister to China. Under normal circumstances, the top bureaucrats of the Ministry of Foreign Affairs would perform these actions. However, because of a lack of normal channels between the two countries, these informal political actors, Takeiri in particular, fulfilled the role of "Japan's Kissinger." The point here is that, although Takeiri performed a similar function as Kissinger, he had no official position either in the government or in the ruling party. However, he was the chairman of an opposition party and a personal friend of the prime minister. This indicates that *yatō gaikō* allowed the opposition camp to play a significant catalytic role in crucial political events. This case has further enhanced the importance of informal political institutions and channels (known here as *kuromaku*) in Japanese political life.

THE INTELLECTUALS AND THINK-TANKS

Intellectual participation in politics began to be noticed in the Meiji period. Almost every circle of society accepted the slogan "a rich country and a strong army" as national goals during the period of Japan's modernization. Mainstream intellectuals of the time were no exception, thereby supporting the government's efforts to achieve the national goals. From the late 19th century to 1945, Japan began to emulate Western colonial behaviors by pursuing an aggressive policy toward its Asian neighbors, notably China and Korea. During those years, a few Japanese intellectuals, including university professors and journalists, began to criticize and oppose Japan's aggressive foreign policy toward its Asian neighbors. This change of attitude corresponded with the introduction of Western democratic ideas into Japan. This critical attitude toward the government was partially a result of the academic independence demanded by intellectuals and partially a result of the fact that intellectuals did have "dissident opinions."[11]

During World War II, owing to the rapid development of new technology and the changing nature of international affairs, the Japanese government began to seek advice from scholars and experts through more cooperative relations with intellectuals. A typical example was the Shōwa Kenkyūkai (the Shōwa Research Association), which was made up of scholars from the imperial universities of Tokyo and Kyoto, and other intellectuals, founded by Prince Fumimaro Konoe.

Nevertheless, intellectuals' participation in the policymaking process was rather limited in both scale and duration, and many intellectuals still continued to criticize governmental policies. The critical attitude toward the government has been inherited by a good portion of the postwar intellectuals, many of whom were in line with opposition parties such as the JSP, CGP, and DSP.[12]

Beginning in the early 1970s, this antiestablishment sentiment began to change among certain intellectuals. A small group of scholars and experts in various fields started to actively participate in the policymaking process.[13] Their new attitude was that, in order to influence policy, one must participate in the process. This attitude was further enhanced by the LDP's de facto one-party domination. Some intellectuals had tired of always being "outsiders" and wanted to become "insiders." This change of attitude, though not very noticeable, was quite significant, for it showed the evolution of mass participation in Japanese politics and the development of a pluralistic society.

The participation of intellectuals in the policymaking process is far from being formal and institutionalized. Although groups of scholars are referred to as *shinkutanku* (think-tanks, or research institutions), normally they do not form their own advisory or consultative institutions as their counterparts do in the United States. They can participate in the policymaking process in three ways. First, they can become private advisers to the prime minister. Almost every prime minister has had a small circle of his own private advisers. These inner groups are usually informal, having various degrees of influence depending on the individuals involved. Several prime ministers, such as Satō, Ōhira, and Nakasone, have deliberately included scholars in their inner groups. Scholars are "selected" as advisers if they share similar political views with the prime minister; if they maintain a good personal relationship with the prime minister; and if they have a scholarly reputation. Once included in the inner groups, scholars retain their close contact with the prime minister. It is not unusual for a scholar-adviser to meet with the prime minister once or twice a month.[14]

The second way is for intellectuals to join various governmental advisory committees. These committees are organized at three different levels: the office of the prime minister, the ministries, and the bureaus within ministries. These governmental services normally carry no remuneration except for reimbursement for transportation expenses to and from committee meetings.

Third, intellectuals can influence national policy by participating in policy seminars sponsored by the news media. Scholars are invited to discuss issues concerning domestic politics or foreign policy together with politicians or high-ranking bureaucrats. It is not unusual for the prime minister himself to appear at such discussions.[15] These seminars, highly publicized through television programs and newspapers, naturally have an impact on public opinion, as well as contribute to achieving consensus within the government.

Most think-tank members are technical experts or economists, and they assist the governmental bureaucrats who lack expertise or technical know-how on specific issues. Because the formation of foreign policy has traditionally been monopolized by political leaders and Foreign Ministry bureaucrats, few outsiders participate in the process of foreign policymaking. However, under certain circumstances, when government agencies need advice on certain issues, they accept help from scholars. This was the case during the process of rapprochement when Japan's China policy was reexamined. Because of the over twenty-year political vacuum between Japan and China, both political leaders and Foreign Ministry bureaucrats had little up-to-date knowledge about China's domestic political system and foreign policy. Therefore, some leading scholars in Chinese politics and international relations were constantly consulted.

In the summer of 1971, under increasing pressure to seek normalization of relations with China and to work out a "correct" policy toward the issue of China's representation in the forthcoming United Nations Assembly, the Satō administration desperately needed advice from such experts. An informal study group was formed; it was composed of thirteen leading specialists on China and international relations, including Professors Shinkichi Etō (University of Tokyo), Tadao Ishikawa (Keiō University), Tadao Miyashita (University of Kobe), Chūzō Ichiko (Ochanomizu Women's University), Tadao Umesao (University of Kyoto), Seiji Imabori (University of Hiroshima), Yonosuke Nagai (Tokyo Institute of Technology and Science), Jun Etō (Tokyo Institute of Technology and Science), Fuji Kamiya (Keiō University), Masakazu Yamazaki (Kansai Gakuin University), Masataka Kosaka (University of Kyoto), and Mineo Nakajima (Tokyo University of Foreign Studies). On August 26, the study group held its first meeting to discuss the China policy. Kosaka and Nakajima were appointed as coordinators, and Chief Cabinet Secretary Noboru Takeshita and Acting Foreign Minister Toshio Kimura participated in this first discussion (Ijiri 1987: 84–85; and Kusuda 1975: 116–117).

Professor Shinkichi Etō of the University of Tokyo, a leading conservative China specialist, became one of the inner-circle advisers to Prime Minister Satō. He was frequently consulted by both the prime minister and the top bureaucrats of MOFA. In December 1970, when Satō disclosed his strategy for a gradual change on China policy to improve relations with the PRC, while maintaining close ties with Taiwan, Etō suggested that the prime minister should be cautious and "pay close attention to public opinion."[16] Since pro-Taiwan political forces were still active at that time, the real meaning of this advice was to let the prime minister slow down the normalization process with Beijing.

There is yet another example of the influence of the group. Prior to LDP Secretary General Hori's request to Tokyo Governor Minobe to communicate his personal letter to Premier Zhou Enlai at the end of 1971, Mineo Nakajima, a China specialist at the Tokyo University of Foreign Studies and author of several books on China, was asked to review the draft of the letter and make some modifications (Ijiri 1987: 106; and Nakajima 1982: 149).

After rapprochement in 1972, the number of bilateral personnel exchanges between China and Japan grew rapidly, making it possible for governmental bureaucrats to increase their knowledge of Chinese affairs. Since then, the role of think-tank in the formation of China policy has not been as prominent as it was during the pre-normalization era.[17]

These examples of the intellectuals' political influence are not extremely impressive. First, the percentage of intellectuals who serve as advisers to political leaders and the governmental bureaucracy has remained small, and the function of such intellectuals has been basically informal. Second, the government bureaucracy has maintained an insulation entity from the "outsiders." There are few personnel exchanges between universities and governmental agencies, whereas in the United States such exchanges are quite common. Third, intellectuals have conflicting opinions about their participation in politics. Many of them are still afraid of being used as "tools" by politicians and of losing academic credibility; therefore, they stay away from politics.[18] Others believe that they must actively participate in "real political life" to fulfill their social responsibilities.[19]

Despite these differences, since the early 1970s the role of intellectuals has become increasingly prominent in Japan's political life. For example, more than two hundred public advisory councils are appointed by and advise virtually all central government ministries and agencies. In 1988 more than one thousand university professors were appointed as members of these councils (out of 4,200 members), followed by about seven hundred trade association officials, six hundred businessmen, and representatives from other groups of the society, such as journalists and labor union (S. Fukai and H. Fukui 1992: 33). Furthermore, these advisory councils, according to Fukai and Fukui (1992: 33), have served as "the main integrator and melting pot for members of the several elites in contemporary Japan" by providing "vital links" both between government and the public and among Japan's political elites.

There are three reasons for this development: First, the development of advanced technology and a complex world economy have required the acquisition of highly specialized knowledge by governmental agencies. Second, an increasing number of scholars believe that participation in the policymaking process is one way to do research in their own fields. In this sense, participation is used as a means of what Shumpei Kumon called "social experiment."[20] Third, owing to the de facto one-party rule since 1955, some intellectuals feel strongly that in order to increase their influence in society, they have to actively participate in the policymaking of the "mainstream" politics.

THE POLITICAL FUNCTION OF THE NEWS MEDIA

An assessment of the function of political institutions in the normalization process cannot be complete without a discussion of the news media, in particular Japanese newspapers. The role of the news media in Japanese political life and their influence on society have increased remarkably owing to their large circulation and active political participation.

There are three categories of newspapers. The first category encompasses

Table 15
The Diffusion Rate of Newspaper Circulation

Rank	Country	Diffusion Rate (copies per 1,000 people)
1	Japan	569
2	East Germany	530
3	Sweden	524
4	Finland	515
5	Norway	483
6	Britain	421
7	West Germany	408
8	USSR	405
9	USA	265
10	France	191

Sources: Japan Newspaper Publishers and Editors Association (as of October 1985) for Japan. UNESCO 1984 statistics for all other countries.

national papers, including five major ones, *Asahi, Yomiuri, Mainichi, Nihon Keizai,* and *Sankei.* They all enjoy a large circulation with *Yomiuri* and *Asahi* at the top; they had a circulation of 8,852,610 and 7,533,727 (morning and evening editions as a set in large cities), respectively, in 1984. The second category includes the block papers that cover Western Japan, Central Japan, and Hokkaido. The third category encompasses regional papers such as *Chūgoku* (Hiroshima), *Kyoto* (Kyoto), *Tohoku shinpō* (Miyagi), and *Niigata nippō* (Niigata) (Haruhara et al. 1986: 33). Japan is number one in the world in terms of the distribution rate of newspaper circulation, maintaining 569 copies per 1,000 people (more than twice the number of the United States), with the average Japanese household receiving more than one paper (see Tables 15 and 16).

Japan's print media also include a large variety of wide-circulation magazines. The most influential and widely read monthlies include the relatively conservative *Chūō Kōron* (with a circulation of between 60,000 and 70,000) representing the "mainstream" of society; and *Bungei Shunjū* (530,000), which is noted for its treatment of controversial political and social issues that the newspapers will not touch. There is also *Sekai* (100,000), which has a strongly antiwar and leftist editorial policy, and has covered a number of controversies including nuclear disarmament, world peace, and the situation on the Korean peninsula in recent years (Haruhara et al. 1986: 74).

Japan has six nationwide television networks: one is publicly operated—NHK (the Japan Broadcasting Corporation)—and the other five are privately owned—NTV, TBS, Asahi, Fuji, and NET. According to recent polls conducted by NHK, despite a slight decline in the last decade, the average Japanese views television at least three hours per day (see Table 17), reflecting the degree of TV network influence.

A strong social influence does not necessarily mean a strong political influence by the media. In order to evaluate the role of the mass media during the normalization process with China, we must examine the actions various news organizations have taken toward this goal.

Table 16
Newspaper Circulation and Distribution, 1960–84

Year	Circulation	Number of Households	Copies per Household
1960	24,438,070	20,656,000	1.18
1965	29,776,465	24,082,000	1.24
1970	36,303,928	27,878,000	1.30
1975	40,512,598	33,320,006	1.22
1980	46,391,096	35,830,857	1.29
1984	47,515,488	37,934,575	1.25

Source: Japan Newspaper Publishers and Editors Association.

Article Twenty-one of the postwar Japanese constitution states that (1) freedom of assembly and association as well as speech, press, and all other forms of expression are guaranteed; and that (2) no censorship shall be maintained, nor shall the confidentiality of any means of communication be violated. This has laid a foundation for the basic principles of the news media community—to maintain impartiality and avoid identification with any particular political party or ideology. In practice, impartiality does not prevent the news media from taking their own stand, especially when facing controversial issues. On many occasions, Japanese newspapers have followed editorial policies that strayed from the official government line. This tendency has made them a powerful political force. In fact, all newspapers had their own political agenda on the China issue during the normalization period.

Japanese newspapers led Japanese political actors in entering into agreements with the Chinese on Chinese terms. They also furnished the editorial support for other political actors to take new positions in furthering relations with China. They created a popular milieu in which formal recognition (normalization) became possible.

Throughout 1971, major national dailies gave extensive coverage to the issue of China's representation in the United Nations and the normalization of relations between Japan and China. Every major national paper carried an average of forty-seven editorials, or about four each month, on the subject (Kim 1981: 151).

In this regard, *Asahi* played a leading role. In a poll conducted by *Asahi* on June 23, 1970, only 19 percent of the respondents agreed with the statement that "in order to establish diplomatic relations, it cannot be helped if ties with Taiwan are severed." Forty-six percent opposed it. *Asahi* then decided to launch an all-out effort to "educate" the public on the China question, and in the January 1971 issue devoted two entire pages to this purpose. *Asahi* called for the termination of efforts to maintain Taiwan's representation at the United Nations and pushed for government-to-government contact with Beijing for the restoration of formal diplomatic relations. After an extensive five-month campaign, *Asahi* took another opinion poll on the China question by making similar statements to the previous ones. This time, 33 percent of the respondents agreed with the statements while

Table 17
Average Television Viewing Time (age 7 and older)

Year	Hours per Day
1976	3 hours 27 minutes
1979	3 hours 16 minutes
1982	3 hours 4 minutes
1985	3 hours 0 minutes

Source: NHK

22 percent disagreed. On June 23, 1971, exactly one year after the first opinion poll, *Asahi* declared in an editorial that, although the great majority of the people wanted normalization of relations with China, the ruling Liberal Democrats and the central bureaucracy were holding stubbornly to the policy of "one China and one Taiwan." Other newspapers during the same period obtained similar results from their polls, although their questions were not exactly the same as *Asahi*'s (Miyoshi and Etō 1972: 97–115).

Asahi made another move a year later. Dissatisfied with Prime Minister Satō's passive position on the China issue, the newspaper went even further and asked for a pro-PRC candidate to replace Satō. In a column article of June 7, 1972, *Asahi*'s Beijing correspondent suggested that a new prime minister of Japan must accept Beijing's three principles for normalization and must demonstrate, by concrete action, that its pledge to do so was genuine. The article went on to argue that Fukuda's assumption of power would make the normalization of relations with China difficult, since he served as Satō's foreign minister and was deeply involved in "unfriendly activities" toward Beijing.[21]

Based on these events, we could argue that the media were trying to influence public opinion in Japan's China policy. On the other hand, as can be seen from numerous opinion polls conducted periodically by the newspapers, the pro-Beijing stance of the newspapers indeed reflected the changing public mood in Japan.

The press clearly benefited from a favorable public image. According to a survey, 64 percent of the respondents expressed an opinion that the press reflected the "feelings" (*kimochi*) of the people, while a mere 8 percent answered this question negatively. The central government did poorly in the same survey, with only 27 percent of the respondents believing the government reflected the feelings of the people and 52 percent saying the government did not represent them. The Diet did not fare much better than the government (Shinohara 1971: 14).

Facing domestic and international pressure, Prime Minister Satō finally announced his intention to resign from office on June 16, 1972. Having for years been portrayed by the newspapers as a reactionary political figure and the incarnation of Japanese militarism, Satō was angry and frustrated with the press. In the conference room where he announced his resignation, he discourteously told reporters, "I don't like the biased press." When reporters protested, Satō said "Please get out." After all the newspaper reporters left, he allowed himself to be covered only by television cameras desiring "to talk to the people directly" (Japan Newspaper Publishers and Editors Association 1973: 39).

Initially, Kakuei Tanaka, the new prime minister, was received warmly by the press. He was praised as "a man of determination and action," "a computerized bulldozer," and he was described as "cheerful and folksy." In return, Tanaka firmly assured the press that "it is natural to seek the understanding of the people through the mass media. I will show respect for the newspapers" (Kusumoto 1976: 122). His stance showed that "voter-conscious" politicians are more careful than bureaucrats toward the news media, because of their tremendous influence on public opinion.[22]

The good relationship between Tanaka and the news media did not last long, however. About a month after his inauguration, Tanaka indicated his real feelings about the news media, regarding them as a potential threat. At a dinner with nine reporters, Tanaka warned them, "Don't pursue any trivial matters. If you don't cross a dangerous bridge, I will be safe. So will you. If I think a particular reporter is dangerous, I can easily have him removed." Ironically, two years later, it was Tanaka who was forced to resign from office, partially due, at least on the surface, to personal scandals, which were investigated and revealed to the public by the news media, led by the monthly magazine *Bungei Shunjū* (Kim 1981: 168–169).

The intellectual community widely admires the news media's tradition of criticizing political leaders, known as "opposition spirit" (Watanuki 1977: 26–27). However, the pro-Beijing stance of the majority of the news media and the actions taken by *Asahi* in particular were not without criticism. Shinkichi Etō, for example, criticized *Asahi*'s reporting of the Japanese-Chinese normalization issue as a display of manipulating public opinion and active advocacy of its own biased opinion (Miyoshi and Etō 1972: 219–224).

Not all Japanese newspapers adopted a pro-Beijing stance. In its editorial of June 14, 1971, for example, *Mainichi* insisted that Beijing governed the mainland but did not rule Taiwan; Taipei ruled Taiwan but did not govern the mainland. This was reality, and a foreign policy must be formulated on the basis of reality, implying a one-China, one-Taiwan policy. Later, *Mainichi*'s attitude did change with the changing international environment and domestic mood toward the China issue.

Press-government relations in Japan deserve close attention. Some intellectuals would like to emphasize the "opposition spirit" of the news media. For example, right after the downfall of the Kishi administration in 1960, a principal editorial writer of *Asahi* said, "If *Asahi* rendered overall support to the JSP, because it judged that the LDP was not good at all—though this is, needless to say, strictly hypothetical, this alone might cause a loss of the majority on the part of the LDP" (Ryu 1961). Although this statement appears to exaggerate the political impact of the newspapers, it nevertheless reflected the critical function of the news media in Japan's political life.

An opposite view holds that a collaboration exists between the news media and the government. In the postwar era, there has been well-established coordination between the news media and the government through the press club system. These clubs are exclusively established, professional organizations that are given such perquisites as rooms, equipment, and staff by major news sources within the government, major industries, and other corporate bodies. The government agencies, such as the Ministry of Foreign Affairs, regularly hold press conferences at the clubs, which a few scholars have described as a "collaboration between the government and the newspapers," and "government control and guidance of the news" (Yamamoto 1989: 371–388).

These differing arguments are examples of the dual function played by the news media in Japanese society. On the one hand, the newspapers will "monitor" the actions taken by the conservative ruling coalition (the LDP and the central bureaucracy). On the other hand, the news media will try to assure a stable social environment and the realization of Japan's "national goals," thereby preventing the society from going in radical directions.

This dual function of the news media can also be described as a valve function, which may be further explained in terms of three aspects. First, the press coverage can affect the career of individual political leaders—for example, the careers of two prime ministers, Satō and Tanaka. Second, the press helped block attempts by the conservative ruling coalition to amend the postwar constitutional frameworks such as the issue of Japan's rearmament. The newspaper attacks on Satō's alleged militarism are a good example. It may also push the conservatives to be aware of new developments, such as calling for normalizing relations with China to follow the new trends in the international community. Third, the press contributed to restraining the left-wing opposition parties and direct mass actions from taking more radical lines (J. B. Lee 1985: 171–176). With this valve function, the news media may help to maintain a moderate climate of public opinion between conservative LDP and left-wing social forces such as JSP and JCP.

INFORMAL POLITICAL ACTORS AND ORGANIZATIONS SHARING POWERS

This examination of the process of Sino-Japanese rapprochement demonstrates that the rapprochement decision resulted from many political and social forces. These forces included LDP politicians, government bureaucrats, business leaders, opposition parties, intellectuals, and the news media in Japan, as well as external factors—China, the United States, the China-related debates at the United Nations, and the changing international environment. Here we have a picture of Japan that is similar to the one described by Richard Neustadt (1960: 26) in his examination of American politics—"a government of separated institutions sharing powers."

What has made this process distinctive in Japan is the *kuromaku* phenomenon whereby so many informal political actors, institutions, and organizations were involved in important political decisions. The catalytic and valve functions of informal political institutions were crucial in the process of normalizing relations with China. This conclusion coincides with Donald Hellmann's conclusion on Japanese foreign policy toward the Soviet Union. Hellmann (1969: 56, 69) argued that the LDP factional struggle became synonymous with the foreign policymaking process, and the party's formal decision-making apparatus "was incapable of constraining the policy formulation process." It can be said that in Japan, political powers are shared not only by the established formal institutions, but also by informal political actors and organizations, such as LDP study groups, the Satō administration's five *ahiru* of duck diplomacy, the opposition parties' informal channels, freedom of action in the business community, the think-tank function of the intellectuals, and the dual role of the news media.

Informal practice is used not only externally but also internally. Informal political actors and organizations often serve as a tool connecting and coordinating activities among various power centers in society. This can be seen in the subtle relationship (rival yet cooperative) between the ruling LDP and opposition parties (in this case the JSP and the CGP) during the normalization process. Such connecting and coordinating functions are important to the effectiveness of the society, making the system work more smoothly and rationally. The process of Sino-Japanese normalization demonstrates that the dynamic activities of informal political actors and organizations have enabled Japan's political system to be highly sensitive to both domestic demands and international changes.

On the other hand, because of its informal nature, the negotiation process often appears "closed." Thus, as I. M. Destler and others (1979: 327–328) point out, it may become "ineffective" because of difficulties for policy implementation. The roles played by informal political actors and informal organizations vary greatly, and are heavily dependent on individual efforts and circumstances, thus making these actors less predictable, if not less reliable. The lack of institutionalization (in a relative sense) in this political process may cause confusion and uncertainty for foreigners, particularly for Westerners.

Informal political actors and institutions can be further explained from the perspective of organizational theories. Informal activities, as Selznick (1961: 22–23) pointed out, are deviations from formal organizations that tend to force a shift away from the purely formal system as the effective determinant of behavior to "(1) a condition in which informal patterns buttress the formal, as through the manipulation of sentiment within the organization in favor of established authority; or (2) a condition wherein the informal controls effect a consistent modification of formal goals, as in the case of some bureaucratic patterns." This is to say, informal actors and organizations tend to support the formal system, while making modifications to formal goals. This trend eventually results in the "formalization of erstwhile informal activities," with the cycle of deviation and transformation beginning again on a new level (Selznick 1961: 23). One obvious example is the LDP factions, which were once regarded as informal organizations within the LDP but over time gradually became formalized, and a part of the formal political institution.

NOTES

1. *Nihon keizai shimbun*, May 11, 1970; and Ijiri (1987: 182).

2. *Peking Review*, January 26, 1971, p. 13.

3. *Keidanren geppō*, January 1972, p. 5; and Ijiri (1987: 203).

4. See "Tanaka seiken to zaikai no mitsugetsu" [Honeymoon of the Tanaka government and the Zaikai], *Sekai*, September 1972, p. 159; and Ijiri (1987: 282).

5. *Renmin ribao*, November 1, 1970; see C. Lee (1976: 93).

6. *Asahi shimbun*, July 17, 1972.

7. *Asahi shimbun*, December 14, 1970; and Ijiri (1987: 169).

8. *Akahata*, November 28, 1969; and Ijiri (1987: 159).

9. Over the years Japan's opposition party diplomacy has been conducted not only with China, but also with North Korea and the former Soviet Union.

10. *Asahi shimbun*, October 17, 1970; and Ijiri (1987: 167).

11. Interview with Junnosuke Masumi, professor of Japanese politics at Tokyo Metropolitan University, October 25, 1985, Tokyo.

12. Interview with Akio Watanabe, professor of international relations at the University of Tokyo, October 31, 1985, Tokyo.

13. Interview with Akira Ishii, professor of Chinese politics at the University of Tokyo, November 5, 1985, Tokyo.

14. Interview with Seizaburō Satō, professor of international relations at the University of Tokyo, October 31, 1985, Tokyo.

15. Interview with Takashi Inoguchi, professor of international relations and Japanese politics at the University of Tokyo, January 12, 1986, Tokyo.

16. *Asahi shimbun*, December 10, 1970; and Ijiri (1987: 62).

17. Interview with Tadao Ishikawa, professor of Chinese politics and president of Keio University, October 1, 1985, Tokyo.

18. Interview with Yoshiie Yoda, professor of Chinese history and politics at Waseda University, July 12, 1986, Tokyo.

19. Interview with Sadako Ogata, professor of international relations and Chinese politics at Sophia University, December 12, 1985, Tokyo.

20. Interview with Shumpei Kumon, professor of international relations at the University of Tokyo, October 31, 1985, Tokyo.

21. *Asahi Shimbun*, June 7, 1972.

22. Interview with Yoshikazu Sakamoto, professor of international relations at the University of Tokyo, January 29, 1986, Tokyo.

PART IV

Consensus-Building and Political Culture
Case Study: Negotiations for the Four Economic Agreements

6

Personal Connection and Informal Consensus-Building

Compared to the terms *tsukiai* (social networks) and *kuromaku* (informal political actors and organizations), phenomena discussed in Parts II and III, the term *nemawashi* is perhaps more familiar to outsiders, scholars and practitioners alike. *Nemawashi*, which literally means "cutting around the roots of a plant before it is transplanted" in Japanese, refers to a behind-the-scenes working style. Edwin Reischauer (1988: 321–322), for example, called *nemawashi* a "system of careful and thorough consultations before a decision is arrived at by general consensus." The Japanese make wide use of the term in their daily lives to refer to a process of informal consensus-building.

In their study of Japanese business corporations and trading companies, James Abegglen and George Stalk (1985: 208) argue that *nemawashi* is a kind of "informal, pre-decision process of discussion and accommodation of views." Jun-ichi Kyōgoku (1987: 69–71) goes deeper in examining the *nemawashi* style by referring to it as a form of implicit communication in which one person can read the other person's mind, although nothing explicit has been said about the matter or problem that has come up. This kind of informal, subtle, and sometimes nonverbal communication and understanding is an important part of Japanese political culture, requiring closer examination in order to better understand the internal dynamics in Japan.

Parts II and III analyzed Japanese politics at the societal and the institutional levels; Part IV (Chapters 6 and 7) examines Japanese policymaking from the third level, namely, to analyze informal preparation and consultation at the personal level, with emphasis on the political culture perspective. It uses the negotiation processes of the first set of post-rapprochement Sino-Japanese governmental economic agreements (trade, aviation, navigation, and fisheries, respectively) as a case study to illuminate the individual-level operation in Japan's policymaking. When I conducted interviews in Tokyo on this case study, the more I learned about the details in the negotiation process the more I felt that *nemawashi* was a distinct working style in Japan's decision-making, and therefore an important part of my thesis of informal mechanisms.

THE IMPORTANCE OF PERSONAL CONNECTION IN JAPAN

According to Chie Nakane (1972: 79–80), three types of personal relations make up the foundation of social organizations. The first, which is common in Japan, is the emotional relationship established through vertical ties. The second is the contrasting horizontal relationship which relies on brothers or other kin rather than outsiders. This kind of personal relationship is prevalent in India and Southeast Asia. The third is contractual relations, which are based on contracts and legalities, and are common in Britain and the United States.

Nakane (1972: 43) further explains that the emotional relationship that emerges from basic interpersonal and intergroup relations in Japanese society is one of vertical linkages through enterprise or school, and not of horizontal stratification by caste or class. The notion of a vertical relationship can be applied to the personal connection in Japan. Many Japan specialists have emphasized the importance of the personal relationship in Japanese politics. Donald Seekins (1983: 286), for example, states that in Japan the political elite is remarkably homogeneous and interconnected, defined by a geography of personal networks built up through the years in college, in work relationships, and even in marriage connections.

Within the vertical system, everyone has his or her own social status, corresponding to the traditional value of group cohesiveness and group homogeneity which is often called groupism. The root of groupism, according to Takeshi Ishida (1983: 7–8), can be traced back to the tradition of rural communities:

> Villagers had to work together very closely during specific periods when a large work force was needed—such as for the gathering of grass for fertilizing and feeding livestock, the securing of irrigation water, the transplanting of rice, and of course harvesting.

Groupism has led to the social pattern of a leader-follower relationship. In their analysis of the LDP's internal factions, Bradley Richardson and Scott Flanagan (1984: 100) argue that the leader-follower factions are "the most important informal elements of Japanese political parties." And the pattern is important to Japan's group activities.

In Japan, one's social status is important. A natural question to ask when introductions are made is: "What is this person's social position, higher or lower?" This distinction in social status is clearly reflected in the honorific forms which are widely used in spoken Japanese. Verb forms, and even basic verb stems, alter sharply depending on the speaker's hierarchical relationship to the person being spoken to. For example, a man who wants to ask his younger brother or a subordinate whether he has already gone somewhere will say: "Mō itta ka?" But he will employ totally different words when addressing his boss with the same question, "Mō oide ni narimashita ka?" (Christopher 1983: 40). A Japanese will adjust his or her own attitude and behavior based on the judgment of what status another person has.[1] This is one reason why the Japanese feel uneasy in dealing with foreigners: it is difficult for them to determine the status of foreigners, especially in comparison to their own status.

Differentiation of social status among members of Japanese society and the operation of personal connection produce a feeling of obligation known as *giri*. A person tends to be guided by *giri* to "behave in certain loosely prescribed ways toward another, to whom the person is indebted" (Smith 1983: 45). Therefore, personal consultation has become an important means of fulfilling the perceived social obligation as well as avoiding open confrontation.

In sum, personal connection and the perceived obligation and indebtedness in Japanese society merit close examination. Individual contact and connection may be casual at the beginning stage and may not necessarily result in obligation. Nevertheless, as personal connection deepens, mutual obligation (*giri*) based on mutual interest begin to mount, and individual consultation becomes necessary. The notions of personal connection and consultation have become norms of behavior guiding social activities in Japan. One of the most distinguishing characteristics of this behavior is that it is often based on informal personal obligations at the individual level rather than on formal rules or contracts.

POLITICAL CULTURE AND JAPAN STUDIES

The study of cultures has long been a focus of social scientists, including political scientists, anthropologists, and sociologists. Many anthropologists, for example, have conducted extensive research on cultural phenomena, linking cultural behavior to social, economic, and political activities. For example, in *Culture and Practical Reason*, Marshall Sahlins (1976: 213) argues that any economic system is "a cultural specification and not merely a natural-material activity." Notions of traditional culture, or "ideology in the proper sense of the term," according to Clifford Geertz (1973: 340), "provide a guide for political activity; an image by which to grasp it, a theory by which to explain it, and a standard by which to judge it." Other studies of culture, such as "talking culture" (M. Moerman 1988), "the link between cultural interpretation and social theory" (J. Brenkman 1987), and "cultural communication" (G. Malone 1988), have also facilitated our understanding of comparative political behavior in the international arena.

Extensive research by political scientists on culture and its relationship to political behavior and development began in the middle of the 1950s, when political culture as a field came into being.[2] Political culture assumes that in any operating political system there is a subjective realm of politics which gives meaning to the polity, discipline to the institutions, and social relevance to the individual acts. In *Political Culture and Political Development*, Lucian Pye (1965: 7) suggests that the notion of political culture assumes that the attitudes, sentiments, and cognition that inform and govern political behavior in any society are not just random congeries, but represent coherent patterns that fit together and are mutually reinforcing. Pye further argues that the concept of political culture suggests that "the traditions of a society, the spirit of its public institutions, the passions and the collective reasoning of its citizenry, and the style and operating codes of its leaders are not just random products of historical experience, but fit together as a part of a meaningful whole and constitute an intelligible web of relations." Political culture studies "tradition," "spirit," "passions and collective reasoning," and "style and operating codes."

Political culture provides a conceptual vehicle to better understand the dynamics of political development by forming an important link between the events of politics and the behavior of individuals in reaction to those events. In Sidney Verba's (1965: 516) words, "although the political behavior of individuals and groups is of course affected by acts of government officials, wars, election campaigns, and the like, it is even more affected by the meanings that are assigned those events by observers." Ronald Inglehart (1990: 432) believes that cultural factors will become "a more crucial influence on human behavior," especially in advanced industrial society.

The importance of a political culture approach has long been emphasized by specialists in comparative politics, especially those in area studies including Japan studies. Personal connection, which is a foundation for consensus-building activities such as *nemawashi*, has been emphasized by several Japan specialists. In *The Political Culture of Japan*, Bradley Richardson (1974: 3–4) suggests that the political culture approach "seems especially suitable for studying the attitudes of ordinary people toward politics in Japan." He further elaborates:

> The fact that Japanese society is community- and group-oriented, that it is consensualistic in its decision-making processes, and that in a residual sense, it is paternalistic in certain social sectors in its personal relationships, can hardly be omitted from an analysis of political socialization processes and their effects. Indeed, much of the scholarly comment on Japanese political experience has paid more than passing attention to these kinds of things.

This suggestion is echoed by Takeshi Ishida, a scholar from Japan. In his book *Japanese Political Culture*, Ishida (1983: 4) emphasizes the importance of examining "the pattern of [a] combination of traditional and new elements both in value systems and organizational structure," and of identifying "the Western influence and the way it was modified to suit Japanese society." Political culture becomes quite complex in transitional and modern societies. It may contain a number of subcultures, which "often indicates latent tensions in values arising from the modernization process" (E. Krauss 1974: 168). Studying Japanese political culture may help us better understand a combination of traditional values and modernized political institutions, leading to a distinctive way of behavior—informal mechanisms.

By examining the negotiation process of the four economic agreements, the focus of this chapter is on the bureaucrats' internal and external *nemawashi* activities (informal preparations at the individual level) during negotiation sessions. To obtain a clear picture of these rather complicated negotiation processes and to gain a better understanding of the Japanese working style, it is necessary first to examine basic settings for the first post-rapprochement Sino-Japanese economic agreements, including the historical background as well as internal and external obstacles.

BASIC SETTINGS FOR THE SINO-JAPANESE ECONOMIC AGREEMENTS

In his historic visit to Beijing in September 1972, Prime Minister Kakuei Tanaka signed a nine-article joint statement with Chinese Premier Zhou Enlai which normalized relations between the two countries. The statement confirmed Japan's new policy on the issue of Taiwan, stating that Japan recognized Beijing as the sole legal government of China. Japan thus broke off official ties with Taipei, thereby terminating "the abnormal state of affairs" between Beijing and Tokyo. It also paved the way for official economic exchanges between the two countries. Article Nine of the Zhou-Tanaka Joint Statement emphasized these exchanges as follows:

> In order to further develop the relations between the two countries and broaden the exchange of visits, the Government of the People's Republic of China and the Government of Japan agree to hold negotiations aimed at the conclusion of agreements on *trade, navigation, aviation, fisheries*, etc., in accordance with non-governmental agreements. [emphasis added][3]

The four economic agreements were the first set of such agreements between the two governments, and they replaced previous nongovernmental agreements such as the "friendly firms" and the memorandum trade agreements.[4]

On the surface, the transition from a nongovernmental setting to a governmental arrangement would not appear difficult since both sides had already treated the memorandum trade offices in Beijing and in Tokyo as semiofficial channels. Earlier, the L-T (Liao-Takasaki) Trade Agreement (later renamed the Memorandum Trade Agreement) had been suggested by Chinese Premier Zhou Enlai when he discussed bilateral relations with Kenzō Matsumura in Beijing during September 1962.[5] In October, Tatsunosuke Takasaki discussed this new idea with then Prime Minister Hayato Ikeda and received his approval. One month later Takasaki visited Beijing and signed the L-T agreement with Liao Chengzhi, a cabinet member of the Chinese government and a member of the party's Central Committee. On the Japanese side, both Matsumura and Takasaki were influential LDP Diet members. Matsumura was leader of the LDP's Miki-Matsumura faction and had served as minister of agriculture and forestry, education, and welfare in the Japanese government. Takasaki had served as minister of MITI and the Economic Planning Agency.[6] From the beginning, these nonofficial trade agreements had the endorsement and blessing of high-level leaders in both China and Japan.

From the Chinese perspective, this arrangement was nongovernmental in name only. In reality, there were virtually no private trading companies in China, as under the socialist economic system at that time the government owned every trading company. For example, the China Council for Promoting International Trade (CCPIT), which was one of the main counterparts of Japanese trading companies, was under the jurisdiction of the Ministry of Foreign Trade, and thus never was a true nongovernmental organization. Chinese representatives in the Tokyo Memorandum Trade Office were mostly officials from the Ministry of Foreign Trade.

The Japanese followed a similar approach toward the memorandum trade agreements. Although the Ministry of Foreign Affairs and the Ministry of Justice were very cautious with regard to the "purely private nature" of these personnel exchanges, the Japanese government knew very well that these were semiofficial arrangements. This point was confirmed by three meetings in October 1962: the Conference of Ministers (politicians) from related ministries such as MOFA, MITI, MOF, and EPA; the Conference of Administrative Vice-Ministers (bureaucrats) from the same ministries; and the Joint Conference of the party-government leaders (politicians and bureaucrats). These three conferences decided to use the liaison office in Beijing as a semiofficial window to communicate with the Chinese government for both economic and political purposes, and to train China experts preparing for future rapprochement (Japan-China Economic Association 1975c: 48–51).

The Takasaki liaison office in Beijing was established in 1964 and was financially supported by MITI and MOF. To fulfill the dual purpose of promoting communication and training personnel, directors and most of the staff members of the Beijing liaison office were governmental officials, usually from MITI. The office members increased from five in 1964 to eighteen in 1972. By the time of normalization in September 1972, the eighteen members of the Beijing office were all governmental officials: eleven from MITI, five from MOFA, one from MOF, and one from MAFF.[7] The strong presence of Japanese governmental bureaucrats in Beijing before normalization made things easier for the transitional process from private channels to governmental agreements.

Bilateral economic exchanges developed rapidly after normalization. Nineteen governmental agreements concerning economic exchanges were signed during the first post-normalization decade from 1972 to 1981.

1. Trade agreement, January 5, 1974

2. Aviation agreement, April 20, 1974

3. Maritime transport agreement, November 13, 1974

4. Insurance agreement for air traffic accident damages, December 2, 1974

5. Agreement on forward exchange transactions between Japanese yen and Chinese renminbi yuan, April 16, 1975

6. Fisheries agreement, August 15, 1975

7. Agreement on the establishment of private-level shipping offices in each country, August 25, 1975

8. Agreement on meteorological cooperation, September 25, 1975

9. First silk trade agreement, May 24, 1976

10. Agreement on the establishment of a meteorological communication link connecting Beijing and Tokyo, September 25, 1977

11. Agreement on trademark protection, September 29, 1977

12. Long-term trade agreement, February 16, 1978

13. Peace and Friendship treaty, August 12, 1978

14. Contract on coking coal under the Sino-Japanese long-term trade agreement, August 14, 1978

15. Maritime arbitration protocol, December 9, 1978

16. Sino-Japanese liner service agreement, January 1979

17. Agreement providing for a Japanese loan of 50 billion yen to China, April 30, 1980

18. Exchange of notes on construction of a China-Japan Friendship Hospital in Beijing, January 26, 1981

19. Agreement by which Japan would provide 50 million yen to China for use in education and research work, March 20, 1981

Although the initial transitional process appeared to go smoothly, serious problems developed during the negotiations over the four economic agreements. From the Japanese perspective, the problems derived from two sources: international constraints and domestic opponents. International constraints came from control of strategic goods trading activities led by the United States, and known as COCOM,[8] and from the issue of most-favored-nation (MFN) treatment. Domestic opposition came from historical legacies on the issue of Taiwan. The background and significance of these issues are closely examined later in this and following chapters. These two elements significantly influenced Japan's negotiations over the four economic agreements. It became clear that the bureaucrats who actually conducted negotiations had to overcome these obstacles in order to get these agreements accomplished. Informal consultation was one of the means the bureaucrats frequently used both externally and internally.

EXTERNAL CONSULTATION

In his study of international negotiations, Glen Fisher made a comparison between Westerners and Japanese. He noticed that Westerners[9] who negotiate with Japanese feel that "the whole idea of holding a formal session specifically to negotiate is somewhat foreign to many Japanese" (1980: 17). *Nemawashi* is one of the most distinctive Japanese negotiation styles, and implies a negotiation method of "informal contact before-hand" or "talks under the table." In this way contacts and mutual trust can be established for all negotiating parties, and disputes can be solved quietly through compromise.

The existence of newly established formal diplomatic relations certainly made the process of economic negotiations easier. Nevertheless, each of the four economic agreements was hampered by international constraints and domestic opponents.

In negotiating the trade agreement along with the other economic agreements (aviation, navigation, and fisheries), the Japanese government strongly felt that the previous nonofficial economic arrangements (trade and fisheries) reflected an unequal relationship. Through the system of "friendly companies," for example, China was able to select Japanese firms based on political conditions. The MITI and MOFA bureaucracies had long been unhappy with this type of trading arrangement.[10] Therefore, the new Tanaka administration believed it was necessary to conclude official and equal bilateral agreements with Beijing as soon as possible. The Japanese government believed that the new agreements should encompass all aspects of the previous nonofficial commercial agreements and include all communication channels between the two countries that operated in the absence of diplomatic relations.

In the absence of a prior formal governmental relationship, the two countries had little understanding of each other's political and economic systems and negotiating procedures. They also lacked personal connections. The Japanese were uncomfortable with this situation. Therefore, informal contact was frequently used for conducting preliminary contact at different levels. Within four months after the establishment of diplomatic relations in September 1972, the Japanese government sent three *nemawashi* teams to visit Beijing in preparation for economic negotiations. The first working team visited Beijing less than a month after normalization.

The team was at division level (comparable to the "desk" level in the U.S. government) and was composed of two groups: three government officials headed by MITI's North Asian Division Director Yoshio Uchida, and three businessmen headed by Japan's representative for the Memorandum Trade Office, Kaheita Okazaki. In Beijing, they were received by their counterparts headed by Wu Shudong, division chief of the Chinese Ministry of Foreign Trade.

Although there were no substantial talks on economic agreements, the Japanese made a preliminary exploration of China's negotiating procedures. In addition, the Japanese officials informed their Chinese counterparts about the Japanese intention to establish a new coordinating trade organization called the Japan-China Economic Association (JCEA) in the following month of November.[11] (For more detail on JCEA, see Chapter 7.)

The second *nemawashi* team arrived in November. This time Japan sent a high-level governmental economic delegation to visit Beijing. This large-scale delegation consisted of thirty-one members from six different ministries: Foreign Affairs; International Trade and Industry; Finance; Agriculture, Forestry, and Fisheries; Transportation; and the Economic Planning Agency. The leader of the delegation was MOFA's Assistant Vice-Minister Fumihiko Tōgō, and the deputy leader was Yogorō Komatsu, director general of MITI's International Trade Bureau. Their Chinese counterparts were Han Nianlong, vice-minister of foreign affairs, and Xi Yesheng, director general of MFT's Fourth Bureau. Again, there were few concrete talks on economic agreements. Instead, focus was placed on each country's trading system, including the custom service and tariff regulations. "This experience was very necessary for us, because we needed time to become familiar with the practice and principles of the Chinese," says Kunihiko Makita, then a young China specialist of foreign affairs who participated in most of the Sino-Japanese negotiations, and who is now director of MOFA's China Division.[12]

The third *nemawashi* visit took place in January 1973 at the ministerial level. This time the Japanese delegation was led by MITI Minister Yasuhiro Nakasone, who was also the first cabinet member to visit Beijing after the Sino-Japanese rapprochement. Nakasone had extensive conversations on bilateral economic relations with Chinese leaders, including Premier Zhou Enlai, Vice-Premier Li Xiannian, and Foreign Trade Minister Li Qiang. Zhou received all delegation members the first time and then twice held separate meetings with Nakasone alone. In the separate meetings, discussion focused on broader political, economic, and international issues.[13] Both Zhou and Nakasone agreed that the Sino-Japanese trade agreement should be concluded by the end of 1973.

These three *nemawashi* trips are quite typical of the Japanese negotiation style. The informal external preparations operated from bottom to top, starting at the level of division chief, progressing up to the level of assistant vice-minister and bureau director, and finally reaching the level of government minister.

In the Japanese bureaucracy, when a decision is about to be reached, a well-informed member of the group (normally starting at lower levels) will draw up a proposal on the matter and circulate it through the organization to get formal approval from other members who affix their seals to the document. This decision-making style is known as *ringisei* (*ringi* means to ask from below), which can be defined as the way to reach consensus at all levels within the bureaucracy (N. Ike 1972: 73), and can be regarded as part of the root in the decision-making process of informal preparation and consultation.

Under this Japanese decision-making procedure, a person initiates and drafts a policy idea, which is then deliberated on by various higher level decision-makers. Sometimes as many as ten different levels of decision-makers are involved before the policy is finalized. The logic behind this system is to allow all members of an organization to participate in the decision-making process: circulation of a draft proposal throughout an organization will facilitate the flow of administrative information; and a high degree of cooperation can be achieved in administering a policy once it is decided, since approval has already been obtained at all levels.

Through this method, Japanese bureaucrats are not only able to reach consensus among themselves, but also gain substantial knowledge about their negotiating counterparts to prevent unnecessary conflicts arising from lack of understanding. In addition, this practice makes it easier to correct mistakes since higher level officials are always able to make course changes, if mistakes are made by their subordinates. Therefore, it is necessary first to examine the background of these international and domestic restraints.

INTERNAL CONSULTATION

Within the Japanese governmental bureaucracy, MOFA and MITI were open rivals, especially over the issue of leadership in the negotiation process. MOFA and MITI were fighting for leadership when the governmental affairs delegation (the second *nemawashi* team) was formed to prepare the visit to China. Since this was a mixed delegation consisting of members of six ministries, a question inevitably arose: Which ministry would be the leader? MITI felt that it should naturally take the responsibility for leadership since this trip covered international trade negotiations. MOFA argued that protocol required important international negotiations to fall under the jurisdiction of MOFA.

After extensive internal consultations within and between the two ministries, including talks at the various levels of division, bureau, and ministry, a compromise of dual leadership was reached. The official leader of the delegation would be MOFA's Assistant Vice-Minister Fumihiko Tōgō, and the deputy leader would be MITI's International Trade Bureau Director Yogorō Komatsu. However, Komatsu would depart for Beijing three days ahead of Tōgō. This meant that for the first three days Komatsu would lead the delegation, followed by Tōgō for the following three days.[14] During the first three days of the trip in November 1972, Komatsu held substantial talks with his counterpart, Xi Yesheng, director of the Fourth Bureau of the Chinese Ministry of Foreign Trade. Three days later, Tōgō arrived. He met with Foreign Trade Minister Li Qiang, Vice-Minister Liu Xiwen, and Foreign Affairs Vice-Minister Han Nianlong. During the discussions, MOFA and MITI officials conducted virtually all the talks to explain Japan's current foreign trade systems. Officials from other Japanese ministries just listened to the discussions without active participation.[15]

The internal consultation within the Japanese bureaucracy (in particular between MITI and MOFA) was successful in preparing for the economic agreements with China. The root-building activities not only solved rival relations, but also coordinated various opinions within different ministries.

MITI's challenge to MOFA's leadership was no surprise in this particular case. At the time of the Sino-Japanese rapprochement, MITI had been the most active and the least conservative governmental agency in the Japanese bureaucracy. MITI had not only made detailed studies of the Chinese market and its economic system, but had also paid great attention to training its own China specialists.

Let us take MITI bureaucrat Yoshio Uchida as an example. A Tokyo University graduate, Uchida entered MITI in 1957. As a junior official, he worked in various MITI divisions over a seven-year period (including a short period at the Economic Planning Agency). In 1964 Uchida was promoted to deputy director of the Third Overseas Market Division, under the Bureau of International Trade. At the time this division covered a broad range of areas including East Asia, Southeast Asia, the Soviet Union, and East Europe. In 1964, MITI started a Chinese language class for a small group of bureaucrats. This class was taught by two well-known China experts from the University of Tokyo, Professors Takeshirō Kuraishi and Akiyasu Tōdō, and two native Chinese speakers. At first, Uchida was too busy to consider his own participation in the Chinese class. One day his immediate supervisor, Yaeji Watanabe, director general of the International Trade Bureau, asked him, "Why don't you join in the group and start your Chinese lessons?" This was a turning point in Uchida's career. From then on, Uchida began to learn Chinese and became a China specialist.[16]

In 1966, six years before normalization, Uchida was sent to Beijing as a private citizen to become one of the five members of the Sino-Japanese Memorandum Office. Uchida and his family spent three years in Beijing. During his stay in China, he further improved his language ability, and he made Chinese friends in political as well as economic circles. Uchida and his wife studied Chinese culture thoroughly, even learning how to cook Chinese dishes with local flavors. Their home became known as "Neitian Fandian" (the Uchida Restaurant) among his Chinese and Japanese friends.

Upon his return to Tokyo in 1969, Uchida was sent to several MITI posts, including one in Hokkaido, that were not directly connected with the China trade in order to broaden his experience. In 1971 he was appointed director of the newly established Fourth Overseas Market Division (later renamed the North Asian Division). This division was mainly in charge of trade with China. Uchida immediately became involved in intensive negotiations with the Chinese on the trade agreement and other economic agreements. His knowledge of China was fully utilized.

Uchida stayed in this China-related position for three years. Later he was transferred to more than five senior trading positions, including three years in San Francisco as director of the Japan External Trade Organization (JETRO) office. In 1983 Uchida decided to take early retirement from MITI, so that he would be able to follow the pattern of *amakudari* (descent from heaven). This was a typical method for Japanese bureaucrats to have second careers after mandatory retirement. His landing post was the Arabian Oil Company, which was Japan's largest overseas oil company. Uchida become senior adviser for the company and concurrently director of a subsidiary company, the Huanan (South China) Oil Development Company, which attempted to set up joint ventures with the Chinese in the exploration of oil resources in the South China Sea. His stint with the private company, however, did not last long. In 1987 Uchida was recalled by the government, and he was appointed executive director of the Information-Technology Promotion Agency.[17]

Uchida's story shows the strength of MITI, which comes from a long-term vision of international relations, and the superbly trained experts who have field experience, language abilities, and special knowledge accumulated over a long period. When the issue is technical and administrative in nature, this strength becomes even more obvious. Similar strengths are found in well-trained MOFA officials as well. All these examples demonstrate the necessity of internal consultation and coordination within the bureaucracy.

GAKUBATSU AND THE GOVERNMENT BUREAUCRACY

Many scholars of the Japanese bureaucracy observed that graduates of the University of Tokyo (Todai) constitute the single most important source of administrative elite in Japan. According to B. C. Koh (1989: 159–170), for example, in 1986 "six out of ten civil servants occupying the position of section chief or higher in the national government were Todai graduates. The proportion increases to 76 percent at the bureau-chief level and to 86.7 percent at the vice-ministerial level." It is not difficult to imagine that the common school background, known as *gakubatsu* (meaning "school clique"), likely provides the basis on which the governmental bureaucracy can enjoy well-established personnel connections and build consensus.

This personal connection based on *gakubatsu* played a significant role in coordinating different internal interests among the various central agencies that were conducting negotiations on Sino-Japanese economic agreements. In one preliminary session for the negotiations, for example, the Japanese delegation was composed of eleven officials at the division-director level from three different ministries: MOFA, MITI, and MOT (Ministry of Transportation). Usually, MOFA officials take charge of foreign trade negotiations to ensure a unified voice toward "outsiders" (foreigners). According to one Japanese official's recollection, the relationship among members of the Japanese delegation was cordial partially because most of the officials were alumni of the University of Tokyo. Furthermore, two key members, MOFA's China Division Director Michihiko Kunihiro and MOT's International Shipping Division Director Chiyoji Tomita, were graduates of the Todai Faculty of Law and had known one another in school. Tomita felt comfortable because he "was three years senior to Kunihiro," while Kunihiro showed respect to him as dictated by traditional behavior. Tomita, in turn, was glad to be cooperative with Kunihiro.[18] This case illuminates the importance of the "old boy" connection as an integral part of Japan's informal mechanisms.

Going to college in Japan is not only an educational experience; it is also, as Susan Pharr points out, "the opportunity to enter into new relationships with peers" (1981: 90). *Gakubatsu* denotes the group consciousness derived mainly from a common university or college background. Graduates of the same university or college share an in-group feeling, a ready familiarity with others. As a means of social bonding in Japan, a common educational background, next to one's institution or place of work, is more effective than either family or local background (Nakane 1970: 128).

More importantly, the entire elite circles in Japanese society (and not just the governmental bureaucracy) are composed largely of graduates from about a dozen top universities. The University of Tokyo, the top of the tops, is considered a combination of three prestigious American universities—Harvard, MIT, and Berkeley. As Robert Christopher points out,

> Half of Japan's postwar prime ministers have been Todai products, as are four out of five [of] the country's ranking bureaucrats and whole battalions of top corporate executives. In fact, even the more "revolutionary" forces in Japanese society tend to be spearheaded by Todai graduates: a number of Communist Party leaders went there. (1983: 85)

Other well-known educational institutions include the state-run universities Kyoto, Kyushu, Tohoku, Nagoya, Hokkaido, Hitotsubashi, and Osaka and private universities such as Waseda, Keiō, and Chuō.

In the central governmental agencies, Todai *gakubatsu* is especially impressive. Table 18 shows that about 80 percent of Japan's high-level bureaucrats are Todai graduates. Todai graduates dominate in the ministries of foreign affairs (95.7 percent), finance (92.2 percent), labor (90.9 percent), and agriculture and forestry (88.1 percent).

As in the United States, the candidate has to pass a foreign service examination in order to be admitted to the Ministry of Foreign Affairs. During the entire forty-year period 1949–89, Todai graduates had a disproportionately higher percentage (559 people) among those who passed the upper level (A-class) foreign service examination. Todai was far head of the rest of the elite universities: Hitotsubashi (94), Kyoto (80), Keiō (40), Tokyo Foreign Studies (30), Waseda (26), Chuō (6), and Osaka (6) (Murakawa 1989:54).

This high concentration of Todai graduates in the bureaucracy may find its roots in history. Todai was established by the Meiji government to train government officials, whereas Kyoto University, for example, was established to train academics or prepare others for nonbureaucratic careers, such as journalism. With a reputation as *kanryō yōseijo*, or a "school for bureaucrats," Todai's domination of the central bureaucracy is unequaled worldwide: it surpasses the combined share for Oxford and Cambridge in the British bureaucracy (A.

Table 18
**Distribution of Tokyo University Graduates as High-level Central Bureaucrats,
by Ministry**

Name of Ministry	1975	1980	1985	Total	Percentage of Total
Foreign Affairs	15	14	15	44	95.7
Finance	17	17	13	47	92.2
Labor	10	9	11	30	90.9
Agriculture	13	14	10	37	88.1
Education	9	9	7	25	86.2
Health & Welfare	11	12	12	35	83.3
Int'l Trade & Industry	12	10	12	34	81.0
Transportation	17	15	17	49	77.8
Home Affairs	5	5	5	15	71.4
Justice	8	7	6	21	67.7
Post & Telecom.	11	9	13	33	66.0
Office of the Prime Minister	5	5	1	11	64.7
Construction	8	8	6	22	62.9
Total	141	134	128	403	80.3

Source: P. Kim 1988: 146.

Kubota 1969: 162), and it exceeds a combination of Harvard, Yale, Princeton, and Columbia in the federal government of the United States. Because of the importance of *gakubatsu* in the Japanese central bureaucracy, the year of graduation of *gakubatsu* members has also become an important criterion for career promotion of governmental officials (A. Burks 1981: 186).

In sum, the Todai *gakubatsu* has proven to be an exceptionally useful personal connection within Japan's central bureaucracy, as well as for networking with other segments of Japanese society.

DISPUTES OVER COCOM AND MFN

Trade restrictions, known as COCOM and the most-favored-nation (MFN) treatment, were central issues of dispute during the negotiations of the Sino-Japanese trade agreement. Therefore, before discussing subsequent developments at the negotiation table, it is necessary to provide a detailed background of these two issues.

A primary objective of this agreement was to promote bilateral economic relations. Since the MFN clause was a key element in facilitating commercial relations and it was previously not included in nongovernmental trade agreements, it became a central concern for both sides.

From the Chinese perspective, before 1949 China had a series of painful unequal treaty experiences with foreign powers in which the MFN clause applied unilaterally to foreigners in China, without providing reciprocal treatment for the Chinese in foreign countries. Therefore, Beijing was determined to obtain the MFN clause as a fundamental principle of its official trade treaties and agreements with foreign countries.

Five basic points of the MFN clause were described in a textbook on foreign trade used in Chinese universities:

- *Conditional vs. unconditional*: The condition form implies that concessions shall be generalized only upon the reciprocal payment of equivalent compensation, whereas the unconditional form lays down no conditions under which concessions, granted by contracting states, should be generalized.

- *Mutual vs. unilateral*: The mutual form consists of the reciprocal grant of MFN treatment, whereas the unilateral form provides one contracting state with MFN treatment while denying it to the other.

- *Limited vs. unlimited*: The limited form confines the application of the clause to certain specified objects or territories, whereas the unlimited form imposes no restrictions on the scope of application.

- *Positive vs. negative*: The positive form requires that both contracting states undertake to grant each other all privileges, favors, and immunities they have granted or may hereafter grant to any third state, while the negative form stipulates that neither contracting state shall treat the other less favorably than it does any third state.

- *Simple vs. complex*: The simple form contains a general statement providing MFN treatment, whereas the complex form defines the clause in greater detail and usually consists of four parts concerning its general purpose, interpretation, limitations, and exceptions.[19]

In reviewing China's past practices with countries from both the Western and Eastern blocs, we can see that China has favored the unconditional, mutual, limited, and positive forms. China has criticized the unilateral, unlimited, and negative forms as unequal, and views the conditional form as obsolete.

When examining the Sino-Japanese trade agreement, several questions merit consideration: Did the agreement have an MFN clause? How was the MFN clause defined? What were the different policies between Japan and China regarding the issue of MFN?

The first two parts of Article One of the trade agreement defined the MFN treatment as the following:

1. The Contracting Parties shall accord each other most-favored-nation treatment with respect to customs duties, internal taxes, and other charges imposed on imported or exported goods, in matters relating to the method of levying such duties, taxes, and other charges as well as customs rules, formalities, and procedures.

2. The conditions of most-favored-nation treatment applicable to the goods mentioned in Paragraph 1 above shall be the same as those granted to third countries by either Contracting Party.[20]

Clearly, MFN treatment in this case was of the mutual and limited form favored by the Chinese. However, it applied only to "duties, taxes, customs rules, and procedures." It did not define what aspects it did not apply to. It would be useful at this point to compare the Sino-Japanese trade agreement with trade agreements between China and other Western countries that had different MFN wording. The Sino-Australian trade agreement is a good example for comparison.

Australia signed a trade agreement with China on July 24, 1973, six months before the Sino-Japanese trade agreement. The MFN treatment was also a central issue of the Sino-Australian trade agreement. Article Four states:

The two Contracting Parties shall grant each other *most-favored-nation treatment in the issue of import and export licenses* and the allocation of foreign exchange connected therewith, as well as in all respects concerning customs duties, internal taxes or other charges imposed on or in connection with imported goods, and customs and other related formalities, regulations and procedures. [emphasis added] (G. Hsiao 1977: 199)

In many aspects, the Sino-Australian agreement was similar to the Sino-Japanese agreement. Both agreements were in mutual and limited forms. They were also in negative and complex forms, which defined the MFN clause in detail, and would not grant one another all privileges, favors, and immunities. In other words, instead of granting complete MFN treatment, the clauses granted limited MFN treatment.

Nevertheless, in a more careful examination of these two trade agreements, it is not difficult to discover differences between the two. One obvious difference is the Australian MFN clause applied to "import and export licenses," whereas the Japanese clause referred to "customs duties, internal taxes, and other charges imposed on imported or exported goods." This MFN clause for import and export licenses provides broader coverage than what the Sino-Japanese trade agreement offered. China badly needed high technology and advanced equipment for its modernization drive and wanted the broader coverage of the MFN clause from

Japan, similar to that of the Australian agreement, which provided for the import and export licenses.

The issue of import and export licenses, however, was subject to export controls set by COCOM. In the case of trade agreements with China, Japan was influenced more by COCOM restrictions than Australia for two reasons. First, although Australia was a member of the Western bloc, it did not become a COCOM member until 1989.[21] Japan, on the other hand, became a member as early as 1952 and, therefore, was more deeply restricted by export controls relating to China. Second, according to an MITI official, the trading items were different. Australia exported mainly minerals and agricultural goods to China, whereas the Japanese exports were composed largely of industrial equipment and machinery which were usually subject to COCOM restrictions.[22] To get a clearer picture of the relationship between Japan and COCOM, it is necessary to review the post–World War II period.

The Paris-based Coordinating Committee (COCOM) was a product of the cold war, originating in the immediate postwar era. In the fall of 1945, the United States implemented an export control policy against communist countries. In November 1948 the United States, together with Canada and the major Western European countries, worked out a multilateral agreement on export controls and established an organization called the Consultative Group, which met quarterly in Paris (hence known as the Paris group). COCOM handled its day-to-day work. The original target of COCOM was the Soviet Union. China was not yet included on the list because at that time the People's Republic was not yet founded. As a defeated and occupied nation, Japan was not eligible for COCOM membership during the early period of its existence.

It was only after the 1949 communist victory in China, and especially after the outbreak of the Korean War in 1950, that the United States imposed a trade embargo on the new People's Republic. This led to the establishment of the China Committee (CHINCOM) in September 1952, which was under the jurisdiction of the Consultative Group, to specifically deal with export controls against areas in Asia under communist rule, excluding the Soviet Union.

Although Japan was not a member of COCOM during the early period, its trade relations with China were strictly controlled by the American occupation authorities, known as the Supreme Commander of the Allied Powers (SCAP). In a *Diplomatic History* magazine article, Yōko Yasuhara (1986: 89) examined the process of Japan's participation in the COCOM and concluded that Japan's export control policy was formulated under instructions and pressures from SCAP. During the occupation period, the United States ordered the Japanese government to maintain export controls on China trade at a much tighter level than those of COCOM members.

Interestingly, the United States originally opposed Japan's admission to COCOM, because the restrictive rules of COCOM were not as strict as those rules imposed by SCAP on Japan's exports. The United States feared Japan would enjoy a "relaxed" control policy under COCOM and that Sino-Japanese trade might expand quickly, thereby damaging U.S. interests. The Americans took several steps to impose a strict export control over Japan's trade with China. In December 1950 SCAP sent a directive to the Japanese government ordering it to suspend exports of strategic (or "controlled") items to Mainland China, North Korea, Hong Kong, and Macao (Y. Yasuhara 1986: 85). This effectively suppressed the Japanese business community's desire to expand Sino-Japanese trade. In the following year, Sino-Japanese trade declined sharply.

The United States rejected Japan's application to enter COCOM, which would have meant the relaxation of Japanese trade controls to COCOM levels. Instead, the Truman administration wanted to establish a separate export control organization for Asia. Other COCOM members, however, supported Japan's COCOM membership for their own reasons. The British, for example, were afraid that if a new organization tightly controlled the expansion of Sino-Japanese trade, it would encourage Japan to move to Southeast Asia, thereby challenging British commercial interests in the region. Under such pressure from its European allies, the United States was compelled to admit Japan. But before doing so, Washington unilaterally discussed the issue with SCAP and the Japanese government. The result of this discussion was the transfer of full export control responsibilities from SCAP to the Japanese government in March 1952, one month before the end of the occupation. In April, an American technical mission was sent to Tokyo to supervise Japanese government officials on security controls and to urge Japan to joint a separate Asian trade control organization.

The United States' demand for control of Sino-Japanese trade was confirmed by an international meeting in Washington in July and August 1952. The United States, Japan, Britain, France, and Canada participated in this conference. A compromise was reached: Japan joined the Paris Group, but a separate Far Eastern Coordinating Committee called the China Committee (CHINCOM) was established under the Consultative Group of COCOM. Thus, Japan became a member of both COCOM and CHINCOM.

At the time of the Washington conference, the United States made a further move to ensure that Japan would stick to restrictions on trade with China. Harold Linder, the chief of the U.S. delegation, put pressure on Ryūji Takeuchi, chief of the Japanese government's Overseas Agency in Washington. Linder insisted on a formal letter from the Japanese promising to control items on U.S. security lists and other goods of strategic importance. Reluctantly, Takeuchi agreed to submit such a letter to the U.S. government.

In September 1952 Linder and Takeuchi reached an agreement entitled an Understanding Between Japan and the United States Concerning the Control of Exports to Communist China. According to this agreement, Japan promised to control all commodities on international control lists, all items on U.S. security lists, and additional items on which the two governments would agree in the future. Meanwhile, the U.S. government gave Japan a list of about 400 items, and Japan agreed to control approximately 280 items. The remaining items were left for further discussion. Thus began U.S. guidance for the Japanese government's policies on export controls under COCOM. Hence, as long as the United States maintained COCOM principles toward China, it was virtually impossible for Japan to abolish COCOM unilaterally. This still holds true today (Y. Yasuhara, 1986: 88).

Besides political pressure from the United States, certain economic considerations motivated Japan to commit itself to COCOM regulations. Japanese officials were afraid that if Japan unilaterally abandoned export controls toward China, it would not be able to obtain advanced technologies from the United States and other Western countries.[23]

Japan's entry into COCOM has enabled Japan to further integrate its economy into the world capitalist system and to develop Japan-U.S. economic cooperation and the U.S.-Southeast Asia-Japan nexus. On the other hand, it has had a long-term negative influence that has severely hindered the development of Sino-Japanese trade. It was inevitable that the COCOM issue became a central point in the negotiations for the 1974 Sino-Japanese governmental trade agreement.

INDIVIDUAL CONTACT DURING THE NEGOTIATION

The exchange of the drafts of the Sino-Japanese trade agreement took place in June 1973. Two months later, the Chinese trade delegation headed by Xi Yesheng, a bureau director of the Foreign Trade Ministry, arrived in Tokyo. The Japanese delegation was led by MOFA's Asian Affairs Bureau Director Masuo Takashima, with MITI's Trade Policy Bureau Deputy Director Toshio Ōishi as number two.

Japanese officials from different ministries had different agendas regarding the coming negotiations. Finance Ministry officials, for example, were concerned about the issues of customs duties and settling accounts between the Japanese yen and the Chinese renminbi.[24] The greatest concern for the Japanese delegation, however, was the issue of MFN and COCOM. Members of the Japanese delegation discussed this issue every night to work out a better position for the coming talks with the Chinese.[25]

Generally speaking, with regard to the issue of COCOM, officials from the Ministry of Foreign Affairs (MOFA) and the Ministry of Justice (MOJ) were more conservative, whereas MITI officials were more open-minded. But MITI had its own problem because of its dual responsibilities. On the one hand, MITI was to promote Japan's international trade; on the other hand, MITI was also responsible for implementing the COCOM regulations. This put MITI in a difficult position. Nevertheless, MITI bureaucrats tried their best to keep a balance between these two functions.[26] Internal consultation, which was conducted to coordinate the different opinions among bureaucrats from various ministries, produced two principles accepted by the Japanese delegation: first, the agreement should be reached as soon as possible; and second, Japan had to maintain the COCOM principles since Japan-U.S. relations were the cornerstone of Japanese foreign policy.

At this stage, Japanese bureaucrats foresaw four possible outcomes of the negotiations:

1. A full MFN treatment, meaning immediate abolishment of the COCOM restrictions.
2. MFN except COCOM, meaning clearly indicating the COCOM restrictions.
3. MFN with specific definitions without mentioning COCOM, meaning that the agreement would sound like full MFN treatment. But since there were specific definitions, both sides would understand that the MFN could not go beyond these definitions, meaning the COCOM restrictions would not be violated by the Japanese government.
4. Failure to reach an agreement.[27]

The first possibility was virtually unacceptable to the Japanese given the existing international situation, and the last possibility was the least desirable. Therefore, the Japanese delegation adopted the second and third alternatives as its negotiating goals.

During the negotiations, both sides agreed to include the MFN clause in the agreement, but found it difficult to decide whether the MFN treatment should be subject to COCOM or not. The Chinese delegation argued that because friendly relations were now being established between the two countries, Japan's discriminatory restrictions against China should be abolished. The Chinese further proposed to reciprocate MFN treatment for export and import licenses, because it would benefit both countries.[28]

The Japanese maintained that all goals could be accomplished except those that involved multinational agreements, meaning COCOM. Before the disagreement developed further, MOFA's China Division Director Kunihiro used the method of individual contact several times by talking to several leading members of the Chinese delegation away form the negotiation table. He specifically explained Japan's difficult position and obtained an understanding from the Chinese.

The Chinese, of course, had known before they went to Tokyo that the COCOM issue would be difficult. Kunihiro's personal contact further clarified the international constraints that Japan had to face. The Chinese, therefore, did not insist on this issue.[29] The surprising flexibility of the Chinese delegation kept the rest of the negotiations moving smoothly.

In January 1974, the two respective foreign ministers, Ji Pengfei and Masayoshi Ōhira, signed the trade agreement. Article One of the agreement concerned MFN treatment. There were specific definitions of MFN treatment without mention of the COCOM restrictions, and the "import and export licenses."[30] This was exactly the third choice previously prepared by the Japanese delegation. Both sides were satisfied with the trade agreement.

The negotiations for the Sino-Japanese Governmental Fisheries Agreement began in late 1973. After almost two years of negotiation, it was signed in August 1975. One of its main points was to replace the existing nongovernmental fisheries arrangement. The first nongovernmental arrangement had been signed in 1955 by the Fisheries Association of China and the Japan-China Fisheries Association. This agreement covered a three-year period and expired in 1958. Prior to this agreement, bilateral fisheries talks were initiated because of successive Chinese seizures of Japanese fishing vessels operating off Chinese coasts in the Yellow and East China Sea areas. In 1958 China decided not to extend such nongovernmental arrangements, primarily because it was unhappy over Japan's "unfriendly" behavior, such as the Nagasaki flag incident (see Chapter 5). This no-relations status lasted until December 1963 when Sino-Japanese relations began to improve and the second nongovernmental arrangement was concluded. The third arrangement started in December 1965 and expired in June 1975 (Hong 1977: 1–3). As the deadline for expiration approached, there was added pressure to continue bilateral talks to complete the agreement as soon as possible.

The prolonged and intermittent negotiations focused on fishing rights and territorial limits in the Yellow Sea and the East China Sea. Since the agreement provided for many measures of the preservation and effective utilization of fishery resources, it involved both technical problems and the issue of territorial limits. The Japanese delegation also needed time to conduct extensive personal contacts with their Chinese counterparts to push for resolving these obstacles.

The Japanese delegation was composed mainly of officials from MAFF and MOFA. The leadership role was taken by MOFA officials. This time, there were no serious disputes between MAFF and MOFA, because a clear division of labor had been arranged beforehand, following internal consultation between the two ministries. MOFA would be in charge of overall principles and the issue of territorial limits, whereas MAFF would be responsible for technical issues such as fishery resources and fishing vessel emergencies.[31] The negotiations over the fisheries agreement produced no rivalry between MOFA and MAFF, in contrast to the dispute between MOFA and MITI during negotiations for the trade agreement.

In both form and substance, the Sino-Japanese government fisheries agreement was quite similar to the previous nongovernmental arrangements (Hong 1977: 22), which further demonstrates how Japan's informal and nongovernmental arrangements often function as a prelude to later formal official agreements.

NON-WESTERN STYLE AND THE AVOIDANCE OF CONFRONTATION

Reflecting Japan's traditional culture and behavior style, *nemawashi* (informal preparation and consultation) often adopts an indirect or implicit way of communication by arranging individual meetings of informal talks outside of official negotiations. This non-Western manner, represented here by *nemawashi*, as Karel van Wolferen suggests (1989: 338), is not the Western "democratic" way of decision-making, because its implicit behavior often "involves talking with the concerned parties so as to prepare them to 'accept a plan,' " without actually providing the option of rejection. Furthermore, the disadvantage of this system is that it is an inefficient use of time. It is also difficult to identify who has real responsibility for a decision (S. Misawa 1973: 30).

On the other hand, this indirect style indeed reflects Japan's traditional cultural emphasis on the importance of maintaining harmony (at least superficially) among the Japanese as well as with foreigners. This tradition makes the Japanese uncomfortable with outspokenness in social gatherings, especially in a formal setting. They use such occasions to ceremonially adopt what has already been worked out in a behind-the-scenes process of consensus-building. To disagree openly at a formal stage is offensive (G. Fisher 1980: 17). Extensive personal contacts and consultations are used to avoid open confrontation and to build consensus through informal means. In this sense, *nemawashi* accomplishes the goal of maintaining harmony and reaching solutions. Moreover, within the governmental establishment, vertical communication is normally more effective[32] than horizontal communication; hence, informal preparation and consultation become all the more necessary for facilitating horizontal communication among various policymaking institutions, such as MOFA and MITI. We may attribute this effective communication not only to regular governmental channels, but also to the frequent use of informal consultation at the personal level for the purpose of consensus-building, as we have seen from the negotiation process for the four agreements.

The next chapter continues our examination of the *nemawashi* working style by looking into the activities of the LDP, the National Diet, and the business community during negotiations for the four economic agreements.

NOTES

1. Some research indicates that since the 1970s this kind of vertical relationship in Japan has recently weakened and has gradually changed toward a more horizontal relationship. See Takao Sofue (1986).

2. The concept of political culture comes from a study by Gabriel Almond, "Comparative Political Systems," *Journal of Politics* 18 (1956). Almond argues that "every political system is embedded in a particular pattern of orientation to political action."

3. For the full document of the Sino-Japanese Joint Statement, see *Peking Review*, October 6, 1972, pp. 12–13.

4. The friendly firms system began in the late 1950s, when the Chinese started to use political criteria to choose Japanese firms that accepted the principle of "no separation between politics and economics." These firms were designated as friendly firms. The memorandum trade agreements (previously the L-T Memorandum) were nonofficial agreements, which were first concluded in November 1962. See "Background of Japan's China Policy and Sino-Japanese Trade" in Chapter 2.

5. See Japan External Trade Organization (JETRO), *How to Approach the China Market* (1972: 78–79).

6. See Yu Qinggao, Hua Jue, et al., eds., *Xiandai Riben Mingren Lu* [Records of notables in contemporary Japan] (1984): 205–206, and 348–349.

7. Ibid., pp. 82–86.

8. COCOM stands for the Coordinating Committee of the Consultative Group, which was created in 1949 by the United States and its European alliances to control the trade of strategic goods with the communist bloc headed by the Soviet Union. A similar committee specially related to China was called CHINCOM, standing for the China Committee of the same Consultative Group. It was established in September 1952 to enforce the control of exports to the People's Republic of China. These two committees were similar and often overlapped. Therefore, for convenience, I will use COCOM to refer to both trade restriction organizations except in specific instances. Japan's relations with COCOM are discussed later.

9. "Westerners" is a vague concept, because there are many differences among "Westerners"; for example, Americans are different from Europeans.

10. Interview with Michihiko Kunihiro, June 4, 1986, Tokyo. Kunihiro served as director of MFA's China Division from 1973 to 1974 and was MOFA's assistant vice minister at the time of interview.

11. Interview with Yoshio Uchida, February 25, 1986, Tokyo. Uchida served as director of MITI's North Asia Division from 1971 to 1974.

12. Interview with Kunihiko Makita, February 19, 1986, Tokyo.

13. Interview with Yoshio Uchida, February 25, 1986, Tokyo.

14. Interview with Yoshio Uchida, March 4, 1986, Tokyo.

15. Interview with Keisuke Inui, March 14, 1986, Tokyo. Inui, as director of the International Shipping Division of the Ministry of Transportation, participated in the governmental affairs delegation in 1972.

16. Interview with Yoshio Uchida, June 20, 1987, Tokyo.

17. Ibid.

18. Interview with Chiyoji Tomita, May 29, 1986, Tokyo. Tomita was managing director and vice-president of the Japan Asia Airways Company at the time of interview.

19. These points were summarized by Gene T. Hsiao, based on a Chinese textbook on foreign trade. See Hsiao, *The Foreign Trade of China* (1977: 125).

20. For the full document of the Sino-Japanese Trade Agreement see Gene T. Hsiao, *The Foreign Trade of China* (1977: 196–198), (*Source*: The Japanese Government).

21. See "U.S. Exports: Strategic Technology Controls," *Gist*, Department of State, November 1989.

22. Interviews with Yoshio Uchida, March 4, 1986, Tokyo. Uchida served as director of MITI's North Asian Division from 1971 to 1974.

23. Interview with former Foreign Minister Saburō Ōkita, July 4, 1986, Tokyo. Also interview with Michihiko Kunihiro, June 4, 1986, Tokyo.

24. Interview with Saemon Ichikawa, March 7, 1986, Tokyo. Ichikawa as an MOF official served in Japan's Beijing Embassy for three years (1974–77), and was director of the JCEA at the time of interview.

25. Interview with Toshio Ōishi, March 6, 1986, Tokyo. Ōishi was president of the Japan Overseas Development Corporation at the time of interview.

26. Interview with Yoshitoshi Munakata, March 14, 1986, Tokyo. Munakata was the first Japanese commercial counselor to the Beijing Embassy (1973–74), and was

commissioner of Japan's Fair Trade Commission at the time of interview.

27. Interview with Toshio Ōishi, March 6, 1986, Tokyo.

28. Interview with Lin Liande, October 28, 1986, Beijing. Lin was one of a few of China's Japan specialists since he graduated from the University of Tokyo in the early 1940s. Before normalization he worked for the CCPIT dealing with Japanese trade. After 1972 he was appointed as the first director of the Japan Division at the MFT, and then was promoted to the level of bureau chief. Lin retired in 1985 after being stationed three years in Tokyo as China's commercial counselor.

29. Ibid.

30. For the full document of the Sino-Japanese Trade Agreement, see Gene T. Hsiao, *The Foreign Trade of China* (1977: 196–198), (*Source*: The Japanese Government).

31. Interview with Yoshihiro Hamaguchi, March 13, 1986, Tokyo. Hamaguchi was first secretary at the Japanese Embassy in Beijing sent by MAFF, and he was director general of MAFF's Forestry Administration Department at the time of interview.

32. In a study on Japanese policymaking at the local level, Steven Reed (1986: 166) has noticed that "communications among various levels of government in Japan are so effective that local governments are seldom surprised by a central policy change."

7

Political Trust and Mutual Understanding

The theme of trust and distrust is emphasized in the study of political culture. Lucian Pye (1965: 22) suggests that political cultures are built either on the fundamental belief that it is possible to trust and work with one's fellows, or on the expectation that most people are to be distrusted and that strangers in particular are likely to be dangerous. Pye believes that "each political culture differs according to its patterns of trust and distrust." Trust is derived from mutual understanding, and understanding is dependent on proper channels of communication. One important channel of communication in Japan is through informal preparation and consultation at the individual level.

In Japan, it is possible to communicate through nonverbal understanding. Informal consultation is an important form of implicit communication (J. Kyōgoku 1987: 69–71); it is often used to explain *tatemae* (public behavior) and to convey *honne* (one's true intention or feeling) to one another through informal ways. Boye De Mente (1987: 19) points out that these contrasting principles in Japan are "used to cloak the truth or reality of situations that might be inconvenient or embarrassing to acknowledge publicly." Each party, therefore, will receive true messages without any misunderstanding or open confrontation. Frequently, informal consultation at the personal level is more important in Japan's political life than formally arranged meetings.

For example, according to Bradley Richardson (1991: 338), there are two kinds of election campaigns—formal and informal—in Japan. In a formal campaign, candidates and party leaders are more likely to give speeches before crowds of citizens or to publish political statements in the mass media. In an informal campaign, "a variety of appeals for support are made via word of mouth through people's social network contact." Personal connections are indeed an effective factor for political mobilization.

To understand personal connection and informal consultation, we may also look deeply at the way in which nonverbal communication affects Japan's social and political life. According to Eiichirō Ishida (1974: 117), even today Japanese politicians approve of mind-to-mind communication known as *ishin-denshin* (tacit or intuitive understanding) or *haragei*. *Hara* literally means stomach or belly, but in this case mind, intention, spirit; *gei* means art, accomplishment. *Haragei* thus means "stomach art," or implicit understanding.

The conceptual significance of political trust and understanding in Japan has been examined by some Western scholars (G. Akita 1967: 139–140). Robert Butow (1954: 70), a historian, stated that "a man who uses *haragei* is a man who says one thing but means another." This statement, however, only scratches the surface of the *haragei* concept. A more accurate explanation is that the two parties involved understand exactly what each other is thinking, but, for political or other reasons, they choose not to say so explicitly. This inconsistency does not necessarily mean that either is lying, but rather that the real intentions can be understood only by those who understand their culture. This inconsistent behavior corresponds to the difference between *tatemae* and *honne*.

This chapter continues to examine Japan's informal mechanisms at the individual level by conducting the case study on the negotiations for the four Sino-Japanese economic agreements (trade, aviation, navigation, and fisheries). The examination is through the political culture perspective. This chapter focuses on political maneuvers within the ruling LDP/bureaucracy apparatus, the National Diet, and the business community.

THE TAIWAN ISSUE AS AN OBSTACLE

As discussed in previous chapters, one of the main obstacles to Sino-Japanese rapprochement and the four economic agreements came from the pro-Taiwan conservative groups within the ruling LDP. When negotiations were held during the 1973–75 period, there were two basic objectives for the mainstream LDP leaders: externally to persuade Beijing to make compromises and to get the agreements signed, and internally to attain an understanding among the various political forces, in particular from the conservative groups, so as to avoid open confrontation. This goal of internal understanding within the ruling coalition became a crucial element for Japan to successfully carry out its new China policy in the post-rapprochement era.

Under the leadership of Prime Minister Tanaka, the LDP established the Council for the Normalization of Sino-Japanese Diplomatic Relations in July 1972. This Council had two purposes: to facilitate the normalization process, and to set up a forum for different opinions, especially for the pro-Taiwan forces to speak out so that they could have an opportunity to show their loyalty to their "old friend" Taiwan. The first purpose was successfully accomplished. The second, however, encountered problems. The fast pace of normalization with the PRC did not allow careful internal consultations with the pro-Taiwan groups, which were becoming increasingly bitter. Although no longer in the party's mainstream (or majority groups), many of the pro-Taiwan conservatives were still strongly critical toward the new China policy. This group became a time bomb for Sino-Japanese relations, and how to deal with them became a headache for those LDP leaders, known as mainstreamers, who wanted to make a rapid change in Japan's China policy.

The negotiation for the aviation agreement, which began in March 1973, was tough and time consuming. At first, the Chinese demanded a suspension of Taiwan's China Airlinés (CAL) flights to Tokyo, arguing that Japan must stop treating Taiwan as an independent country as had been clearly stated in the Zhou Enlai-Tanaka Joint Statement. If Japan continued to allow Taiwan's airlines to use the name of "China" and to carry Taiwan's flag, it would create the problem of "two Chinas," which Beijing firmly opposed.

China demanded that Japan cancel the Japan-Taiwan route operated by CAL and Japan Airlines, or at least reroute Taiwan's flights to other Japanese airports such as Nagoya and Okinawa, instead of Tokyo; that use of Taiwan's flag by CAL not be allowed; that Taiwan's airline be officially called another name, such as the Airlines of Taiwan rather than China Airlines; and that Taiwan airline branch offices in Japan be transferred to local agencies run by the Japanese.

Thus, the Taiwan issue became a major obstacle for the economic agreements, particularly for the aviation agreement. A deadlock existed for some time— neither side was willing to make concessions. Although the Taiwan issue[1] itself was not a domestic problem in Japan (rather, it was China's domestic problem), there were pro-Taiwan forces within Japan's political circles, particularly within the conservative ruling LDP, which made the Taiwan issue a battlefield of Japanese internal politics. Politically, Japan's pro-Taiwan forces shared the anticommunist ideology of the Taiwan government. Large-scale Japanese business interests, which maintained intimate relations with conservative factions, were deeply involved in trade with Taiwan and had over $100 million of investment in Taiwan.[2] It is easy to understand why the conservatives worked hard to oppose any movement to break off relations with Taiwan, and instead discouraged expansion of trade relations with Mainland China.

In August 1963 the Japanese government under Prime Minister Hayato Ikeda approved the financing of the Kurashiki Rayon Company's sale of a vinylon plant (worth $20 million) to China on a five-year credit term through the government-owned Export and Import Bank of Japan. Taipei viewed the sale as economic aid to Beijing, and it resulted in Taiwan's recalling top diplomats from Tokyo to press the Japanese government.

In March 1964 Ikeda sent Shigeru Yoshida, a former prime minister and a senior LDP statesman, to Taipei to discuss Japan-Taiwan relations with Chiang Kai-shek, Taiwan's Nationalist Party's (KMT) leader. Shortly after this visit, Yoshida wrote a letter to Taipei's presidential secretary-general Zhang Qun (Chang Chun), dated April 4, 1964, that confirmed a five-point agreement he had reached with Chiang and assured Taiwan that the Japanese government would not allow Japanese exporters to use Export-Import Bank funds for the purpose of financing sales to China. This letter was later referred to as the Yoshida Letter, and became a well-known pro-Taiwan document during the pre-normalization era.

The Yoshida Letter immediately prompted the Japanese government to cancel several sales to China that were already signed into contracts, including another vinylon plant contracted for by the Dai Nippon Spinning Company, a $3.7 million freighter contracted for by the Hitachi Shipbuilding and Engineering Company, and fertilizer plants of The Tōyō Engineering Company. As a result, China had to turn to other advanced countries to purchase plants. During 1964–65, for example, out of twenty-one orders that China placed with industrialized countries, only two were with the Japanese.[3] The Yoshida Letter, therefore, became a major obstacle in the expansion of Sino-Japanese trade.

The Yoshida Letter also included several political references, such as re-covering Mainland China through the joint effort of Taiwan and Japan, and the rendering of Japanese moral support for the KMT. Beijing bitterly criticized the letter's obviously pro-Taiwan stand as casting a "dark shadow over Sino-Japanese trade."[4]

In Japan, as a result of the changing international environment and the growth of pro-Beijing forces, a strong lobby against the Yoshida Letter gradually emerged in the early 1970s among the business community. Nevertheless, the letter remained effective until July 1972 when the new prime minister, Kakuei Tanaka, approved a $48 million sale to China, using the credits of the Export and Import Bank of Japan. This occurred only two months before the establishment of formal diplomatic relations between Japan and China.

Sino-Japanese rapprochement did not put an end to activities by the pro-Taiwan forces within the LDP. There were "old hawks" and "young hawks." The support of Taiwan by many old hawks (leaders of the Asian Studies Group such as Kishi and Kaya, and later the Satō-Fukuda leadership) partially came about as a result of their memory of the KMT's treatment of Japanese soldiers in China after 1945, when Chiang declared that China would not retaliate against the Japanese for what they did to the Chinese and assured the safe return of most soldiers. These old hawks, who had shown loyalty to "old friends in Taiwan" during the pre-normalization period, gradually retreated to the back stage. But the so-called young hawks remained quite active. The most notable organization of the young hawks was Seirankai (the Blue Storm Society or Young Storm Association) which was comprised of thirty-one youthful, nationalistic, and conservative LDP Diet members. In particular, these young hawks presented strong opposition during negotiations for the Sino-Japanese aviation agreement.

CONSERVATIVE MANEUVERING AND THE "UNWRITTEN RULES"

While the Japanese delegation continued the negotiations with China, pro-

Taiwan forces in the LDP strongly opposed the pending aviation agreement. Takeo Fukuda, minister of finance since November 1973, openly argued that since representatives of Beijing and Taipei could coexist in Washington, it would not make sense for Beijing to demand that Taiwan's airplanes use a different airport.[5] Nevertheless, the activities of the old hawks were not as extreme as those of the younger ones.

At the time of the Sino-Japanese rapprochement in 1972, the old hawks were mostly senior statesmen. Their leader Nobusuke Kishi, for instance, was already seventy-seven years old. But the Seirankai was made up mainly of young LDP members coordinated by both Ichirō Nakagawa, aged forty-seven, and Michio Watanabe, aged forty-nine. Other activists were all under sixty. For example, Shintarō Ishihara was forty, Masayuki Fujio was fifty-five, Kōichi Hamada forty-seven, Shin Kanemaru fifty-eight, and Masaki Nakayama forty. This group of conservatives strongly challenged the position of the Kakuei Tanaka-Masayoshi Ōhira mainstream by arguing that continued cooperation with Taiwan was a matter of life and death to Japan's security, since Taiwan played an important function of containing "Red China." They also stressed the traditional Japanese ethics that Japan should not betray an old friend.[6]

There were also economic reasons behind continued links to Taiwan. In 1973 Japan Airlines had thirty-seven weekly Tokyo-Taipei flights carrying over a thousand passengers per day on an average, with estimated annual sales totaling $45 million, whereas there were only three to four proposed Tokyo-Beijing flights per week. Facing this challenge from the Seirankai, both the LDP mainstreamers and the governmental bureaucrats (MOT and MOFA officials in particular) were worried about the fate of the aviation agreement.[7]

Even though Seirankai members threatened to block the passage of the new aviation agreement both in the LDP's policymaking organs (such as the Policy Affairs Research Council) and in the National Diet, they were constrained by the LDP's explicit code of actions (party discipline) and implicit internal understanding of behavioral norms. Party regulations stipulated that those who did not vote the party's official line would be expelled from the party. However, the party members' political actions are more often controlled by compromises reached via implicit internal understanding.

There was an unwritten rule within the ruling party: LDP Diet members could not participate in street demonstrations and other violent protest activities to express factional or dissident opinions.[8] The regulations and pressures from their colleagues prevented the Seirankai from taking more severe actions such as was taken by non-LDP right-wing groups which initiated demonstrations outside government buildings where the Sino-Japanese negotiations were occurring.[9]

These "unwritten rules" are quite significant in Japan's political life. The formation of these rules is the longtime practice within the party; observation of these rules is almost entirely dependent on mutual trust and understanding among party members. This can be understood as a form of *haragei*, or implicit understanding. In this case, both mainstreamers and pro-Taiwan forces understood each other's stance and knew how far they could go.

The main body of government bureaucrats rapidly switched their position from pro-Taiwan to pro-Beijing once normalization was achieved. Then they supported wholeheartedly the new China policy, providing strong support for and cooperation with the Tanaka-Ōhira leadership. It was clear to them that failure to conclude the aviation agreement would mean a devastating blow to the newly established relations with China.

To ensure the passage of the agreement, MOFA officials tried their best to persuade the LDP conservatives. Several divisions and committees under the LDP's Policy Affairs Research Council were involved in the deliberation of guidelines for the aviation agreement, including the Division on Foreign Affairs, the Division on Transportation, and the Special Committee on Aviation Affairs. According to Michihiko Kunihiro, director of MOFA's China Division at that time, Foreign Ministry bureaucrats constantly went to LDP headquarters to attend committee and division meetings. More importantly, these bureaucrats frequently contacted the members of Seirankai. "For a period of three months, I went with Seirankai members and other related Diet members for breakfast virtually every morning. Through this kind of intentional consultation (*nemawashi*), both sides enhanced mutual understanding," says Kunihiro.[10]

Some Seirankai members, such as Masayuki Fujio and Ichirō Nakagawa, were difficult to persuade. They found it emotionally difficult to accept the fact that Japan had already broken its diplomatic relations with Taiwan. Others, like Michio Watanabe, for example, listened to explanations from senior bureaucrats with a certain understanding. Kunihiro and his colleagues conducted extensive one-to-one individual consultations with pro-Taiwan members asking for understanding of the mainstreamers' stand. They argued that cooperative relations with China were in Japan's "real national interest" and that politicians should fully understand that a one-China policy was the basic prerequisite of the PRC to establish diplomatic relations with any country.[11]

These consultations initiated by the bureaucrats also emphasized that Japan's connection with Taiwan was based on economic, ideological, and moral grounds. Few military and strategic concerns existed between Japan and Taiwan, as existed between the United States and Taiwan.[12] Thus, to go along with Beijing was in line with Japan's international interests and its general foreign policy. Japan's new policy toward China was necessitated by the drastic changes in the position of the United States and the United Nations toward China. The Japanese government had tried its best, though unsuccessfully, to reserve Taiwan's seat in the United Nations and had worked hard to maintain nonofficial links with Taiwan as long as possible after break off of diplomatic relations. All these efforts should have been enough to satisfy Japan's international obligation to Taiwan.

The mainstreamers further argued that the Taiwan issue was of little concern to the majority of the Japanese people and that politicians should pay closer attention to public opinions.[13] In the early 1970s the country was in a "China fever." The majority of Japanese welcomed any move toward expanding bilateral exchanges with China. So in terms of attracting votes, politicians had little incentive to work in the pro-Taiwan direction. In sum, during that period, the momentum for Sino-Japanese political and economic rapprochement was strong, and the pending aviation agreement was expected and desired by the majority of Japanese, including the economic and financial communities.[14]

The efforts of the Foreign Ministry on the aviation negotiations received significant support from the mainstream LDP politicians. The Tanaka-Ōhira leadership repeatedly confirmed their determination to conclude the aviation agreement as soon as possible. Foreign Minister Ōhira even threatened to resign should the aviation accord with China fail. On many occasions, Ōhira directly gave instructions to the China Division and its director Kunihiro. Many leading LDP members, such as Masayoshi Itō (who later became president of the Diet members' League for Japan-China Friendship) and Katsushi Fujii (who at that time was chairman of PARC's Division of Foreign Affairs) firmly supported the mainstream position. All these efforts ensured a significant majority of pro-Beijing forces within the ruling party–bureaucracy apparatus.

This majority position permitted the Japanese negotiating team to make some compromise with the Chinese: Japan held that the flag and the emblem carried by Taiwan's China Airlines were private company symbols and did not imply any Japanese recognition of Taiwan as a state. The PRC's CAAC (Civil Aviation Administration of China) aircraft would use the new international airport in Narita, and CAL aircraft would use the old international airport at Haneda.

After the aviation agreement was finally signed in April 1974, Taiwan immediately suspended all flights operated by Japan Airlines and CAL on the Japan-Taiwan air route. The route was not reestablished until July 1975, when Foreign Minister Kiichi Miyazawa made a face-saving statement for Taiwan indicating that the Taiwanese flag would continue to be regarded as a national flag by those countries that still had diplomatic relations with Taiwan, even though Japan no longer recognized the flag as an official one.

As the international and domestic political environments changed, some of the Seirankai members and conservative politicians gradually moved toward Beijing. In 1980 Nobusuke Kishi, one of the major leaders of the pro-Taiwan forces, agreed to be an adviser for the LDP's Nitchū Kenkyūkai (Association for Japan-China Studies), which was to promote Sino-Japanese friendship. In 1983, when China's top Japan hand and a party politburo member, Liao Chengzhi, passed away, Kishi (then himself eighty-seven years old) went to the Chinese Embassy to offer his condolences.[15] Another important conservative activist, Takeo Fukuda, later became Japan's prime minister and conducted peace talks with the PRC. While serving as prime minister, Fukuda completed and signed the Sino-Japanese Peace and Friendship Treaty in December 1978, officially ending the state of war between the two countries. Michio Watanabe, a Seirankai member, later became minister of MITI in the Nakasone administration in the mid-1980s and foreign affairs minister in the Miyazawa government in the early

1990s, and the leader of a major LDP faction. There, he became an active promoter of Sino-Japanese relations. For example, Watanabe was clearly a pro-China figure in China-related political issues such as the Japanese textbook controversy[16] and Japan's governmental loan package to China after the 1989 Tiananmen incident (see Chapter 8).

The Sino-Japanese Navigation Agreement encountered a similar problem—the Taiwan issue. This agreement involved a number of complex and technical issues such as provisions for guarantees on revenue remittances of shipping enterprises, confirmation of cargo transport rights, cooperation in rescue operations in the event of accidents, and approval of certificates of nationality of ships.[17]

The main obstacle for negotiations was the Taiwan issue again. At first, China insisted on the removal of Taiwan's flag from Taiwanese vessels calling at Japanese seaports. With full awareness of the opposition from the LDP's Seirankai and other conservatives, the Japanese delegation was reluctant to accept this proposal. Following the pattern of the aviation agreement, in which the flag of Taiwan had been identified as a private company symbol, would very likely result in a similar consequence—stopping Taiwan's shipping lines with Japan. The Japanese side argued that the Tanaka-Zhou Joint Statement had clearly delineated Japan's relationship with Taiwan, and it was not necessary to place this clause into every agreement. The Chinese, however, insisted that the Taiwan issue should be clearly stated because it was China's basic principle.[18] Because of this deadlock, negotiations were suspended for almost a year.

During this period, the mainstreamers worked hard to break the stalemate. Transportation Minister Masatoshi Tokunaga gave specific instructions to MOT bureaucrats that the agreement with China must succeed. MOT officials used under-the-table consultation to communicate in two directions: the LDP Seirankai members and the Chinese delegation. Japan's position was repeatedly clarified to the Chinese through both informal and formal channels.[19]

The mainstreamers' quiet efforts were fruitful. The LDP pro-Taiwan forces promised they would stop interfering in negotiations if China as well as Japan made concessions. The Chinese gradually realized (partly as a result of personal explanations from the Japanese side and partly because of their own recognition of the international situation with regard to Taiwan) that the key to the Taiwan issue lay in the United States, not in Japan, owing to Washington's leadership in the Western world and its ties with Taiwan. In addition, with the passage of time, Beijing became more confident that its claim to Taiwan had won worldwide recognition. Therefore, the Chinese withdrew their insistence on the removal of Taiwan's flag and the agreement was finally signed in Tokyo in November 1974.[20]

Based on these examples, we can make a number of observations. First, the mainstreamers in the LDP were in much stronger positions than the ultra-conservatives with regard to the China issue. The battle between the pro-Beijing forces and the pro-Taipei forces had been largely concluded by the time of normalization. Nevertheless, the mainstreamers could not take the conservatives lightly and needed to work hard to gain the conservatives' understanding for finalizing the Sino-Japanese economic agreements.

Second, despite the factionalism (in this case, mainstreamers versus pro-Taiwan forces), the LDP was a unified party. Party discipline guided the voting direction by LDP Diet members, thereby guaranteeing the party's majority position in the National Diet. More importantly, there were also implicit codes of behavior, which created an important unspoken understanding or *haragei* within the party: a person could have a dissident opinion from the party's mainstream but could not take extreme measures against the party's official line. This *haragei* prevented the Seirankai members from acting more obstructively and going beyond understood limits.[21]

Third, internal consultation played a key role in adjusting and coordinating opposing opinions within the ruling LDP-bureaucracy apparatus. Without frequent communications through personal connections and consultations, a mutual understanding among the various political forces would not have been reached, *haragei* would not have been confirmed, and the party may have faced more severe problems in negotiations.

MUTUAL UNDERSTANDING IN THE DIET

Part Three of Article seventy-three of the Japanese constitution states that the cabinet can "conclude treaties and agreements" with foreign governments but must "inform the National Diet in advance," and the treaties and agreements must be "approved by the National Diet after the conclusion" of negotiations.[22] Generally speaking, as a result of the long-term ruling position of the LDP, committee chairmen and majority members of the Diet committees have been LDP Diet members.

There was an unspoken understanding in the Diet: challenges to governmental policies and bills normally came from opposition parties, and not from the ruling Liberal Democrats. During the committee hearings, LDP Diet members either kept quiet or showed their support for certain policies.[23]

Since opposition parties (as discussed in Part II) actually pushed the LDP to promote relations with China, there did not appear to be any problem with their approval of the agreements with Beijing after normalization, and no serious challenges were expected from opposition parties.[24] But although in the end the passage of these agreements was expected, the hearings held by the related committees in the Diet were often heated.

Seven weeks after it was signed by Masayoshi Ōhira and Ji Pengfei in Beijing, the documents of the Sino-Japanese Trade Agreement were sent to the Diet on February 26, 1974. On March 28, the Foreign Affairs Committee of the Lower House held a hearing on the agreement presided over by Committee Chairman Toshio Kimura and attended by nineteen Diet members. Foreign Minister Ōhira, together with six senior government officials from MOFA and MITI, attended the hearing to testify.

At the hearing, three opposition Diet members, JSP's Tamio Kawakami, CGP's Ichirō Watanabe, and JCP's Zenmei Matsumoto, took turns questioning Ōhira and the government bureaucrats. The questions focused on COCOM restrictions. Kawakami demanded that the government officials explain why Japan had still maintained COCOM restrictions toward China. He argued that "COCOM has been a major obstacle for the expansion of Japan-China trade," and "since the international situation has greatly been relaxed, the COCOM restrictions should be removed." Matsumoto asked the foreign minister whether Japan planned to withdraw from COCOM, once the Sino-Japanese Peace Treaty was completed. Watanabe recalled the history of COCOM, calling it "a product of the cold war." He gave examples of Western Europe's trading practice with China—Britain and France had sold China advanced airplanes, and West Germany had sold China sophisticated machinery—and asked, "Why could the EEC countries on many occasions ignore the COCOM regulations and expand their trade with China, whereas Japan has continued to be COCOM's *yūtōsei* (the best student)?" Japan's policy, he further argued, not only discriminated against China, but also damaged Japan's own national interests.[25]

Ōhira retorted that Japan, as a member of COCOM, had responsibility to fulfill its international obligation. If Japan withdrew from COCOM, Japan's international position and relations with Western countries would be adversely affected. Nevertheless, Japan had been working hard to reduce and relax the COCOM restrictions over its trade with China. Ōhira confirmed that in the future "Japan would work as hard as possible to abolish the COCOM regulations and to return to the pattern of free trade."[26]

Despite the stormy questions raised by opposition parties concerning COCOM, the trade agreement was passed by the committee unanimously. The opposition parties apparently accepted their role in the Diet—that is, to voice different opinions but not to block the vote. A month later, the House of Councilors also passed the Sino-Japanese Trade Agreement. Thus, the legislative process was successfully completed.

Because the Seirankai members within the ruling party strongly opposed the Sino-Japanese Aviation Agreement, the mainstreamers exhibited greater concern about the Diet hearing held on May 7, 1974. The controversial nature of the agreement drew a big crowd of both political leaders and governmental bureaucrats. The hearing was held jointly by the House Foreign Affairs and Transportation Committees and was chaired jointly by Toshio Kimura and Makoto Miike, respectively. Fifty members of the two committees showed up at the hearing. Foreign Minister Masayoshi Ōhira and Transportation Minister Masatoshi Tokunaga, together with one vice-minister, eight bureau director-generals, and two division directors from the two ministries, were also in attendance.

Two Seirankai members, Shintarō Ishihara and Takami Etō, also attended. Previously, they had strongly opposed the aviation agreement. Before the start of the hearing, some people were shouting and booing from their seats, saying such things as "Why hasn't the MOFA's administrative vice-minister come?" The disturbance indicated a sense of tension in the Diet conference room, but the discussions went smoothly. Ishihara remained silent throughout the entire hearing. Etō pointed out that Japan should not abandon "the old friend—Taiwan," and argued that this could cause distrust in the international community, especially in Southeast Asian countries.[27] Nevertheless, none of the LDP members, including those from Seirankai, voted against passage of the aviation agreement. The restrained attitudes of Ishihara and Etō were strong evidence of how the LDP's implicit code of behavior was observed by dissident party members.

Opposition party Diet members were concerned with other aspects of the aviation agreement. JSP's Saburō Kubo inquired in detail about the airline routes. CGP's Chūsuke Matsumoto was concerned about the selection of the airline company chosen by the Japanese government—the agreement mentioned that each side would choose one airline company to cover the newly established Japan-China air route. Matsumoto argued that since All Nippon Airway (ANA) had been friendly with China, it should be selected. (Soon after the conclusion of the hearings, the Japanese government chose Japan Airline, Japan's biggest airline which had maintained close relations with Taiwan, to open the Japan-China route; ANA did not acquire permission to fly to China until thirteen years later, in 1987.) The DSP's Katsu Kawamura criticized the internal disputes of the LDP. He maintained that conflicting messages sent to the outside world over the Taiwan issue from different factions of the ruling party only confused the international community (including the Taiwanese people) and aggravated the situation.[28]

The two cabinet ministers explained their positions repeatedly. Tokunaga concentrated on technical issues, whereas Ōhira answered the political questions. Ōhira gave a detailed account of his negotiations with Chinese leaders, especially those that took place during his trip to Beijing earlier that January. He confirmed that through his conversation with Mao Zedong, Zhou Enlai, and Foreign Minister Ji Pengfei, he had tried his best to obtain China's understanding of Japan's position and had eventually reached a compromise with the Chinese. Ōhira expressed his regret that the Taiwan authorities could not understand Japan's position.[29]

The two hearings on trade and aviation agreements were controlled by the ruling LDP and its *zoku*. Both committee chairmen were *zoku*-type veteran LDP politicians. Foreign Affairs Committee Chairman Toshio Kimura was an experienced *zoku* in both foreign affairs and transportation. His political experience followed the typical pattern of "bureaucrat turned politician": a graduate of Todai Law faculty—MOT's Division Director—LDP Diet member. By 1974 Kimura had already served thirty-five years in the National Diet. During this long period, he alternated between governmental positions and Diet committees, with concentration on transportation and foreign affairs. After two ministerships (Cabinet Secretariat and the Economic Planning Agency) in the late 1960s and the early 1970s, Kimura assumed the chairmanship of the

Diet's House Foreign Affairs Committee. In July 1974, two months after the aviation agreement hearing, Kimura became foreign minister of the second Tanaka cabinet.

Transportation Committee Chairman Makoto Miike was a career politician turned LDP *zoku*. He had cultivated influence mainly within LDP organizations and the Diet's committees. He assumed the chairmanships of a broad range of Diet committees. In the 1950s and the 1960s, he served as chairman for the construction, transportation, financial, and cabinet committees. During the early 1970s he was appointed deputy chairman of the LDP's General Council, and then posts and telecommunications minister in the Tanaka cabinet. Finally, as a transportation *zoku*, Miike returned to the Diet Transportation Committee to resume its chairmanship.

Under the firm control of the LDP mainstreamers, the Diet committees worked for the interest of the party, making bills sponsored by the government pass through the Diet. But without negotiation with and cooperation from the opposition parties, the passage of bills would not be smooth. The National Diet is an important place for opposition parties to voice dissenting opinions and to challenge the ruling party's position. Opposition parties may also resort to radical means, such as boycotting parliamentary debate on annual budget, to ensure their political demands; yet, their actions are normally within an understood limit that they will not paralyze government operations.

Here is an example. In February 1992, opposition parties held a two-week boycott of the parliamentary debate on Japan's 1992 budget in attacking Prime Minister Kiichi Miyazawa over the involvement of a close political associate in a bribery scandal. The boycott ended after the ruling party promised that former prime minister Zenkō Suzuki, among others, would testify on a bribery scandal.[30] Opposition parties have indeed helped assure democratic operation in Japanese politics.

Dissident opinions within the ruling LDP are seldom expressed at the hearings, however. Rather, the party solves internal disputes by behind-the-scenes maneuvering through personal consultation known as *nemawashi*. This implicit understanding of the division of labor within the Diet and among various factions of the ruling party, as well as among different parties, is indeed quite a significant aspect of Japanese political life.

Passage of the trade and aviation agreements in the National Diet was assured in this political environment of mutual understanding. Passage of the other two China agreements on fisheries and navigation followed a similar pattern, gaining approval from the Diet without serious challenge.

THE BUSINESS COMMUNITY'S DUAL POSITIONS

Leaders of the business community have paid close attention to Sino-Japanese economic relations—both before and after the establishment of formal diplomatic relations between the two countries in 1972. Even though business leaders had little direct involvement in the negotiation process for the four agreements, they had to deal with controversial issues in their own dealings with the Chinese similar to what the LDP-bureaucracy apparatus faced, with the Taiwan issue and COCOM restrictions.

In addition, because of the close ties between the business community and the ruling conservatives, the attitude of the business leaders influenced policymakers. Government bureaucrats also consulted closely with business leaders before and during the negotiations. There were frequent behind-the-scenes preparation activities between major government agencies (MITI in particular) and the headquarters of Keidanren and other economic organizations. Although there was no regulation stating that the two entities should provide information to one another, detailed information about the negotiation progress was communicated extensively throughout the period of negotiations.[31]

This kind of close communication between the government and the business community is not unusual in Japan, since there is a tradition of cooperative relations between the two. But as discussed in Part II, business leaders went one step further than the government and set up nonofficial trade arrangements with Beijing during the pre-normalization period. After rapprochement, the Japanese government was not satisfied with the existing nonofficial trade channels such as the friendly firms system and the memorandum trade agreements, inasmuch as these arrangements placed Japan in a passive position.[32] The government thought it necessary to establish a new business organization immediately after normalization to coordinate Sino-Japanese trade, in which the government would be able to exercise administrative guidance over the business community.

The new organization was arranged in early 1972 and was formally inaugurated in November 1972, with the name the Japan-China Economic Association (JCEA). JCEA is a nonprofit organization that coordinates trade relations with China and conducts research on the Chinese market. JCEA replaced Japan's Memorandum Trade Office. JCEA's initial operational budget was 5 billion yen, 3 billion of which came from MITI and the rest was provided by Keidanren and other business organizations.[33] Therefore, JCEA was closely supervised by both MITI and Keidanren. For instance, during his visit to China in January 1973, MITI Minister Yasuhiro Nakasone led a fourteen-member delegation consisting of governmental officials and business leaders like Yoshihiro Inayama, president of the newly established JCEA and president of Nippon Steel, who later became president of Keidanren. Nakasone introduced JCEA President Inayama to Premier Zhou Enlai, Vice-Premier Li Xiannian, and Foreign Trade Minister Li Qiang.

The Japanese business community's change from a pro-Taipei to a pro-Beijing position has been examined in Part II. With regard to the issue of COCOM, business leaders had much more ambivalent feelings, which led to an ambiguous attitude, or dual position, over the issue.

Generally speaking, Japanese businessmen were in favor of a free trade policy in the international trade system because of Japan's export-oriented development pattern.[34] This was especially true for the trading companies that were deeply involved in trade with China. This group of business leaders opposed the trade restrictions imposed by COCOM.

A good example is the lawsuit relating to the Japan Industrial Exhibition in 1969. To promote bilateral trade, the Japan Council for Promotion of International Trade (hereafter the Japan Council) and the China Council for the Promotion of International Trade (hereafter the China Council) agreed to mutually hold industrial exhibitions. The Chinese exhibitions were held in Tokyo and Osaka, and the Japanese in Beijing and Shanghai. Before the 1969 exhibition, four Japanese industrial exhibitions were held in China (in 1955, 1958, 1963, and 1967). In January 1969 MITI informed the Japan Industrial Exhibition Office that 19 items were not being allowed for exhibitions in China because of COCOM restrictions. This decision provoked strong protests from the Japan Council and trading companies that participated in the exhibition. The decision was criticized as a symbol of the government's hostile attitude toward China. LDP Diet member Tokuma Utsunomiya, who was vice-chairman of the Japan Council, protested to MITI. Diet member Takeo Tanaka began a heated debate around this issue in the Diet (Japan-China Economic Association 1975c: 145–146). The protesters held several demonstrations in front of the MITI building. Once they even held MITI's economy bureau director hostage for two hours.[35]

In February a civil-law case was brought to the Tokyo District Court by the Japan Industrial Exhibition represented by Shigeo Shirane, a Japan Council official, against MITI. The point of dispute was whether export controls based on COCOM were illegal. Shirane contended that since COCOM was based on political principles, it was an abuse of power for the MITI minister to issue export controls based on the principle of COCOM. He further demanded compensation of 1 million yen from the government. The governmental representative argued that, if Japan did not observe the COCOM rules, it would be punished by other advanced countries in terms of high-technology transfer. Therefore, Japan's national interests would be damaged (Japan-China Economic Association 1975c: 146–150). In July 1969 the Tokyo District Court ruled that the COCOM regulations had no legal basis for limiting Japanese exports to China. The next month, MITI removed 79 items from the COCOM list but added 23 new items to it (C. Lee 1976: 159). This event elicited strong dissatisfaction from the business community toward the government's China policy.

It would be wrong, however, to assume that the business leaders had a unified view on the COCOM issue. Some Japanese businessmen were afraid that the Chinese would eventually compete with the Japanese economy if China received advanced technologies from the industrialized countries. In 1985 a leading Japanese economist Kiichi Saeki, director of the Nomura Research Institute, openly expressed this view when he attended the Sino-Japanese Symposium on Exchanges of Economic Knowledge in Shenzhen. Saeki stated that "the precondition for Japan to open its domestic market to China is to keep Japan's leading position in technology at least five to ten years ahead of China"; this was "an internal understanding of Japan's national interests within the business community."[36] This demonstrated the reluctance of Japanese business to transfer advanced technologies to China. In this view, export controls based on COCOM restrictions might serve as a good weapon against the flow of technology to China. Business leaders in this group were quite willing to follow the government's lead to restrict China trade.

This dual position of the business community reflected an implicit understanding of Japan's national interests regarding the issue of COCOM among the political and economic elites. This understanding served as a mechanism to coordinate various interests when Japan conducted negotiations with China.

CHINA'S POSITION AND SINO-JAPANESE NEGOTIATIONS

During the negotiations for the four economic agreements, the Chinese showed a combination of principles and flexibility. This performance was highlighted by the manner in which the Chinese dealt with COCOM restrictions and the Taiwan issue.

China had long opposed the COCOM restrictions. As early as 1955, the Chinese issued a joint statement with a Japanese delegation of nonpartisan Diet members then visiting Beijing. The first point of the joint statement was to realize normalization of relations between China and Japan at an early stage; the second point stated clearly that the COCOM restrictions should be abolished as soon as possible. In 1958, after discussions between China Council Chairman Nan Hanchen and Japan Council Chairman Kumaichi Yamamoto, the minutes of the meeting were published. The first point of the minutes was that "Japan should completely abolish the COCOM and all other man-made restrictions that have damaged Japan-China trade" (Japan-China Economic Association 1975c: 6–15).

During the 1969 lawsuit between the Japan Industrial Exhibition and the Japanese government, the Chinese gave full moral support to the Japan Industrial Exhibition Office and other Japanese trading companies that made strong protests to MITI. But during the official negotiations, anxious to sign the agreement, the Chinese delegation did not insist on an immediate abolition of the COCOM restrictions, although initially it did raise the demand. This also showed flexibility on the part of the Chinese in understanding Japan's difficult international position, particularly in relations with the United States.

The Taiwan issue followed a similar pattern. Regarding basic principles, such as "Taiwan is part of China" and "the PRC is the sole legal government of China," the Beijing government has always stood firm. China's strong reactions to the 1958 Nagasaki flag incident, its severe criticism of the 1964 Yoshida Letter, and its bitter denouncement of the 1969 Satō-Nixon Joint Statement, not to mention Zhou Enlai's three political conditions and four trade conditions, demonstrated China's firmness on the issue of Taiwan.

During the first round of negotiations in 1973 over the navigation agreement, for example, the Chinese delegation insisted that ships under Taiwan's flag should not be allowed to call at Japan's seaports. When they were unable to push this issue through, the Chinese suspended negotiations. A year later, when the negotiations were resumed, the issue of the flag was not raised at all.[37] The navigation agreement was concluded smoothly. This time China's concession was mainly due to a broad strategic consideration with regard to the changing international environment (G. Hsiao 1977: 62–63). At the same time, it may also have reflected Beijing's increased knowledge (partially as a result of Japan's personal consultation activities) about international and domestic constraints, such as COCOM and pro-Taiwan forces, that Tokyo had to face.

China's decision to invite President Nixon to visit Beijing in 1972 and to normalize relations with Japan represented drastic changes of direction in China's foreign policy. These decisions, due to China's vertical administrative system, were made directly by the top Chinese leaders Mao Zedong and Zhou Enlai. During the Cultural Revolution of the late 1960s and early 1970s, Mao and Zhou were the architects of virtually all major foreign policy decisions.

Because of the delicate nature of the new relationship with Japan and because of the domestic and international political significance, Zhou was in charge of virtually every detail of Sino-Japanese negotiations and the preparation of bilateral documents, such as the joint statements, communiques, treaties, and agreements (including the four economic agreements). In many respects these agreements would set precedents for similar negotiations with other countries.

Premier Zhou Enlai met with virtually every visiting Japanese governmental delegation that visited Beijing for political and economic negotiations. During that period there was a rule called *yishi yibao* meaning "one matter, one report (to the top leaders)," for the Chinese foreign affairs and foreign trade officials.[38] According to Toshio Ōishi, deputy leader of the Japanese delegation for negotiating the trade agreement in Tokyo, the Chinese delegation stopped several times during the negotiation to place phone calls to Beijing and to await instructions. Ōishi says, "I was told that they had to wait for instructions from Premier Zhou himself."[39] Ōishi's recollection was confirmed by his Chinese counterparts. Lin Liande, then director of the Japan Division of the Chinese Foreign Trade Ministry, recalled that the premier was in charge of every detail of the negotiation, and that he read negotiation drafts word for word inserting some corrections in his own hand.[40]

Several times, when the bilateral negotiations were deadlocked and the governmental officials were not able to handle the situation, Mao Zedong and Zhou Enlai broke the deadlock by pushing the negotiations forward.[41] Such was the case in negotiating the Sino-Japanese Aviation Agreement in the summer of 1973. The two sides could not reach a compromise on the name, flag, and landing airport of Taiwan's airline. To put more pressure on the Japanese on this issue, the Chinese economic delegation that was currently in Tokyo to conduct negotiations for the Sino-Japanese Trade Agreement delayed the start of their talks for several weeks to show the unhappiness of the Chinese side.[42] The Japanese government, on the other hand, under pressure both domestically (the LDP conservative wing) and externally (the Taiwan authorities), was in a serious dilemma over whether to make further concessions.

The situation remained unresolved until Foreign Minister Masayoshi Ōhira's visit to Beijing in January 1974. Ōhira had two goals: to sign the trade agreement which was ceremonial, and to seek a breakthrough on the aviation agreement. The first mission was accomplished with great fanfare. Ōhira was received by both Mao and Zhou, and his picture appeared on the front page of *Renmin Ribao* (People's Daily), China's leading official newspaper, signifying the success of the visit.[43] But the second goal hit an impasse: both sides were unwilling to make further concessions. In Ōhira's (1979: 115) recollections, the negotiations were very tough: "despite three meetings, we had not moved a single step forward."

On the last day of Ōhira's visit, the two sides decided that, instead of continuing to work against the deadlock, they should take a relaxed break in the morning, primarily because Ōhira had caught a cold and had a high fever, and he and his delegation were to return to Tokyo in the afternoon. Ōhira felt tired and discouraged over not being able to accomplish his second mission. Several hours before his departure to return to Japan, Ōhira had a final talk with Ji Pengfei, the Chinese foreign minister. A Chinese official walked into the conference room and asked Ji Pengfei to receive a telephone call. Twenty minutes later, Ji returned and brought back a new Chinese proposal, which was very close to the one proposed by the Japanese delegation. Within two hours, a compromise over the aviation agreement was reached. Everyone at the meeting knew that it was Premier Zhou Enlai who had called and made the breakthrough.[44]

Negotiations and their formal signatures of the four economic agreements were concluded during the early part of the 1970s. At that time, China was still under the shadow of the Cultural Revolution's radical policy and had just started to open its doors to the outside world. Some Chinese policies during that period were influenced by leftist (or radical) ideas. For example, Japan had a practice of special favor treatment (SFT) specifically for developing countries that gave them reduced taxes and easier access to export goods to Japan. Taiwan was on the SFT list. During the negotiations for the trade agreement, the Chinese delegation only inquired about the nature of the SFT and asked for an explanation of Taiwan's status with regard to the SFT arrangement. The Chinese did not ask for SFT for their own goods, because they felt that China's reputation might be damaged if it received the SFT from Japan and was regarded as a less developed country. In other words, the Chinese had difficulty accepting the fact that China might need to receive special favor treatment from Japan.[45]

On some subjects, China, lacking experience or knowledge about the international trade system, was not ready to conduct negotiations with the Japanese. One of the Japanese concerns over the trade agreement was the issue of patent and trademark protection. They were afraid that the lack of agreement on these issues might discourage Japanese businessmen from conducting trade with China and that Japan's interests might not be properly protected. In the 1973 trade agreement negotiations, the Japanese raised this issue at the negotiation table. But the Chinese were not yet ready to discuss it.[46] The issue of patent and trademark protection was not resolved until 1977 when a Sino-Japanese trademark protection agreement was signed.

Following traditional values, the Chinese emphasized the importance of maintaining ties with "old friends." The first paragraph of the trade agreement, for example, made a clear statement that the two governments, "having a regard for the achievements thus far accumulated through existing non-governmental trade relations" and "through friendly negotiations," reached the trade agreement. The Chinese designed this peculiar clause to show those "old friends," especially "friendly companies," that China would continue to do business with them under favorable conditions.

Another clause in the trade agreement is also noteworthy. The MFN treatment "shall not apply to special favors accorded to neighboring countries by either Contracting Party for the purpose of facilitating border trade." The Chinese insisted on this clause because China maintained special border trade relations with some of its neighboring countries and provided preferential pricing systems to those countries. Notably, China exported its oil to North Korea for a special price as a gesture of friendship and a form of economic aid (C. Lee 1984: 14–15).

On many occasions, formal negotiations were not sufficient to communicate key information and real intentions. Therefore, informal means such as under-the-table consultations at the individual level became more important.

CONFUSION AND BUILDING TRUST

A goal of the policymaking process in Japan is to seek points of compromise, so that all involved parties can protect their interests in the internal bargaining. At the same time, the possibility of open conflict will be reduced to a minimum, and political harmony will more likely be maintained. This case study has provided a picture of maneuvers within and outside the ruling party/bureaucracy apparatus. Morton Halperin (1974: 312) described this process as "pulling and hauling" among various political forces and interest groups.

Political trust and mutual understanding are key elements in this pulling and hauling process. As we have noticed from the above case study, individual behavior may have to be within the limit of the societal constraint, namely socially acceptable "beliefs, values, and cultural norms" (M. Jeremy and M. Robinson 1989: 3). The LDP's implicit internal code of behavior which prevented the Seirankai members from taking more drastic actions, the opposition parties' acceptance of their role in the Diet, and the business community's dual positions toward the COCOM restrictions are important factors contributing to Japanese policy toward the four economic agreements.

This trust and understanding is closely related to the notion of *giri* (obligation) that was discussed earlier. In the widest sense, the character *gi* signifies that each individual acts according to the understanding of how he should behave.

The word *giri* simply means the reason for *gi* (right-doing). Therefore, *giri* is a promise to act in a fitting manner according to where one stands in relation to others in the social structure. And the promise, unlike modern obligation, is not grounded in rights. Rather, *Giri* (obligation) is a promise of a certain attitude or conduct that the surrounding people would expect. This becomes a basis of the norms for individual behavior in Japanese society. As Karel van Wolferen (1989: 43–44) argues, "The Japanese are rarely allowed to forget the existence of socio-political arrangements that are infinitely stronger than any kind of might the individual could ever bring to bear on them." A result of the deepened personal obligation is that "a sense of trust is built up" (H. Minami 1971: 157–164).

On the other hand, it takes time to build up this political trust both internally and externally. Internal implicit understanding through informal consultation (*nemawashi*) at the individual level may not be understood by outsiders. People from other political culture backgrounds may not be able to see through *tatemae* (open statement) and learn about *honne* (real intention). Even though both Beijing and Taipei shared apparently similar cultural heritages with the Japanese, sometimes they all had difficulties understanding Tokyo's real intention—a confusion caused by conflicting messages (such as the Seirankai controversy) coming from Japan's ruling circles. This misunderstanding by outsiders may not only cause confusion externally, but may also delay Japan's internal policymaking process. But once political trust and mutual understanding are built up, things will proceed more smoothly. In his examination of a local community in Tokyo, Theodore Bestor (1989: 189) has noted this general pattern of Japanese decision-making—"discussion may continue for years; once a group attains consensus, however, action may be almost immediate."

In sum, behind-the-scenes consensus-building through personal connections and consultations is a distinctive Japanese working style that is used to convey information and to exchange true intentions and ideas through informal means. The ultimate goals are to build up political trust and to achieve mutual understanding. Nevertheless, this non-Western working style may cause confusion among outsiders who do not necessarily understand *haragei*—"the art of stomach."

NOTES

1. For detailed discussions on the issue of Taiwan, see PRC-Taiwan related articles in Quansheng Zhao and Robert Sutter, eds., *Politics of Divided Nations: China, Korea, Germany and Vietnam* (Baltimore: University of Maryland School of Law, 1991).

2. See R. K. Jain, *China and Japan* (1981: 71).

3. See Colina MacDougall, "China's Foreign Trade," *Far Eastern Economic Review*, January 27, 1966, p. 124.

4. *Peking Review*, February 19, 1965, p. 31.

5. *Japan Times*, May 25 and 26, 1973.

6. Interview with Michihiko Kunihiro, June 4, 1986, Tokyo.

7. Interview with Tōru Nakamura, June 3, 1986, Tokyo. Nakamura was director of MOT's International Aviation Division from 1972 to 1975, and was director of MOT's Aviation Control Department at the time of interview.

8. Interview with Motoji Suganuma, a veteran LDP member and the former president of the Tokyo Municipal Assembly, March 3, 1986, Tokyo.

9. Interview with Toshio Ōishi, March 6, 1986, Tokyo.

10. Interview with Michihiko Kunihiro, June 4, 1986, Tokyo, who was MOFA's assistant vice minister at the time of interview and recalled these days vividly.

11. Ibid.

12. Interview with Seizaburō Satō, professor of international relations at the University of Tokyo, February 20, 1986, Tokyo.

13. Interview with Heishirō Ogawa, March 8, 1986, Tokyo.

14. Interview with Heishirō Ogawa, February 13, 1986, Tokyo.

15. See Yu Qin, Hua Jue, et al., *Xiandai Riben Minren Lu* (1984: 217–218).

16. In 1982, 1985, and 1986, Japan's Ministry of Education was sharply criticized by both domestic progressive forces and Japan's Asian neighbors, including China, North and South Korea, Thailand, and Hong Kong, for revising the description of Japan's past war behavior in school textbooks. For detailed accounts, see Allen Whiting, *China Eyes Japan* (1989: 46–59).

17. *Japan Times*, November 3 and 14, 1974.

18. Interview with Chyoji Tomita, May 29, 1986, Tokyo. As MOT's International Shipping Division Director, Tomita participated in the negotiations for the Sino-Japanese Navigation Agreement. Tomita was managing director and vice-president of the Japan Asia Airways Company at the time of interview.

19. Ibid.

20. *Japan Times*, November 14, 1974.

21. Interview with Yukio Nakamaru, staff member of LDP's Foreign Affairs Division, August 28, 1986, Tokyo.

22. Constitution of Japan, 1947.

23. Interview with Tomomitsu Iwakura, staff member of LDP's PARC, August 11, 1986, Tokyo.

24. Interview with Haruo Okada, a veteran JSP Diet member, February 27, 1986, Tokyo.

25. The 72nd House of Representatives, Records of the Hearings of the Foreign Affairs Committee, #15, Tokyo, March 1974.

26. Ibid.

27. The 72nd House of Representatives, Records of the Joint Hearings of the Foreign Affairs Committee and the Transportation Committee, #1, Tokyo, May 1974.

28. Ibid.

29. Ibid.

30. Robert Delfs, "Scandal Tactics: Opposition Resists Temptation on Paralyze Government," *Far Eastern Economic Review*, February 13, 1992, pp. 11–12; and "Japan Parties End Parliamentary Boycott," *Far Eastern Economic Review*, February 27, 1992, p. 14.

31. Interview with Yoshio Uchida, February 25, 1986, Tokyo.

32. Ibid., March 4, 1986, Tokyo.

33. Ibid., February 25, 1986, Tokyo.

34. Interview with Junichi Amano, general manager of Mitsui Bussan's Iron Ore Division, July 4, 1986, Tokyo.

35. Interview with Yoshitoshi Munakata, March 17, 1986, Tokyo.

36. Interview with Peng Jinzhang, deputy director of the Institute of Japan Studies, Chinese Academy of Social Sciences, October 29, 1986, Beijing. Peng attended the Shenzhen symposium and listened to Saeki's talk.

37. Interview with Choji Tomita, May 29, 1986, Tokyo.

38. Interview with Wu Xuewen, July 15, 1986, Fukuoka.

39. Interview with Toshio Ōishi, March 6, 1986, Tokyo.

40. Interview with Lin Liande, October 28, 1986, Beijing.

41. Interview with Liu Yanzhou, April 12, 1986, Tokyo. Liu was one of the first group of Chinese journalists who was allowed to be stationed in Japan in 1964. Altogether he was in Japan more than fifteen years over three different periods.

42. *Japan Times*, August 31, 1973.

43. *Renmin Ribao*, January 6, 1974.

44. Interview with Heishirō Ogawa, March 8, 1986, Tokyo. As the first Japanese ambassador to the PRC, Ogawa was a member of Ōhira's delegation. Also see Ōhira (1979: 113–115).

45. Interview with Lin Liande, October 28, 1986, Beijing.

46. Interview with Yoshio Uchida, March 4, 1986, Tokyo.

PART V

Empirical Summary
Case Study: Japan's Aid to China Before and After Tiananmen

8

Informal Mechanisms in Dealing with International Crisis

Part V continues to examine informal mechanisms in Japan's policymaking process by means of an empirical summary. This summary has two purposes. First, it studies Japanese policymaking and external behavior from all three levels of analysis that were treated separately in the previous chapters: the societal level (the social environment and networks); the institutional level (informal political actors and organizations); and the individual level (consensus-building through personal connections). Second, since the previous three case studies have concentrated on internal policymaking mechanisms, this empirical summary attempts to look at how policymakers in Japan utilize informal mechanisms to conduct external activities, that is, to deal with an unexpected international crisis. This summary is presented through a case study on Japan's official development assistance (ODA) to China and its aid policy before and after the Tiananmen incident of June 4, 1989, when the Chinese military suppressed student-led demonstrations at Tiananmen Square in Beijing.

At the economic summit of seven major industrialized nations held in July 1990 in Houston, Texas, Japanese Prime Minister Toshiki Kaifu announced that "Japan will gradually resume" its third package of government loans to China valued at 810 billion yen (U.S. $5.4 billion), thereby ending its more than one year long economic sanctions against China.[1] This soft loan package to China was designed to last five years, and about 15 percent (120 billion yen, or $0.8 billion) of the total amount was expected to be disbursed in the 1990 financial year.

Observers of Asian affairs have noticed that, "While other world leaders kept their distance, it is notable that it was Japan which moved furthest and mostly quickly to restore friendly relations with Beijing in the aftermath of Tiananmen, and that it was Japanese Prime Minister Toshiki Kaifu who undertook to act as the spokesman for China's interests at the Group of Seven meeting in Houston."[2]

Even though the United States and other Western economic powers approved Japan's decision, they did not immediately follow Japan's lead in changing their policies toward China.[3] Washington, for example, did not soften its position until December 1990 when it abstained in the vote for the World Bank's first "non-basic human needs" loan to China since Tiananmen. In exchange, Beijing abstained from voting on the crucial United Nations Security Council resolution authorizing military action against Iraq.[4] In May 1991 the United States dropped its opposition to resuming the Asian Development Bank's (ADB) loans to China.[5] Clearly, the Japanese action in regard to aid issues with China was significantly ahead of other Western countries, particularly the United States.

This example of Japan's ODA to China before and after Tiananmen can be used to further examine Japan's informal mechanisms within the framework of the making of Japanese foreign policy toward China.

Immediately after the Tiananmen incident in June 1989, Tokyo decided to join in the economic sanctions imposed on China by Western industrialized countries, putting a hold on its government loans. Yet, the Japanese government was cautious with the aid issue. Instead of calling it a sanction, Tokyo initially described the holding back of loan disbursements as necessary in protecting Japanese aid officials in China amidst the violent military actions in Beijing.

Tensions between the two countries eased somewhat in early May 1990 when the Japanese government extradited a Chinese hijacker who seized a Chinese airliner on a flight from Beijing to Fukuoka in western Japan in late 1989. The hijacker claimed to have been involved in the pro-democracy movement. Some foreign observers saw the return of the hijacker to China as China's only major "diplomatic victory since June 4." China's next objective, according to an Asian diplomat, was "to persuade Japan to restore its official loans and so end sanctions by Western governments."[6]

For more than a year after Tiananmen, Japan refused to restore the loans, arguing that Tokyo's hands were tied by public opinion and international obligations.[7] Japan's action, in line with Western economic sanctions (including the suspension of World Bank loans worth $750 million),[8] continued to sour relations between Japan and China, despite Tokyo's gesture of goodwill in the hijacker incident. It became increasingly clear that Japanese ODA to China not only possessed economic significance, but was also a crucial part of Japan's diplomacy toward China, directly affecting overall bilateral relations. In this sense, Japan's aid to China may be called aid diplomacy.

JAPAN'S ODA TOWARD CHINA

There are several forms of Sino-Japanese economic cooperation, such as trade, foreign investment, Export-Import Bank loans, and ODA. Japan's ODA programs include government loans, grants, and technical aid. To get an overall picture of Japanese ODA to China, we need first to look at some basic factors that influence this aid.

As early as 1961, Japan became a member of the Development Assistance Committee (DAC) under the Organization of Economic Cooperation and Development (OECD), which was a coordinating organization of the world's donors (P. Trezise 1990: 35). Although at that time, and up until the mid-1960s, Japan was also the World Bank's second largest borrower after India, since the mid-1960s Japan has actively been involved in foreign aid programs. Asia has remained the single largest area receiving Japanese aid (for example, 71 percent in 1980 and 65 percent in 1987).[9]

Japan's ODA goals have undergone several changes over the past three decades. In the 1960s ODA was used to promote Japan's exports. After the 1973 oil shock, Japan's aid policy switched to securing raw-material supplies—during this period China was one of the source countries (together with Indonesia and the Middle East). Entering the 1980s, Japan tried hard to boost aid to strategically important countries that did not necessarily have close links with Japan, such as Egypt, Pakistan, and Turkey.

China was a latecomer in joining Japan's list of aid recipients. Although the 1972 Sino-Japanese rapprochement and the 1978 Sino-Japanese Peace and Friendship Treaty laid the foundations for the rapid development of bilateral relations, it was not until 1979 that China received any Japanese foreign aid. At that time, Beijing signed an agreement with Tokyo to receive a governmental loan.

Despite the late entry to Japan's list of aid recipients, China's aid from Japan grew substantially throughout the 1980s. From 1982 to 1986, China was the largest recipient of Japanese aid, and in 1987 and 1988, China was second only to Indonesia.[10] Japan is the largest ODA donor to China. For example, Japan's ODA to China accounted for 45 percent of the total amount of aid that China received from DAC members and international organizations during the period 1979–84. During the same period, the International Monetary Fund was second (14 percent), with U.N. agencies third (12 percent) and West Germany fourth (9 percent) as aid donors to China (T. Ōkubo 1986: 5). Japan's share of total aid to China reached nearly 70 percent before the Tiananmen incident.

Japan's ODA to China has a distinct characteristic: there is a high concentration in loan aid, which has accounted for 85 to 90 percent of the total bilateral ODA. The primary reason for this type of aid is the Chinese emphasis on funds for large-scale infrastructural projects, such as railways, ports, and hydroelectric power plants. From the Japanese perspective, these large-scale projects normally have high feasibility status and receive better publicity in the international community, and are therefore more desirable.

Since 1979, there have been three major packages of Japanese government loans to China. The first government-to-government loan was 350 billion yen (U.S. $1.5 billion) for China's five-year plan (1979–84), which was pledged by Prime Minister Masayoshi Ōhira during his visit to China in December 1979. This was followed by a 470 billion yen (U.S. $2.1 billion) package agreed to by Prime Minister Yasuhiro Nakasone in March 1984 for the five-year period

1985–90. The third package is the 810 billion yen (U.S. $5.4 billion) loan covering 1990–95 that Prime Minister Noboru Takeshita promised during his visit to Beijing in August 1988. These government loans, known as soft loans, follow the international standard of providing longer payback periods and lower interest payments. This means the loans are repayable over thirty years at 3 (or a little more than 3) percent interest, with a ten-year grace period. In 1988 the Japanese government announced an interest reduction on yen loans to developing countries to approximately 2.6 percent, and China was one of the first countries to receive this new low rate.[11]

Although this chapter focuses on Japan's government loans, China can obtain loans through a number of other channels. The most notable are short-term and higher interest private commercial loans and the Export-Import Bank loans. For example, in May 1979 the Export-Import Bank of Japan agreed to a loan of $2 billion with a fifteen-year term at 6.25 percent interest. Three months later, China obtained two commercial loans for a total of $8 billion at a higher rate and with shorter payment periods of six months and four and a half years, respectively (Whiting 1989: 121–122). No doubt, the government loans have much better terms than the commercial and Export-Import Bank loans.

Japan clearly considers economic factors when it formulates its aid policy toward China. Although trade with China accounts for less than 5 percent of Japan's total trade, China is economically important to Japan in terms of natural resources and potential markets. For years Japan, alternating with Hong Kong, has been China's leading trade partner, accounting for approximately one fourth of China's total foreign trade. However, Japan's leading position in the China market has constantly been challenged by other industrialized countries, making foreign aid an area of competition between Japan and the Western states.

In 1979 China began its economic reform and open door policy. For the first time since the late 1950s, China showed a willingness to accept foreign aid, including loans and grants. The first loan request was for a package of eight infrastructure construction projects that included three hydroelectric power plants, three railroad lines, and two ports. When China began to explore loan possibilities for these projects in the summer of 1979, Tokyo was well aware of the competition from other industrialized countries. There were several private commercial loan offers from France ($7 billion), Britain ($5 billion), Sweden, and Canada. The Japanese also knew of U.S. Vice-President Walter Mondale's promise of $2 billion Eximbank credits to China when he visited Beijing in 1979. The Japanese government understood that these project loans would be a convenient and useful way to enhance Japan's long-range economic benefits. It would allow Japan, as Lee (1984: 116–119), a longtime observer of Sino-Japanese relations, pointed out, "to establish a firm foothold in China's economic infrastructure, and induce a spillover effect to other areas of Sino-Japanese economic cooperation."

From the first loan package (1979), Japan agreed to provide six (out of eight) construction projects for government loans. Railroad line and seaport projects were selected, and two hydroelectric power plant projects were dropped. This selection clearly reflected Japan's economic interests. The two ports, Shijiusuo and Qinhuangdao, were important exporting ports of energy supplies (in particular coal) to Japan. Two of the three railroad lines, the Yanzhou-Shijiusuo Railway and the Beijing-Qinhuangdao Railway, directly connected the two ports. Japan provided 62 percent and 100 percent of requested loan amounts, respectively. On the other hand, the third railroad, Hengyang-Guangzhou Railway, was irrelevant to Japan's energy supply route and thus received only 16 percent of what China asked for. The Japanese rejected the two hydroelectric power plant projects (Longtan and Shuikou) because they were in conflict with Japan's economic interests. The Longtan Hydroelectric Power Plant would have had the capacity to supply electricity to a large aluminum refinery with an annual production capability of 600,000 tons, which was in conflict with Japanese joint venture interests in aluminum production in Indonesia and Brazil.[12] These examples demonstrate that the actual selection from the requested projects reflected, as Greg Story suggested, "the needs of the donor rather than the recipient, that is, it followed Japanese rather than Chinese economic priorities" (G. Story 1987: 35).

The economic benefits of Japan's aid diplomacy to both Japan and China are obvious. Japan has not only ensured itself of a long-term supply of raw materials (energy in particular),[13] but has also broadly and deeply enhanced its position in the China market. No other country can match the degree of Japan's involvement in China's economic affairs. The large-scale aid programs have also enhanced Japan's international reputation as a top donor in the world. From the Chinese perspective, Japan's ODA programs have provided cheaper capital than private banks for China's modernization drive, particularly its large-scale infrastructural construction projects. This interdependence between China and Japan will be a long-term phenomenon.

Despite its relative success, Japan's aid programs are not without fault. To the contrary, one may hear such criticism of Japan's ODA projects as having bureaucratic red tape and tough conditions for the beneficiaries (R. Drifte 1990: 75). Many people within and outside of Japan complain that there is a lack of "a grand design for lending."[14] Generally, Japanese ODA, as aid expert Robert Orr points out, is not strictly aid but rather *keizai kyōryoku* (economic cooperation). Thus, Japanese aid is inevitably more commercial than Western aid.[15] As will be discussed later, Japan's post–Tiananmen performance demonstrates that Japan's aid decisions are heavily influenced by Western countries, particularly the United States. There has been confusion over controversial decisions, such as when and how the economic sanctions toward China should be lifted, and what kind of aid projects can or cannot be advanced.

TOKYO'S DUAL POSITION TOWARD TIANANMEN

Japan's initial reaction to the Tiananmen incident reflected its two diplomatic goals: to be in line with Western democracies by strongly criticizing the military suppression, and to ensure that cooperative Sino-Japanese relations, developing since the early 1970s, would not be damaged permanently.

Immediately after Tiananmen, Prime Minister Sōsuki Uno and top foreign affairs officials deplored Beijing's armed suppression and called it "morally intolerable."[16] Domestic Japanese reactions to the Tiananmen incident were also strong. Economic sanctions were frequently called for and received a wide range of political and public support. This support came not only from the ruling Liberal Democratic Party (LDP) and the highest government bureaucrats, but also from opposition parties. LDP's Foreign Affairs Department Chairman Kōji Kakizawa openly called for economic sanctions, saying that Japan should make clear that it was a nation that respected the principles of democracy, freedom, and human rights. The Japan Communist Party (JCP) Secretariat Chief Mitsuhiro Kaneko demanded to "immediately halt economic assistance to China," because it is "paid for by the sweat of the Japanese people's brows." Japan's largest labor organization, the Japanese Private Sector Trade Union Confederation known as *Rengō* (with 5.4 million members), and the 4.5 million-strong General Council of Trade Union, announced that they would suspend exchanges with China to protest Beijing's action.[17]

Japan was the only Asian country that went along with Western industrialized countries in imposing economic sanctions against Beijing's suppression of the pro-democracy movement that left hundreds dead.[18] One measure Japan took was to freeze its government loan of $5.4 billion which had been scheduled for release in April 1990. In the immediate post–Tiananmen period, because of a lack of clear direction, Japanese aid officials followed a case-by-case review process for approving current loans and grants to China.[19] Other measures included the suspension of high-level government contacts and several scheduled economic and cultural exchange meetings, including the inauguration of an investment-promotion organization for China and a Sino-Japanese meeting on high technology transfer.[20]

Because of the fall of China's international credit rating since June 1989, some bankers raised the possibility that China might have to reschedule some of its $44 billion foreign debt, if it was unable to sign new loans. About half of China's debt is owed to Japan, China's largest creditor, and the World Bank's outstanding loans to China come to about $8 billion. Even before the crackdown, Japanese big business (industry and commerce in particular) had already shown less enthusiasm about China as a marketplace (W. Arnold 1985: 114). For example, Japan ranks a poor third in overseas investment in China (after Hong Kong and the United States), with about 8 percent of the total foreign investment China received in 1988.[21] After Tiananmen, commercial bankers became increasingly reluctant to extend new loans to China. Japanese bankers were deeply concerned about China's current economic situation which was affected by the political chaos. "The downhold on loans from Japanese banks has nothing to do with politics," a Japanese banker claimed in early 1990. "It just doesn't look profitable for us at this time."[22]

Despite its reluctance to extend the loans, the Japanese government is cautious to avoid pushing China into further isolation. Some Japanese officials privately argued that sanctions were likely to strengthen Chinese hard-liners and heighten a nationalistic reaction, and that political instability and economic stagnation on the mainland jeopardized a peaceful and prosperous Asia-Pacific region (A. Whiting 1992: 43).

Immediately after the crackdown, the chief spokesman for the Ministry of Foreign Affairs, Taizō Watanabe, emphasized that "What the government is taking into account most is the fact that relations between Japan and China are naturally different from those between the U.S. and China" (referring to Japanese military behavior in China during World War II). He also warned that Japan must be cautious because Beijing might launch a harsh attack against Tokyo's economic sanctions in order to distract domestic attention in China from the current unrest. The government's view was supported by many business leaders. For example, after the Beijing crackdown, Bank of Japan Governor Satoshi Sumita advocated a "wait and see attitude."[23]

Japan's dual position was highlighted by a *Japan Times* editorial on the first anniversary of the Tiananmen incident. On the one hand, it condemned Beijing's repressive policy and on the other claimed that "outsiders' one-sided perceptions of China have played an excessively great role in isolating China in the international community." It also stated that it was time "to try to pave the way for China's full-fledged return to the international community." Equally important was the fact that, as time passed, Japan's business community began to complain that the hold on loans had seriously affected exports to China; the business community wanted the government loans resumed.[24]

This dual position inevitably produced a diplomatic dilemma and created confusion in Japanese policy toward China. The controversy forced Tokyo to search for a balance among various options, trying to confirm to both the West and China that Japan (1) would continue to be in line with the West, and (2) would prevent pushing China into further isolation. Therefore, Japan needed to work on two different diplomatic fronts—China and the West—in its post–Tiananmen policy toward China.

CULTIVATING A WARM SOCIAL ENVIRONMENT

The Japanese have attached great importance to building "a multilevel network of cooperative relations in the international community at both the governmental and private levels" (M. Kosaka 1989: 73). Through various social activities, known as *tsukiai* (as examined in Part II), the Japanese are clearly trying to cultivate a warm social environment in foreign countries for broader political access. In the long process of Sino-Japanese relations, the Japanese have indeed carried out extensive *tsukiai* activities including ODA programs, thereby expanding their political access in China. This ability to maintain political access would in turn make it easier for Japan to handle international crises such as Tiananmen.

Let us briefly review how Japan has utilized ODA as a weapon to promote a friendly social environment between the two countries. Emotional ties with China have played a part in formulating Japanese aid policy. In the public opinion polls taken for the past several years, China has consistently been second only to the United States as the most friendly nation. Both of China's nationalist and communist leaders, Chiang Kai-shek in 1951 and Zhou Enlai in 1972, respectively, foreswore Japan's war reparations as goodwill gestures. Many Japanese felt Japan could use government loans as surrogate reparations for Japan's past war behavior in China. As one experienced foreign banker in Hong Kong suggested, "Financially these loans make no sense. Politically they are really disguised reparations" (Whiting 1989: 123).

More importantly, Article Nine of Japan's postwar constitution renounces "the right of belligerency." As a *Far Eastern Economic Review* article points out, Japan "cannot use military might in pursuit of its overseas policy."[25] This leaves economic means, including ODA, as one of the prime ways available to the Japanese government to exercise political influence in the international arena.

To further promote the bilateral relationship and increase mutual understanding at the public level, Japan has directed most grants toward humanitarian purposes and cultural exchanges to China. One of the most important projects was the China-Japan Friendship Hospital in Beijing, which cost 16.4 billion yen and accounted for 57 percent of all grants to China in the 1980–85 period. Other smaller projects included a Sino-Japanese youth exchange center in Beijing (1985),[26] a rehabilitation center in Beijing for the physically handicapped (1986), water purification facilities in Changchun (1986), forest resources restoration (1988), an experimental fishery station in Hebei Province (1988), a national library and a foreign language college in Beijing (1988), and preservation of the Dunhuang Mogao Cave on the historic Silk Road (1988). The one billion yen grant in aid to the Mogao Cave was pledged by Prime Minister Noboru Takeshita when he visited China in 1988; he indicated that the grant was to "appeal to the hearts of the Chinese people."[27] Economic assistance to China has also come in the form of technical and training assistance. For example, of ten thousand "foreign experts" in China in 1986, about 40 percent were Japanese, and a management training center funded by the Japanese was opened in Tianjing in 1986.

Japan's aid diplomacy and the efforts to "appeal to the hearts of the Chinese people" were fruitful. U.S. journalists noticed that the Japanese maintained better access to top leaders in China than other Western leaders and diplomats did. Social network activities between the Chinese and the Japanese were helpful in cultivating political ties. For example, in 1984 Chinese Communist party Secretary General Hu Yaobang invited visiting Japanese Prime Minister Yasuhiro Nakasone to a rare private family dinner. In early 1985 Hu dined with Japanese Ambassador Yōsuke Nakae three times in one week, whereas

American Ambassador Arthur Hummel during his entire four-year posting met with Hu only once.[28]

There is another good example. After signing the agreement transferring Hong Kong to Chinese sovereignty in 1997, British Prime Minister Margaret Thatcher proudly announced that the Chinese officials agreed to receive a British trade delegation. But when the mission of ten top British industrialists arrived in February 1985, they found themselves outdone by a visit of one hundred members of the Japanese Chamber of Commerce. The Japanese delegation met with Deng Xiaoping; the British did not. A Western journalist concluded, "No other country can compete with Japan for access in China."[29] This greater access to the Chinese leadership can largely be explained (in addition to cultural affinity) as the result of Tokyo's longtime network activities with Beijing.

ODA has also been used to reduce friction between the two countries. While basically maintaining cordial relations since normalization in 1972, Sino-Japanese relations did experience friction. As mentioned previously, the most notable issue of contention was Japan's so-called revived militarism. In 1982 and 1985–86 large anti-Japanese demonstrations took place in Beijing and other major cities. These demonstrations were led by university students who were inspired by Beijing's sharp criticism of the Japanese government's revision of Japan's past war behavior in school textbooks (known as the textbook controversy) and by an official visit by Prime Minister Yasuhiro Nakasone to the Yasukuni Shrine to honor the war dead. Other problems included a territorial dispute over Diaoyu Island (or *Senkaku* in Japanese), and a controversy between China and Taiwan over ownership rights of a student dormitory in Kyoto, resulting in a Japanese court decision in favor of Taiwan. During these frictions, Japan's political leaders pledged large-scale soft loans to China. Although there were no direct connections between the controversies and the loans, the Japanese used government loans as goodwill gestures to smooth over the friction and to promote better ties with the Chinese.

Tokyo's strong desire to cultivate close political ties with Beijing can also be traced to economic considerations. Since normalization of diplomatic relations, China has remarkably increased its importance to Japan in economic terms. China's natural resources, in particular energy resources, are desirable for Japan. After the oil shock of 1973, Japan became aware of political instability in the Middle East that could jeopardize its assurance of that region's energy supply to Japan. (Japan imports 75 percent of its oil from the Middle East.) With rich natural resources such as coal and oil, and safer, cheaper, and closer sea routes, China is an ideal source from which Japan can import its energy supplies. Thus, maintaining a cordial relationship with Beijing was one of the top priorities in Japan's energy policy as well as its overall foreign policy.

In the aftermath of Tiananmen, Japan was careful to preserve the social environment between the two countries as much as possible. Tokyo took every opportunity to show goodwill to Beijing. For example, although Japan refused to implement new loans, it lifted its freeze on ongoing aid projects in

August 1989.[30] In October 1989 the World Bank began to resume its lending to China for humanitarian aid, including a $30 million loan for earthquake relief (October 1989) and a $60 million credit for agriculture projects (February 1990).[31] Following the World Bank lead, the Japanese government, for the first time after the Tiananmen incident, released a new grant aid of $35 million in December 1989 for improving facilities at a Beijing television broadcasting station and a Shanghai hospital.[32]

Finally, Japanese Prime Minister Toshiki Kaifu paid an official visit to Beijing in August 1991, the first by a leader of a major industrialized nation since Tiananmen. Economic relations, including the issue of Japanese aid, were a major topic during the visit, and Kaifu promised to provide $940 million of ODA loans to China in 1991.[33] All these efforts further confirmed the belief of Chinese leaders that Japan's attitude toward China was different from that of Western industrialized countries.

ACTIVITIES OF INFORMAL POLITICAL ACTORS AND ORGANIZATIONS

Following the decision to suspend high-level official contacts between the two countries, the Japanese government banned current Japanese leaders from visiting China. But this ban applied only to those who held formal official positions, and not to private citizens. During the immediate post–Tiananmen period, in an urgent need to keep channels open, Tokyo often utilized informal political actors and organizations, or *kuromaku* (see Part III), in its contacts with Beijing.

There are two types of informal political actors: (1) scholars and businessmen who are private citizens with close ties with the government, and (2) politicians of both ruling and opposition parties, who do not hold government positions so that they can be regarded as private citizens, but have considerable influence because of their high positions within the political parties.

Isami Takeda, a Dokkyō University professor who participated in the first post–Tiananmen informal group visit to China, gave a detailed account of activities of the first type of informal political actors and organizations.[34] In early August 1989, two months after Tiananmen, a Japanese delegation that included Takeda quietly visited Beijing for one week. At that time, few Japanese would visit Beijing: while government officials were banned from visiting by their government, the Foreign Ministry advised tourists not to visit China for safety reasons. The delegation was organized by the Forum of Liberal Society (FLS) and therefore was considered a private visit.

The FLS was a Tokyo-based, foreign policy-oriented think-tank (*shinkutanku*), with a membership of more than a dozen LDP young Diet members (*wakate*) from virtually every LDP faction. The Forum's chairman was Takujirō Hamada, a former parliamentary vice-minister of foreign affairs, who specialized in foreign policy issues. The Forum conducted research on a wide range of issues in foreign affairs and maintains close ties to both MOFA and the LDP's PARC. The FLS had a sizable research staff and ran such programs as Asian Forum and Japan-China Policy Dialogue.

The delegation was composed of six members: two senior FLS policy staff members, two university professors, and two businessmen. Of the two professors, one was a specialist in East Asian affairs and the other was an expert on Japanese foreign aid programs. The two businessmen were from All Nippon Airway (ANA) which had contributed funds to the Forum and had a keen interest in China. One of the businessmen had been the head of the ANA Beijing office and spoke fluent Chinese. During his years in Beijing, he had made many Chinese friends, especially among sons or daughters of high-level officials. Before their departure, the two FLS staff members visited MOFA. Although many scheduled China trips, official and private alike, were canceled, MOFA gave a clear green light to this visit. The mission of this delegation was to assess Beijing's situation, to pass nonofficial messages, and to conduct free discussions with the Chinese.

Upon arrival in Beijing, the first problem the delegation encountered was the high level of publicity the Chinese press desired to cover the visit. In contrast, the Japanese delegation wanted to keep a low profile.

Considering the relatively low-level and nonofficial nature of the FLS delegation, its activities during the Beijing visit were surprisingly extensive. It also seemed that the delegation had remarkable access to foreign affairs and other political institutions in Beijing. After a detailed briefing at the Japanese Embassy in Beijing on the current Chinese situation, the delegation was welcomed by Fu Hao, former Chinese ambassador to Japan, at the Great Hall of the People, a place usually reserved for high-level official activities. Then, the two FLS staff members were received by a vice-minister of the Chinese Foreign Ministry for a lengthy discussion on post–Tiananmen Sino-Japanese relations. In addition, the delegation was initially scheduled to meet with Deng Rong, the daughter of China's paramount leader Deng Xiaoping (which was regarded as rather unusual), but the meeting was canceled at the last minute without any explanation.

The formal host of the delegation was the Chinese Institute of Contemporary International Relations (CICIR), a research institution directly under the supervision of the State Council of China, believed to have access to the party-government leadership. Despite considerable pressure on intellectuals at that time (for example, the office building of the Chinese Academy of Social Science was still under military control), the Chinese participants appeared confident. The Chinese side was headed by the CICIR's director and a deputy director as well as about a dozen researchers. The Japanese were told that it was rare for the director to attend this kind of discussion with foreign visitors because of his high-level government position and busy schedule. Thus, from the beginning to the end, his involvement showed the importance the Chinese attached to this visit.

The discussions focused on post–Tiananmen Sino-Japanese relations, particularly the release of the third package of Japanese government loans. The Japanese expressed their personal opinions to explain Japan's domestic constraints and international obligations. They raised three possible preconditions necessary for Japan to resume the suspended loan: (1) the lifting of martial law in Beijing; (2) the release of loans by the World Bank; and (3) signs of improvement in relations between China and the United States. The Japanese explained that the change in American attitude would be a key issue because of the United States' global influence and that relations with the United States formed the foundation of Japanese foreign policy. The Japanese also helped the Chinese understand the difference in terms of China policy between the U.S. Congress and the Bush administration.

The extensive and lengthy discussions lasted three days, and were frank and cordial. In Beijing, the Japanese were treated as if they were official state guests. After returning to Tokyo, the Chinese Embassy invited the delegation members to a welcome-back banquet. The two FLS staff members not only gave a detailed report to their own institution, but also paid a visit to MOFA and reported on the China trip to the vice minister of foreign affairs.

In summing up this trip to Beijing and the informal actors function that he and other members played, Isami Takeda stated that "informal contact is always important in Japanese foreign policy," because mutual understanding is more likely developed through informal channels. He further explained that as informal envoys the Japanese members could discuss many issues with the Chinese as frankly as possible without official obligation. At the same time, however, various Japanese government options and opinions were passed on to the Chinese.

As was seen in the process of the 1972 Sino-Japanese rapprochement, opposition parties once again played an active role (the second type of informal political actors and organizations) in Japan's aid diplomacy toward China. Whereas the Democratic Socialist Party and the Japan Communist Party remained uncompromising toward Beijing, the Japan Socialist Party and the Clean Government Party were ready to push for releasing the loans. Before his eight-day visit to Beijing in mid-May 1990, JSP Secretary General Tsuruo Yamaguchi paid a visit to Prime Minister Kaifu and urged him to lift the freeze on the loan package as soon as possible. Kaifu told Yamaguchi that he could tell the Chinese leaders that "Japan will certainly honor its promise" in the $5.4 billion loan, but that there were "difficulties in resuming aid immediately."[35]

Discussing the loan issue with Chinese Communist party Secretary General Jiang Zemin and Politburo Standing Committee member Song Ping, Yamaguchi promised that "the JSP would continue to work hard to resume the third loan package."[36] Less than two weeks later, a CGP delegation headed by its founder, Honorary President Daisaku Ikeda, went to China. Ikeda was warmly received by Jiang and Premier Li Peng, with whom he discussed bilateral relations.[37]

Some old politicians, who played the role of informal political actors about twenty years earlier for the Sino-Japanese rapprochement, continued to play an active role. In May 1990 eighty-eight-year-old ex-LDP Diet member Yoshimi

Furui visited Beijing and met with Li Peng. During this meeting, Fukui and Li once again emphasized that "the Sino-Japanese friendship that was established by older generations should not be damaged [by the loan issue]."[38] Interestingly, in 1972 Furui worked as an informal envoy between Tokyo and Beijing in building bilateral relations for the Tanaka administration (see Chapter 5).

NEMAWASHI AND PERSONAL CONTACTS

It was not easy for Tokyo to strike a balance between Beijing and Washington (and other Western countries) in its post–Tiananmen foreign policy toward China. To work on an agreeable solution in its contacts with both Beijing and Washington, Japan utilized behind-the-scenes consensus-building activities, known as *nemawashi* (examined in Part IV). Prominent political business leaders either worked on internal preparations for lifting economic sanctions or quietly visited Beijing to discuss the loan issue and other bilateral problems with Chinese leaders.

In November 1989 Eishirō Saitō, chairman of the Federation of Economic Organization (Keidanren), visited Beijing. Because of his influential position in Japan and the timing of the visit, Saitō was able to see Deng Xiaoping, who seldom received foreign visitors. During the discussion, Deng reportedly "showed great expectation of Japan," and Saitō expressed goodwill in terms of aid to China.[39] In mid-April 1990, LDP Secretary General Ichirō Ozawa consulted with Foreign Minister Tarō Nakayama to prepare for the loan release "even if countries like the United States do not take a similar action."[40] Michio Watanabe, head of one of the LDP's largest factions and former chairman of the LDP's Policy Affairs Research Council, visited China in early May and met with Party Secretary General Jiang Zemin and Premier Li Peng. Watanabe pledged to implement the loans as soon as possible, saying, "I can say this clearly, after having conferred with other leaders in Japan." Li thanked Japanese leaders for their efforts to have the loans made available, but also warned of the harm that could come to Sino-Japanese relations "if the loans are delayed too long."[41] Such face-to-face maneuvering helped to convey Japan's real intention to the Chinese that eventual lifting of economic sanctions was only a matter of time and would take place in the near future.

Japan's concern over the aid issue toward China was also due to Tokyo's sensitivity to reactions from Western countries. Clearly, it has political ramifications in international relations. ODA reflects a country's international status. As a member of the OECD's Development Assistance Committee (DAC), Japan has been sensitive to its status within the group. In terms of total value of foreign aid, Japan ranked fourth in the club as early as 1968 and contended for second place with France for several years. In 1989 the appreciation of the yen gave Japan the top donor position, replacing the United States.

Although Japan's total foreign aid spending has risen rapidly, the percentage of ODA to gross national product (GNP) remains low. Japan spent just 0.32

percent of GNP on foreign aid in 1988, ranking twelfth among the eighteen DAC members. The DAC average was 0.35 percent of GNP in 1988 despite a United Nations guideline of 0.7 percent for industrialized countries.[42] To keep its international standing, Japan is being pressed to increase its aid spending. By successfully including China on the list of less developed countries (LDCs) drawn up by DAC's Statistics Commission, Japan was able to include its ODA to China as part of its total ODA contribution.

Tokyo has always been aware of international sensitivity to Japan's aid diplomacy toward China. To smooth other countries' concerns, the Ministry of Foreign Affairs in September 1979 released the Ōhira Three Principles of aid policy to China. These principles were aimed at cooperation with the United States and other Western nations (primarily the European Economic Community [EEC]); to ease fears expressed that Japan might move to monopolize the China market; balancing aid to China with aid to other Asian countries, especially the Association of Southeast Asian Nations (ASEAN); and avoiding loans to China's defense-related industries. The last principle was included to deflect criticism from the former Soviet Union, Vietnam, and South Korea.[43]

After Tiananmen, Japan was deeply concerned over U.S. and other Western reaction to its approach to China. This concern, however, was much less influenced by human rights issues. Tokyo's lower priority on human rights was demonstrated not only by its sending back the hijacker to China (as described earlier), but also by the reluctance to defend Chinese students in Japan who were allegedly intimidated and harassed by the Chinese Embassy there.[44] Tokyo was waiting for clear signals from its Western partners, notably the United States, before deciding policy on China. Many observers believed that, if Japan had not taken a tough stand on condemning China's military crackdown, Tokyo "might find itself internationally isolated."[45] As late as the end of 1990, the atmosphere in Washington remained quite negative toward Beijing. Even though President Bush extended China's most-favored-nation (MFN) status, the U.S. Congress was getting tougher in its policy toward China. U.S. lawmakers were determined to step up their efforts to limit World Bank loans to China by exercising their influence over the World Bank.[46] Under such circumstances, Japan appeared to be careful in its own policy toward China.

Tokyo was also aware that Washington had been ambivalent toward Japanese aid to China. On the one hand, the United States itself was explicitly prohibited from extending ODA to China by the Foreign Assistance Act because China was "a member of the international communist movement" (U.S. Congress. House and Senate 1986: 171). Moreover, conservative lawmakers and the Commerce Department viewed Japan's aid presence in China with suspicion, worrying about China's human rights issues and the possibility that Japan might become dominant in the Chinese market. On the other hand, the U.S. State Department and foreign aid agencies had consistently encouraged Japan to take the lead in the West's relations with China through foreign aid, with the view that a moderate and open China would better serve U.S. interests (R. Orr 1990: 73).

In light of the mixed international responses to China, Japan frequently used *nemawashi* to remind the United States and other Western countries that it was best not to impose heavy sanctions on China. For example, before the Paris summit of seven major industrialized countries in July 1989, Japan sent envoys to Washington and other capitals to express its reluctance to criticize China openly. The message to the West sent through *nemawashi* was that the prospect of a wealthy Japan facing an isolated, chaotic China had long been a nightmare for Japanese decision-makers, and prompted Japan's willingness to act as mediator between China and the Western world. A Japanese economic official put it this way: "Japan should take one step ahead of other nations in improving its relations with China. Japan can help create a climate for other nations to improve their relations with Beijing."[47] Prime Minister Toshiki Kaifu's statement at a 1990 New Year's news conference further confirmed Japan's concern; Kaifu claimed, "To isolate China will not be good for world peace and stability."[48]

Personal contacts that were in advanced preparation also helped Tokyo to understand Washington's true intentions. As a key LDP leader and former Japanese foreign minister, Hiroshi Mitsuzuka was sent to Washington in May 1990 to discuss policy toward China with the Bush administration, in particular the loan issue. Mitsuzuka learned from U.S. National Security Adviser Brent Scowcroft that the United States did not want to see the loans to China being restored "too quickly."[49] Japan's sensitivities to the international community slowed the process of lifting economic sanctions against China, and resulted in some confusion over when and how Japan should resume government aid to China. In December 1989 a Japanese government source indicated that Japan would extend the $5.4 billion loan once the World Bank lifted its freeze on new loans to China. Then in early January Finance Minister Ryūtarō Hashimoto promised that Japan would unfreeze the loan programs to China if Beijing lifted martial law.[50] Another possible timing for the loan release, according to a Japanese foreign minister official, was the resolution of the Fang Lizhi issue. Fang, a well-known Chinese dissident and physicist, had taken refuge in the U.S. Embassy in Beijing after the crackdown.[51] Despite these announcements, Tokyo, owing mainly to its concern over its international obligations, let several opportunities pass without lifting its freeze on the $5.4 billion loan, such as Beijing's lifting of martial law in January 1990, the resumption of World Bank humanitarian aid to China, Beijing's release of several hundred prisoners in the first half of 1990, and China's decision to allow Fang Lizhi to go abroad in June 1990.

In sum, Japan's *nemawashi* activities (behind-the-scenes preparation) in the post–Tiananmen period had two functions. Beijing received a clear confirmation that it was only a matter of time before the Japanese would release the loan, despite a delay of more than a year; and Tokyo was also able to clarify its position to Washington that Japan had a keen interest in lifting economic sanctions against China, but would not do so without a clear signal from the United States. Indeed, Japan's decision during the Houston summit in July 1990 to resume aid to China received a "tacit blessing" from President Bush.[52]

BEIJING'S ATTITUDE TOWARD JAPANESE LOANS

Having experienced Western intervention in the latter part of the nineteenth and the beginning of the twentieth centuries, China has been sensitive to issues of national sovereignty and foreign intervention. After the communist victory in 1949, Beijing was isolated from the West. Yet, China was able to receive $1.5 billion in government loans from the former Soviet Union and East European socialist countries during the period 1953–60. After the normalization of relations between China and Japan in 1972, Tokyo, on several occasions, raised the issue of government loans as a form of economic cooperation, but Beijing unequivocally rejected the loans (C. Lee 1984: 113). As late as 1977, a *Renmin Ribao* (People's Daily) editorial still insisted that China should not allow any foreign interests or jointly managed companies to develop domestic primary resources and should not accept any foreign credits.[53]

China's domestic and foreign policy changed drastically after the end of 1978 when Beijing began its open door and reform policy to promote modernization. Beijing gradually realized that the practice of foreign loans in the capitalist world was a necessary way to obtain cheap capital which China badly needed for its economic development. Beijing keenly recognized the enormous economic gap between China and Japan. With barely one tenth of China's population, Japan's 1990 GNP of 4.3 trillion yen (U.S. $31.6 billion) was almost eight times larger than China's GNP.[54] Japan's low-interest capital, advanced technology, and markets have become increasingly attractive to China's decision-makers.

While commercial loans were needed, foreign government soft loans proved more useful as fiscal crises repeatedly threatened China's key projects. In 1979 Japan became the first noncommunist government to offer government loans to China. Other Western countries, such as Belgium and Denmark, and international organizations, including the World Bank, quickly followed suit. Through its experience with the Japanese, China gained valuable knowledge of obtaining entry into the international financial community. A senior U.S. official commented, "Very clearly, China's most important international relationship is with Japan."[55]

The increasing importance of Japanese government loans prompted Deng Xiaoping in 1988 to state publicly that Japanese loans were "extremely significant" when he received Prime Minister Noboru Takeshita, who had just pledged the $5.4 billion loan package to China. Deng claimed, "I want to build a new era like that which we enjoyed during the days of former prime ministers Kakuei Tanaka and Masayoshi Ōhira."[56] Deng's remarks clearly reflected the successful momentum of Sino-Japanese relations brought about by Japan's aid diplomacy.

With the benefits that aid has brought, China has also faced a potentially serious problem—international debt. This concern was reflected in a remark made in 1987 by Lu Zhongwei, deputy director of the Chinese Institute of Contemporary International Relations. He said that "Yen-denominated loans make up 90 percent of Japan's ODA to China. China's future debt problems with Japan will therefore be alarming."[57]

The debt problem grew after June 1989. Up to the end of June 1990, China's international debt stood at $45 billion, with peak repayment periods averaging $5 billion a year until 1996.[58] Much of the debt will go to Japan. In 1990, the Tiananmen incident and the political uncertainty that followed it caused much of the capital that had previously flowed through Hong Kong to China either to shift back to Japan, Taiwan, and Singapore or to be re-routed to Thailand, Indonesia, Malaysia, and the Philippines.[59] Japan is also prepared to turn its ODA programs toward Eastern Europe to support democratic changes there.[60] According to a report in mid-1990, more than $3 billion in foreign loans to China's hotel industry were already in trouble and the Chinese were asking for a reschedule of payment. About 90 percent of foreign hotel loans were rescheduled or were in need of restructuring. Several Japanese commercial banks were involved, such as Sumitomo Bank (a $110 million loan made in 1987) and the Bank of Tokyo (a $73 million loan made in 1989).[61]

Nevertheless, although Beijing openly stated in early 1990 that the foreign debt of some $40 billion was within China's "repayment limit,"[62] some foreign observers had serious doubts. Tomoo Marukawa, a Japanese economic official, for example, believed, "China may manage to get by on a short-term basis, but it will be in serious trouble in the long run."[63] With its centrally controlled financial system and slow but steady economic growth, it is unlikely that China will encounter a major economic crisis in the near future.

Alarmed by the deteriorating situation in late 1989 and early 1990, Chinese leaders pushed hard for Western nations to lift imposed economic sanctions. Beijing was in urgent need to know the intention of Japan, China's largest creditor and leading foreign trading partner. And information on Japan's intention was not in short supply. Owing largely to Japan's informal mechanisms, known as *tsukiai*, *kuromaku*, and *nemawashi*, Beijing was fully aware of the subtle differences between Japan and Western nations and the special role Tokyo could play. Just before the Paris summit of July 1989, Chinese Premier Li Peng praised Japan for its reluctance to condemn China.[64] In November 1989, in his comments on Western economic sanctions, Li Peng predicted that the sanctions would be lifted sooner or later. He said, "Some will go first and other later. We'll wait and see which country will make the first move. The country which does so is brave and praiseworthy."[65] The country Li was referring to as making the first move was clearly Japan.

But Tokyo did not live up to Beijing's expectations of softening its stance over the $5.4 billion loan package, and it only made a small grant ($35 million) "for humanitarian reasons" in December 1989. In the same month, Chinese Vice Premier Wu Xueqian showed his disappointment with Japan by criticizing Tokyo as lagging behind Washington in its China policy, referring to the recent visit of U.S. National Security Adviser Brent Scowcroft who had been sent to Beijing by President Bush.[66]

In his ten-day visit to Japan in January 1990, Minister of the Chinese State Planning Commission Zou Jiahua (the highest Chinese official to visit

Japan since the Tiananmen incident) conducted extensive diplomacy aimed at improving bilateral relations, focusing in particular on the government loan package. He held talks with Prime Minister Toshiki Kaifu and Foreign Minister Tarō Nakayama on the $5.4 billion loan issue. However, except for a goodwill gesture that Japan would soon send an aid study mission to China, there was no change in policy toward "an immediate extension of pledged loans to China."[67] In a March 1990 statement, Chinese Foreign Minister Qian Qichen emphasized "the historical background, geographical location and cultural heritage" between the two countries and called for better relations.[68] Yet the annual bilateral subcabinet-level talks held shortly after Qian's statement did not lead to any progress in lifting Japan's economic sanctions.[69]

Shortly after the economic summit in Houston in July 1990, Japan finally decided to resume its third ODA package to China. The government action further stimulated private sectors to resume loans to China. In 1991, for example, China's giant foreign investment arm, China International Trust and Investment (CITIC), received a $50 million loan from a Japanese syndication and a $113 million five-year, floating-rate note from a group of Japanese lenders with "exceptionally good terms."[70]

With foreign aid as an important diplomatic tool, Japan now has more leverage in its dealings with China. One reason behind Beijing's lifting of martial law in January 1990 was concern over negative international reactions and economic sanctions from Western countries. Japan was an important part of this concern. Even though Japan decided in July 1990 to gradually resume its government loan package, the fact that it imposed economic sanctions for more than a year demonstrates "Tokyo's increasing efforts to translate economic clout into [political] influence and participation."[71] In October 1990, two months after the resumption of ODA to China, Japan's Foreign Ministry issued a White Paper on ODA, outlining the political criterion for allocating aid funds. The White Paper stated, "We as a nation which supports liberty and democracy as its basic values should consult an international framework to help promote democracy and fully support through aid countries making efforts to democratize."[72] This gesture can be regarded not only as a response to pressure from Washington, but also as a clear signal indication of Tokyo's political motivation behind its aid programs.

Tokyo's political motivation was no secret to Beijing. The Chinese leadership may also use politics as leverage to press Japan for more economic assistance. For example, in early 1992, Chinese Premier Li Peng pressed Japan for more yen-denominated loans, indicating that Beijing could assist Tokyo in bringing about full diplomatic relations with Pyongyang in exchange for such financing. This request was made during Li's talk with Makoto Tanabe, chairman of Japan's major opposition party, the Social Democratic Party of Japan (formerly the Japanese Socialist Party).[73]

Japan's aid diplomacy has its limitations. Even though Japan has been urged to follow the example of the United States' Marshall Plan carried out in the postwar period,[74] the size of Japanese aid to China has never reached that level. More importantly, Japan's position today is quite different from that of the United States more than four decades ago. As Bruce Koppel and Michael Plummer (1989: 1055) pointed out, "while Japan's influence in Asia through economic cooperation is enormous, levels of interaction in ODA have not advanced to a point where Japan can extract predictable policy outcomes from the commitments."

Furthermore, loans bring debts that can become a serious problem. These problems may be transferred to Chinese domestic politics. Japan could again be blamed for an economic invasion as it was during the Chinese student demonstrations in the mid-1980s. Although economic sanctions have political leverage, they may also produce a backlash. They may stimulate nationalist feelings in China, creating a new bout of anti-Japanese sentiment. Indeed, Japan was in the difficult position of searching for a balanced role in the post-Tiananmen period. On the one hand, the Western countries and Chinese dissidents criticized Japan for not being tough enough;[75] on the other hand, Tokyo was hard pushed by Beijing to take a lead in improving relations with China.

The large-scale bilateral economic exchanges and government aid from Japan have created economic interdependence between the two countries. They also have far-reaching political implications. As long as China pursues its goal of economic modernization and its political future remains uncertain, Japan's aid diplomacy will continue to play a crucial role in Sino-Japanese relations both economically and politically.

A TRIPARTITE POLICYMAKING MECHANISM

With a more than ten year long history, Japan's aid diplomacy toward China has become an integral part of Sino-Japanese relations. Aid diplomacy has enabled Japan to utilize fully its superior economic strength. The unexpected political turmoil in China—the Tiananmen incident—and Japan's quick, yet cautious, reaction further demonstrate the importance of Japan's foreign aid to Tokyo's political goals. Aid diplomacy has helped promote Japan's international status and smooth relations with neighboring countries, in this case, China. It also demonstrates that Japan has given priority to maintaining its role as a faithful partner to the West, and the United States in particular.

This case study, together with the previous ones, has further revealed the salient patterns in Japan's policymaking process—informal mechanisms—in dealing with international crisis. Informal mechanisms contain three interrelated levels of analysis: social environment and network (tsukiai), informal political actors and organizations (kuromaku), and personal connections and behind-the-scenes consensus-building (nemawashi). We can draw many other interesting questions from this case study, such as why Japan's view of China was so different from that of other Western nations and how Japan uses ODA politically. These are important issues and deserve further examination. But since this book does not focus on these issues, they will not be discussed further.

Tsukiai provides necessary and appropriate social environments for both formal and informal activities. More importantly, in cultivating a cordial relationship, it creates a sense of *giri* (obligation), thereby enabling political access. One of the major political considerations of Japan's aid to China was, as former Prime Minister Takeshita said, to "win the hearts of the Chinese people." This strategy has given the Japanese greater access to China's political leadership.

The importance of *kuromaku* lies in maintaining open channels through informal political actors and institutions. *Kuromaku* are used to convey *honne*, or true intentions, to related parties, as we have seen from the secret trip of the Forum of Liberal Society delegation to Beijing two months after the Tiananmen incident. Such missions could not be accomplished through official channels, given the uncertain political situation in China at that time.

Nemawashi, as a working style, is often used to facilitate mutual understanding among the parties involved. It is a form of informal consultation that aims at avoiding open confrontation, and thus makes it easier to reach compromise. In the post–Tiananmen period, for example, Tokyo conducted extensive behind-the-scenes personal contacts with both Beijing and Washington. These activities have facilitated better understanding of Japan's position in international relations.

In sum, the three dimensions of informal mechanisms are intertwined in the actual decision-making and bargaining process. The activities and functions of informal mechanisms are particularly noteworthy in a delicate situation or in an international crisis, such as the Tiananmen incident.

NOTES

1. *Japan Times*, July 12, 1990, p. 1.

2. *Far Eastern Economic Review*, August 23, 1990, p. 32.

3. *Far Eastern Economic Review*, July 19, 1990, pp. 57–58.

4. Susumu Awanohara, "Mutual Abstainers," *Far Eastern Economic Review*, December 13, 1990, pp. 10–11.

5. "ADB US$70 Million Loan Ends Boycott of China," *Far Eastern Economic Review*, June 1, 1991.

6. *Japan Times*, May 3, 1990, p. 7.

7. For a detailed account, see "Sino-Japanese Relations Remain Far from Normal—Ties on Hold," *Far Eastern Economic Review*, May 10, 1990, pp. 16–17.

8. *Japan Times*, May 10, 1990, p. 6.

9. See Robert Orr, "The Rising Sum: What Makes Japan Give?" *The International Economy*, September/October 1989, p. 81.

10. See Ministry of Foreign Affairs (Japan), *Japan's Official Development Assistance 1989 Annual Report* (Tokyo: Association for Promotion of International Cooperation, 1990), p. 61.

11. See, for example, *Bangkok Post*, July 21, 1988, p. 28.

12. *Asahi Shimbun*, December 1, 1979; Chae-Jin Lee (1984: 121).

13. In the early 1990s, Japan re-emphasized its focus of ODA on energy-related projects. See Anthony Rowley, "Naked Power: Japan Looks to Reduce Its Dependency on Oil Imports," *Far Eastern Economic Review*, December 12, 1991.

14. James Sterngold, "Japan's Foreign Aid Problem," *New York Times*, November 5, 1989.

15. Anthony Rowley, "Lending a Hand," *Far Eastern Economic Review*, October 10, 1991, pp. 68–69.

16. *Japan Times*, June 8, 1989, p. 1.

17. *Japan Times*, June 25 (p. 1), 27 (p. 3), and July 1 (p. 3), 1989.

18. *Journal of Commerce*, November 30, 1989, p. 5A.

19. *New York Times*, June 7, 1989, p. A8.

20. *Japan Times*, June 6, 1989, p. 12.

21. *Journal of Commerce*, August 16, 1988, p. 7A.

22. *Japan Times*, February 2, 1990, p. 10.

23. *Japan Times*, June 6 (p. 12) and 7 (p. 10), 1989.

24. *Japan Times*, May 3 (p. 7), and June 4 (p. 20), 1990.

25. Nigel Holloway, "Aid in Search of a Policy," *Far Eastern Economic Review*, November 9, 1989, p. 64.

26. *Japan Times*, October 14, 1985.

27. *Japan Times*, May 7 (p. 7), and August 25 (p. 1), 1988.

28. Amanda Bennett, "Japan Excels in Relations with China, A Fact That Washington Finds Useful," *Wall Street Journal*, April 13, 1984.

29. Jim Mann, "China and Japan: How They Buried Centuries of Hate," *International Herald Tribune*, May 6, 1985, p. 6.

30. Steven Weisman, "Foreign Aid Isn't Easy for Japan," *New York Times*, August 20, 1989, p. 3E.

31. *Sing Tao International*, May 11, 1990, p. 15.

32. *China Daily*, December 6, 1989, p. 1. Also see *Japan Times*, November 29, 1989, p. 3.

33. Tai Ming Cheung and Louise do Rosario, "Seal of Approval: Kaifu's China Visit Lessens Peking's Isolation," *Far Eastern Economic Review*, August 22, 1991, p. 10.

34. Interview with Isami Takeda, June 6, 1990, Honolulu.

35. *Japan Times*, May 11, 1990, p. 1.

36. *Renmin Ribao*, May 19 and 21, 1990, p. 1.

37. *China Daily*, June 1, 1990, p. 1.

38. *Renmin Ribao*, May 14, 1990, p. 1.

39. *Japan Times*, November 14, 1989, p. 1.

40. *Japan Times*, April 17, 1990, p. 1.

41. Henry Cutter, "Politicians Prepare to Restore China Aid," *Japan Times* (weekly international edition), May 28–June 3, 1990, p. 1; also see *Renmin Ribao*, May 4 and 5, 1990, p. 1.

42. *Japan Economic Institute Report*, No. 1B (January 5, 1990), p. 13.

43. *Asahi Shimbun*, September 3, 4, and 9, 1979; also see Greg Story (1987: 34), and Chae-Jin Lee (1984: 118–119).

44. For the full account, see Mutsuo Fukushima, "Chinese Students Find Tokyo Government Deaf to Their Pleas," *Japan Times*, June 5, 1990, pp. 1 and 2.

45. *Japan Times*, June 7, 1989, p. 10.

46. Susumu Awanohara, "No More Favors: U.S. Lawmakers Expected to Maintain Anti-China Stand," *Far Eastern Economic Review*, June 7, 1990, pp. 56–57.

47. *Japan Times*, July 5 (p. 1), November 9 (p. 12), and December 15 (p. 1), 1989.

48. *New York Times*, January 15, 1990, p. 5.

49. Cutter, "Politicians Prepare to Restore China Aid."

50. *Japan Times*, December 23, 1989, p. 9; and January 11, 1990, p. 1.

51. Cutter, "Politicians Prepare to Restore China Aid."

52. When asked by reporters on Japan's plan to resume aid to China, George Bush answered, "Japan is a sovereign nation that can make up its own mind on a lot of questions." See *Japan Times*, July 9, 1990.

53. *Renmin Ribao*, February 1, 1977; See Laura Newby (1988: 39).

54. Robert Delfs, "Sense or Sensibility: Historical Mistrust Hampers Marriage of Capital and Cheap Labor," *Far Eastern Economic Review*, April 25, 1991, pp. 52–55.

55. Bennett, "Japan Excels in Relations with China."

56. *Japan Times*, August 27, 1988, p. 1.

57. *Asahi Evening News*, July 7, 1987, p. 3.

58. Elizabeth Cheng, "Guarantor's Market: Foreign Lending Makes a Comeback in China," *Far Eastern Economic Review*, June 20, 1991, pp. 94–95.

59. Editorial, "Cold Wind from the North," *The Japan Economic Journal*, September 16, 1989, p. 10.

60. *Japan Times*, December 23, 1989, p. 3.

61. "Ill-starred Ventures: China's Hotel Industry Faces a Foreign Debt Crisis," *Far Eastern Economic Review*, April 26, 1990, p. 54.

62. "China Expands Economic and Trade Co-operation with Other Countries," *Beijing Review*, 33, no. 17 (April 23–29, 1990): 30–31.

63. *Japan Times*, November 9, 1989, p. 12.

64. *Japan Times*, July 4, 1989, p. 1.

65. "Li Peng on Domestic and World Issues," *Beijing Review*, 32, no. 49 (December 4–10, 1989): 12–14.

66. *Japan Times*, December 30, 1989, p. 1.

67. Ibid., January 24, 1990, p. 1.

68. "Foreign Minister Qian Meets the Press," *Beijing Review*, 33, no. 15 (April 9–15, 1990): 17.

69. *Korea Herald*, March 28, 1990, p. 1.

70. Jonathan Friedland, "Borrowings, Samurai Welcome," *Far Eastern Economic Review*, November 7, 1991, pp. 64–65; and Elizabeth Cheng, "Guarantor's Market: Foreign Lending Makes a Comeback in China," *Far Eastern Economic Review*, June 20, 1991, pp. 94–95.

71. "Japan's New Gospel: Kaifu Signals Tokyo's Desire for Influence in Asia," *Far Eastern Economic Review*, May 17, 1990, p. 13.

72. Anthony Rowley, "Japanese Aid: Bonus for Reform," *Far Eastern Economic Review*, October 18, 1990, p. 76.

73. "Peking Links Yen Loans to Tokyo-Pyongyang Ties," *Far Eastern Economic Review*, January 23, 1992, p. 59.

74. The original idea of Japan's "Marshall Plan" was floated by former Foreign Minister Saburō Ōkita: See Hobart Rowen, "Japan Puts Forward Its 'Marshall Plan'," *Japan Times*, October 21, 1986, p. 8. Also see James Robinson, "For a Japanese Equivalent of the Marshall Plan," *New York Times*, May 3, 1986, p. 19.

75. Editorial, "Friendly Advice on Human Rights," *Japan Times*, July 19, 1989; also see Gerald Segal, "Why the Japanese Are Keeping Quiet," *International Herald Tribune*, July 3, 1989, p. 6.

PART VI

Conclusions

9

Theory and Practice of Informal Mechanisms

This study has explored informal mechanisms in Japan's policymaking through a series of case studies. The basic analyses are from three different levels: the societal level, the institutional level, and the individual level. Special emphasis has been placed on Japan's policymaking mechanisms and the interrelationships among political, social, and cultural variables. These characteristics are critical in assessing and understanding contemporary Japanese politics and policymaking.

Because of the increased complexity in the making of foreign policy in pluralistic democracies, we should examine not only why an action was taken, but also, as Morton Halperin (1974: 313) points out, "what were the motives, interests, and sources of power of the various participants . . . which led to the decisions and then to the actions." Concentrating on an examination of informal practice in Japanese politics, this study can be regarded as an effort to study policymaking mechanisms "which led to the decisions and then to the actions."

INFORMAL MECHANISMS AND POLICYMAKING

Informal mechanisms contain several theoretical components: the notion of political pluralism, organizational theory, and political culture. By conducting three levels of analyses, this study has revealed the critical role of the social network, informal political actors and organizations, and behind-the-scenes consensus-building in Japan's policymaking process.

Let us first look at social environment and networks, or *tsukiai*. Social networks are some of the most effective mechanisms by which to coordinate different interests and to achieve consensus among political elites. According to a general anthropological theory on norms of behavior, in a given society the growing child soon comes to realize the advantages of conformity in regards to his comfort and in his early struggles for status. He finds himself caught in a net of social relations within which he receives generously only by giving willingly; if he fails to fit into the norms of behavior, he loses out correspondingly. This social give-and-take, often called reciprocity or equivalence, continues throughout life (F. Keesing 1958: 311). In Japan, the norm of conformity and the social give-and-take phenomenon are reflected in the ideas of *tsukiai*.

The result of the confrontation between silkworm farmers and small- and medium-sized businesses in favor of silkworm farmers demonstrates the importance of special networks between organized farmers and the LDP (Part II). Social networking is also used to cultivate political ties internationally, for Tokyo tried hard to "win the hearts of the Chinese people" through its foreign aid programs throughout the 1980s (Part V). We can also see from the example of coordination within the Japanese negotiation team for the Sino-Japanese economic agreements that the University of Tokyo network, or *gakubatsu*, helped create a valuable cordial atmosphere among the Japanese delegates (Part IV).

A noteworthy phenomenon is the rising influence of a group of highly specialized powerful Diet members, knows as *zoku*, as examined in Chapter 3. With their long service within the party, *zoku* have cultivated their own sphere of influence over one or several particular fields. Once a person has established himself as a top-ranking *zoku*, he has significant influence over his policy field, regardless of whether or not he has had a formal position. The special relationship between the agricultural bureaucrats (MAFF) and the LDP agricultural *zoku* who were backed by farmers was effectively cultivated by silkworm farmers in the raw silk protection.

Next, we should look into the structure of the system at the institutional level. As in any political system there are formal powers and informal powers. This is particularly true in Japanese politics (T. Inoguchi 1985: 14), where there are many informal organizations. Bradley Richardson and Scott Flanagan (1984: 100) define the informal organizations within political parties as "interpersonal networks of friendship and mutual ideological agreement and other relationships or groups which come to exist within parties and which are not called for by the party's formal organizational plans." Therefore, they are often "more important than the parties' formal structures."

In addition, the leader-follower (or interfaction) relationship is particularly important within the LDP, for interfactions are main vehicles for selecting the highest leadership of the party and the state: the party president (also Japan's prime minister). In addition, issue-oriented organized coalitions or groups in Japanese political parties are temporary, and they dissolve after each issue is solved. Based on the case studies on the process of Sino-Japanese rapprochement and the four economic agreements, we have seen that some of the most active players in the policymaking process were informal political actors and organizations. Satō's duck diplomacy, the opposition parties' *yatō gaikō* (diplomacy), and a secret Japanese nonofficial mission to Beijing after the Tiananmen incident are good examples of informal political actors in action.

Many informal or ad hoc organizations of the LDP were involved in formulating China policy. They included the Asian Study Group, the Afro-Asian Study Group, Sōshinkai, Seirankai, and several less formal investigative and special committees, such as the Special Committee on the Silk and Silk Yarn Industries which was organized for raw silk protection. In the early 1970s the LDP's subcommittee on China and the Council for the Normalization of Japan-China Diplomatic Relations also served as bodies of policy deliberation and forums for opposing opinions. All these organizations held debates within the party and had influence over the party's directions. None of these groups were formal organizations within the LDP. Rather, their members were from cross-sections of the party, many of whom belonged to different groups at the same time. More importantly, the political influence of these ad hoc informal organizations within the LDP is often greater than formal institutions such as the Diet committees owing to the de facto one-party rule.[1]

Informal organizations are deviations from formal organizations. They tend to force political activities to shift away from the purely formal system, and in turn they may often support the formal system, while making modifications to formal goals. This trend may eventually result in the formalization of informal organizations, as we can see in the case of LDP factions that have gradually been recognized as a normal part of LDP political life. Informal settings have the functions of catalyst and safety valve for formal political actions.

The third component of informal mechanisms is *nemawashi*, behind-the-scenes consensus-building. This working style has deep roots in Japan's political culture. In Japan's political life, *nemawashi* is widely used within and outside of the ruling party and bureaucracy apparatus to coordinate different positions. *Nemawashi* can also be applied to external relations. As in the case of the Sino-Japanese Trade Agreement, Japanese officials made several prenegotiation *nemawashi* to the Chinese from the division level up to the bureau level, and then on to the ministry level. The duck diplomacy used by Prime Minister Satō for trying to open relations with China is a good example not only of informal political actors, but also of *nemawashi* activities. As explained by the term duck diplomacy, Japan's action was akin to a duck's: appearing to look calm on the surface while busily using its feet under water. Personal contact and connection are also used to convey Japan's real intentions to related parties, as Tokyo did to both Beijing and Washington during the post–Tiananmen period, when Japan was facing an international dilemma over economic sanctions against China (including Japan's third loan package of $5.4 billion).

In Japan, this phenomenon is called the difference between *tatemae* (open statements or expected roles) and *honne* (actual thoughts and intentions). While openly at odds with Beijing over the issue of Taiwan, the Satō administration sent five "ducks"—a top politician, a MOFA bureaucrat, an opposition party Diet member, a nonmainstream LDP leader, and a businessman—to contact Beijing.

Such a maneuver would have been impossible through formal and regular chan-nels. *Yatō gaikō* (opposition party diplomacy) also illustrates *nemawashi* at work in Japanese foreign policy. From the first three Diet members' visit to Beijing in 1952 to the episode of the Takeiri Memo of 1972, opposition parties played a constructive role in normalizing relations with China.[2]

The behind-the-scenes preparations use both explicit and implicit ways of communication. One of them is *haragei*—stomach art or nonverbal communi-cation—which is an intuitive way to convey messages and to achieve mutual understanding. This was clearly reflected in the case of the LDP's unwritten rules that kept the conservative young hawks from going to extremes and in the implicit understanding in the National Diet between the ruling and opposition parties. The idea is based on implicit norms of behavior and an unspoken political trust.

In sum, informal mechanisms in Japan's policymaking have a tripartite character: *tsukiai* contributes an appropriate social environment for political activ-ities; *kuromaku* provides political actors and institutions who will informally carry out politically difficult tasks; and *nemawashi* facilitates mutual understanding and establishes political trust at the individual level. A combination of the three constitutes a special political process that gives decision-makers broader options, provides more flexibility for bargaining and compromise, and reduces the risk of offending the domestic or international actors involved. Informal contact has often become a prelude for later formal exchange and decisions, and thus may act as both a catalyst and a safety valve. We may conclude that Japanese politics cannot function well without informal mechanisms. At the same time, it is important to note that in reality there are often no clear boundaries between formal and informal settings, and the lines between the two may appear blurred.

Informality in Japanese politics may be interpreted in various ways. First, informal mechanisms may be regarded as a reflection of Japan's own pattern for political development. As a latecomer in the world economy, Japan adopted an economic growth-oriented policy which may be referred to as the "catch-up mentality" (G. Rozman 1992: 10). Politicians and bureaucrats alike believed that political stability was the basis for economic growth. To achieve this goal, it is necessary to provide enough channels so that the input of different or even opposite opinions can reach the policymaking organs. Yet pluralistic politics must not lead to social instability and political chaos.

The subsequent path of development for a latecomer, as D. Westney (1987: 216) argues, will "diverge from that of the advanced countries." Late modernizers like Japan, according to Krauss and Muramatsu (1988: 210), may have to adopt the traditions of a strong government bureaucracy and state power to an increasingly pluralistic society with democratic and consumer-oriented values, a differentiated and powerful interest group structure, and a viable principled opposition. Therefore, less formal and more flexible political mechanisms have become necessary to adjust various political forces to concentrate on the nation's modernization. Although recent political development toward further pluraliza-tion has indicated that the broad public consensus on rapid economic growth "has given way to a much less uniform set of goals that reflects a growing pluralism and a fragmentation of political interests" (G. Curtis 1988: 245), the informal patterns of Japanese policymaking have largely remained intact.

One other explanation lies in the structural characteristics of Japan's parliamentary system which forces participants to resort to informal ways. The funds provided by the Japanese government for each Diet member to hire aides are only enough to cover two or three parliamentary aides' salaries. These aides are equivalent to administrative assistants in the U.S. Congress, not legislative assistants. They normally have neither the time nor the expertise to draft legislation. Their main tasks are to take care of constituents and to make sure their bosses get reelected in the next campaign. Diet members often hire more aides using their own political funds from both their Tokyo offices and the district offices, but almost all the aides are engaged in administrative work. Because of this structural limitation, Diet members rely heavily on the bureaucracy in drafting legislation, and yet organize their own research institutions in policy research, if they are powerful enough. One such example is the LDP Diet member Takujirō Hamada's Forum of Liberal Society, which runs such programs as the Asian Forum and the Japan-China Policy Dialogue.

Another structural characteristic is what Junnosuke Masumi called the 1955 political system of longtime one-party (LDP) domination.[3] The LDP has been in power since its establishment in 1955. The party elders and policy-oriented *zoku*, as shown in my case studies, have accumulated great power to handle and influence all major decisions during this time. In a political system where one-party dominance makes consensus relatively easy to achieve, Japanese leaders often can afford to wait for consensus to materialize before announcing a new policy. Although seeking consensus is a widely used strategy by political leaders, the Japanese leaders' inclination toward consensus and their understanding of this process and intentional use of it make it particularly conspicuous there (R. Ward 1978: 72).

From the organizational perspective, Japan's longtime one-party domination may also have an impact on the party itself. The influential position of party elders may discourage junior LDP Diet members from hiring their own legislative staff. The political reality of the elders' leadership within the ruling party, the strong bureaucracy, and insufficient funds and incentive for junior Diet members to become experts in legislation all contribute to the informal nature of policymaking in Japanese politics.

Informal mechanisms may also be regarded as a reflection of Japan's political culture, which has been examined by a few Japan specialists (B. Richardson 1974: 2–4). In traditional Japanese society, harmony is the ideal, even if this means compromise or ignoring a possible controversy. Emphasizing harmony would mean emphasizing harmonious personal relationships, making informal contacts and using informal organizations all the more important. After having examined Asian political culture, Lucian Pye (1985: 285) concludes that "formal structures are given vitality largely through informal relationships, which usually are highly personalized."

Conflict resolution is an important objective of the informal system. In his comparative study of the budgeting process, Aaron Wildavsky (1986: 119) notices that in Japan, "Ministries can practice avoidance. They can sidestep outright conflict by rarely dealing directly with one another." Indirect communication is used to avoid face-to-face confrontation. In Japan, avoidance normally comes through compromises and consultations among related parties. In the case of negotiations for the Sino-Japanese Trade Agreement, behind-the-scenes bargaining took place between MITI and MOFA over the leadership of the Japanese delegation to Beijing. The bureaucrats of the two ministries made compromises by dividing the six-day trip into two parts: each holding the leadership for three days.

Three dimensions of Japan's informal mechanisms have been analyzed here: social environment, political institution, and personal connection and consensus-building. A study of the nature of policymaking can give us "a better understanding of the diversity and seeming inconsistency of the goals that national policy must serve" (R. Hillsman 1967: 13). Public policy, as Pendleton Herring (1965: 30) defines it, is a concept that "implies a plan of governmental action for promoting the welfare of the whole community."

This discussion demonstrates that the Japanese policymaking process derives benefits from these mechanisms. A system of informal mechanisms would facilitate a variety of channels for policy and information inputs in the making of public policy. As John Kingdon points out (1981: 277), the pattern of information inputs into a decision "both affects that decision and determines what kinds of information will not be considered." Therefore, this input pattern is crucial for determining whether or not various opinions can be presented to policymaking organs. Obviously, there are many channels for such inputs in Japan's political system as demonstrated in the case studies of the formation of foreign policy toward China. By adopting an informal way, decision-makers also enjoy a wide range of channels. Informal settings may also be "an important element in the way democracies can listen and hear what they might otherwise ignore" (Apter and Sawa 1984: 241).

The informal mechanism also has its limitations and disadvantages. Since it is informal, there is no fixed method of operation; it depends heavily on various individuals and different situations. The duck diplomacy, the oppositions parties' *yatō gaikō*, the secret nonofficial trip to Beijing two months after Tiananmen, and the different ways of using think-tanks by prime ministers are good examples. While informal methods may encourage more individuals and groups to participate in the policymaking process, informality, based on social connection, as Frank Upham (1987: 166) points out, normally stresses "specific issues rather than universal principles," and hence may also limit the scope of participation. The result of the imbalanced political influence caused by different networks within the ruling party and bureaucracy apparatus may protect the interests of certain groups (such as silkworm farmers), but it may also be at the expense of other groups (such as the raw silk industry and import companies). This system may not be open enough for those individuals or groups who do not have appropriate social networks with policymakers.

The idea of consensus-building through informal means has often slowed the process of coordinating positions within the policymaking apparatus such as the ruling party and the bureaucracy. Subordinates must brief endlessly while their superiors use their networks of personal associations to learn the positions of the other players, or try to persuade without confrontation (G. Fisher 1980: 34). Ultimately, this process may delay decisions and miss opportunities. It takes time to build up political trust both internally and externally. Internal implicit understanding through personal connection and behind-the-scenes preparations can often not be understood by outsiders. Negotiators from other political cultures are unlikely to see through *tatemae* (public statement) in order to understand *honne* (true intention). The informal way of maneuvering may sometimes provide mixed and uncertain messages externally, thereby creating confusion in communication with foreigners.

Informal communications may also make it difficult for the Japanese to deal with foreigners in the international setting. As Takao Suzuki (1986: 156–157) observes, the Japanese have difficulty when their addressee is not Japanese, making Japan's position hard for foreigners to understand. "That is why Japan is always getting a late start in its foreign negotiations, whether diplomatic, political or economic." The fact that Japan was at one time criticized from two different directions—Beijing and Washington—regarding its policy toward China in the post–Tiananmen period illustrates Japan's diplomatic dilemma in defending its true intention in the international community. Furthermore, the Japanese system, in which "each participant anticipates the actions of the other, no one, not even those directly involved, can say who makes the decisions" (A. Wildavsky 1986: 129). It may also create an image in the international community of Japan's policymaking process as ambiguous and irresponsible.

Informal mechanisms may also be used to pursue special interests by political and social groups. Because of its informal nature, the operational process of this system is not open enough to the public. *Giri* (obligation) may provide a basis for structural corruption, which has drawn increasing public attention to recent political developments in Japan. It may also help create an image of what Kent Calder (1988: 470–471) called "a deeply rooted antipluralist bias to much of Japanese political structure and culture." The highly personalistic factors of the policymaking process may have retarded "the development of the concept of politics and policies as public goods and inhibited the rise of power of politicians with a broader vision of national interest in the perspective of an increasingly interdependent international community" (S. Fukai and H. Fukui 1992: 35).

As Japan's economy develops further, the society will advance in the direction of greater political pluralization and internationalization. Popular demand for more active political participation is expected to continue to grow. As the influence of opposition parties and the mass media increases and there are more diversity and individualistic actions by LDP members, Japanese politics will move toward a more inclusive direction. Policy debate in open forums will become more frequent, and special interest groups will be more active and skillful, thereby increasing their political influence. How to respond to the increasing demand from within and outside of the party will be a real test for the LDP.

As a younger and more assertive generation arises in the political world, a large-scale realignment of political parties is viewed by some observers as a likely next step for Japan's political future. Many Japanese voters are no longer satisfied with the traditional lopsided political party structure. According to a public opinion poll of *Nihon Keizai Shimbun* held in June 1992, nearly 60 percent said they hoped to see some kind of coalition government incorporating both LDP and opposition politicians, and only 16.8 percent supported a continuation of the LDP's one single party rule.[4]

Contemporary voters demand more from their political representatives, and their demands will vary widely as the society undergoes more complicated changes in values and expectations. This may facilitate political reforms in the National Diet, allowing Diet members and their aides to spend more time and energy on legislative issues. To respond to the voters efficiently, there may emerge a more structured or formal system to absorb different views from voters and to debate issues in the Diet hearings, rather than heavily relying on behind-the-scenes negotiations. On the other hand, change in political structure and political culture is a long process. Informal practice and its role as policymaking mechanisms are expected to continue to be a distinguishing characteristic in Japan's political life well into the future.

POLITICAL PLURALIZATION AS A FOUNDATION

Let us now return to some basic considerations. Informal practice in Japanese politics, the focal point of this study, is not an isolated concept. The foundation of informal mechanisms, as discussed in Chapter 3, is political democratization and pluralistic politics.

Today no single force dominates in Japan's political life. It is highly unlikely that the Self-Defense Force of Japan might, like the prewar Japanese military, come to claim an independent position free from the cabinet's control. The freedom of expression and the election system have provided guarantees for the operation of political parties. This political setting has provided an institutional base in Japan for social groups and networks to play their political function. Many less developed or developing countries still lack this key element.

Democracy is a process of political development, and although certain criteria (such as effective participation, voting equality at the decisive stage, and control of agenda priorities) measure this process, a perfect democratic process and a perfect democratic government might never exist in actuality (R. Dahl 1989:

109). A variety of models and forms of democracy have developed,[5] but one principle is common to all of them: antitotalitarian/authoritarian rule and political pluralism.

Although the characteristics of informality and the concepts of *kuromaku*, *tsukiai*, and *nemawashi* have existed in Japan for a long time, informal mechanisms did not develop fully until after 1947 when the new constitution came into effect. Only with a democratic base could Japan gradually move away from its authoritarian legacy. It is believed that a democratic movement that resorts to authoritarian methods to gain its objective may not remain a democratic movement for long. In other words, political pluralism cannot last long if the policymaking norms, values, and patterns are authoritarian.

Political pluralism in Japan began to blossom as the bureaucratic dominance on policymaking began to weaken. Both the ruling party and interest groups have gradually increased their influence in the policymaking process. For example, with regard to the Statute on Centralized Control on Imported Raw Silk, interest groups from opposite sides—silkworm farmers and the small- and medium-sized businesses—launched lobbying activities and pressed their demand on the LDP and top bureaucracy. The result in favor of the farmers reflected the imbalance of political influence through the players' social connections with key decision-makers. The shift on policies also involved internal negotiations among government agencies such as MAFF, MITI, and MOFA. The final settlement of the raw silk importation issue could be regarded as a compromise by various forces.

The role of the ruling LDP is becoming increasingly prominent in the policymaking process. Leaders of the ruling party played a crucial role in Sino-Japanese normalization. An interview with a veteran MOFA official confirmed that during the latter period of the Satō administration, considerable pressures arose from within and outside the government bureaucracy to reexamine Japan's China policy, but "everything was meaningless unless Satō and other top politicians came to a decision on the government's basic policy line."[6] It is therefore not too early to assume that the influential role of the LDP, vis-à-vis the bureaucracy, has become entrenched in contemporary Japanese politics. There are five reasons for this entrenchment.

First, ever since its establishment in 1955, the LDP has maintained its de facto one-party rule. The party continues to hold the highest executive power: the prime ministership and the cabinet. This allows senior LDP politicians to play a decisive role in making decisions on highly political and often controversial issues, such as normalizing relations with China. These factors have made Japan different from other democracies like the United States and Great Britain, in which two major parties share power.[7]

Second, because of its longtime majority or near-majority position, it is relatively easy for the LDP to control the legislative branch, the National Diet, as demonstrated in the case of the ratification of the four Sino-Japanese economic agreements. This has also made it possible for the LDP's own policymaking organs, notably PARC, to become more powerful than the policy committees of the Diet itself (F. Valeo and C. Morrison 1983: 29).

Third, it is necessary to pay close attention to the rising influence of *zoku*, powerful LDP Diet members who sit on key committees and other organizations as chairmen, and have developed seniority on the committees, accumulating expertise and political influence over certain policy areas. Thus, the gap between LDP politicians and the bureaucracy in terms of access to information and specialization has been gradually and significantly reduced. Until recently, the bureaucracy dominated information and expertise on virtually all policy matters, and Diet members had to rely heavily on the bureaucracy in drafting legislation owing mainly to the lack of expertise and legislative staff.

The negotiation over the raw silk policy has also demonstrated the close relationship between the bureaucracy and the LDP: more *zoku* members become ministers or parliament vice-ministers, and retired ex-bureaucrats continuously join the party by running for office, and they themselves eventually become *zoku*. For example, in the 1970s 30 percent or more of the LDP Diet members were ex-bureaucrats; and over 40 percent of the cabinet members had bureaucratic backgrounds (Jiyūminshutō 1977: 90). Ex-bureaucrats often serve as informal intermediaries between the ruling party and the government bureaucracy. It is therefore not enough to push through a policy proposal by only going through the government bureaucracy; one must also persuade the LDP and especially its appropriate *zoku*. As Yung Park (1986: 192) argues, "no agency action can be undertaken" without the blessings of the LDP and its *zoku*.

Fourth, internal rivalry within the bureaucracy has also contributed to the LDP's increasing power. As Japan entered the age of industrialization, socio-economic life became increasingly complex. Many more issues and interests are involved in the policymaking process, further intensifying internal rivalry among bureaucrats. It is not unusual for one policy to fall into several different jurisdictions. This has forced bureaucrats to turn to outside forces for arbitration. On most occasions, the LDP can fit this role. Despite the traditional fear of the politician's interference among the governmental bureaucrats, the conflict between MOFA and other ministries increased the possibility that MOFA officials would seek support from politicians, particularly the ruling party's Diet members. The involvement of LDP's leading members in foreign policy issues became more visible in the 1990s. LDP party elder Shin Kanemaru's private negotiations with North Korea in September 1990, and then LDP Secretary-General Ichirō Ozawa's attempt to cut an aid-for-islands deal in Moscow in March 1991 just prior to Soviet President Mikhail Gorbachev's visit to Tokyo are two primary examples.[8]

Finally, for many years, the LDP has received steady support from the two largest conservative forces in Japanese society: organized business and the farmers. In turn, the LDP has implemented various policies such as the protectionist policy over raw silk importation to protect the two groups. This has made it possible for the LDP to maintain a strong conservative alliance. The traditional weak position of labor unions and the decline of influence of socialism have also helped the conservative LDP remain politically dominant. The LDP's landslide victory in the double elections in the summer of 1986 and the comeback victories in February 1990 and July 1992 (a recovery from the setback of the 1989 loss of LDP majority in the Upper House) have all demonstrated the LDP's strength in Japan's political life.

This support from conservative groups has enhanced the LDP position in elections and political fund raising. A primary goal of political parties in any democracy is to win elections (R. Fenno 1973: 1). The LDP is no exception. Thus, politicians must listen to the voice of their constituents to get reelected. To receive financial backing, politicians must also be sensitive to the interests of big business. Organized business and farmers provide both votes and funds to the LDP. The continuity of the Statute on Centralized Control (protectionist raw silk policy) under the leadership of Fukuda and Nakasone, both of whom came from the top silkworm production area of Gunma Prefecture, is a typical example of influence from agricultural constituencies.

According to Jōji Watanuki (1977: 21–22), the rise of the LDP to political eminence has several merits. The most important one is the close coordination among the ruling tripod: the LDP, the higher elite corps of the bureaucracy, and the business community. The second merit is that the LDP's effective *kōenkai* (the association of supporters for Diet members) have played a major role in LDP's longtime rule. Through *kōenkai*, "various demands—personal, regional, and occupational—of the populace have been absorbed and satisfied." The third is that LDP Diet members have enjoyed a wide range of freedom to express divergent policy views and even behavior concerning both domestic and foreign policies. This point is demonstrated by the case study of the process of Sino-Japanese rapprochement, during which the pro-Beijing and the pro-Taipei groups had sharply opposing views.

The rising influence of the ruling party gradually broke the policymaking dominance of the bureaucracy. This development has provided more channels for policy input. With regard to highly controversial issues like Japanese foreign policy toward China, there is a division of labor between political leaders and the civil services: the LDP gives the general direction or sets the tone, whereas the initiation and implementation of these policies depend primarily on the government bureaucracy (J. Kyōgoku 1987: 220). The LDP is unable to fulfill the latter function—in 1986 there were only three staff members, for example, in PARC's Division of Foreign Affairs.[9] In contrast, the bureaucracy is an independent entity with first-rate personnel and excellent executive and informational systems. Its traditional influence over policymaking, though diminished, is still strong, and the LDP's rising influence has not damaged the pluralistic direction of Japan's political development. The overall relationship between the LDP and the bureaucracy is not necessarily one of instruction from LDP to bureaucrats, as one MAFF official suggested, but rather one of consultation.

We can see further interdependence of the LDP and the bureaucracy (M. Takabatake 1978: 11–14). The interdependence between the two has moved toward what Yung Park (1986: 186) describes as a "party-bureaucracy collaboration and symbiosis." This can be seen from the secret trip to Beijing which the delegation of the Liberal Society Forum took during the post–Tiananmen period: throughout the trip, there was a well-coordinated relationship between the LDP-led Forum and the Foreign Affairs Ministry bureaucrats. All these institutional settings have provided greater room for informal practice to operate.

One of the key elements of the pluralistic nature of Japanese politics is the function of political parties and the National Diet. As Roger Benjamin and Kan Ori (1981: 78–79) argue, the political party system in Japan "is the major vehicle for the exercise of political influence." It can be said that the Japanese political parties' leadership function in the political process has replaced the military authority of the prewar period.

In the 1989 election, the LDP for the first time lost majority seats in the Upper House, though it managed to maintain its dominant position in the Lower House. Because of this situation, the LDP has had to compromise with opposition parties on several of its policies, especially in legislative and fiscal matters. Although it is still quite difficult for opposition parties to defeat bills from the LDP, their power to check and to openly criticize the LDP's policies remains undiminished. As we can see from the case study on Sino-Japanese trade negotiations, opposition parties voiced concerns over COCOM trade restrictions during the Diet hearings of the Sino-Japanese Trade Agreement (see Part IV). Therefore, the Diet has become a forum for different opinions.

From the discussion of the opposition parties' role in Sino-Japanese relations, we see that opposition parties can perform four functions. First, they can provide a different perspective on foreign policy which has often opened new horizons to push the ruling party and foreign affairs bureaucrats to change their minds, as they did in the Sino-Japanese rapprochement. Second, opposition parties provide information and informal channels which the LDP and the bureaucracy may not have. Third, they use public means such as the press and Diet hearings, which are televised and broadcast, to change the mood over controversial issues among the public, the bureaucrats, and the ruling party. Fourth, they can evaluate and criticize the results of government policies, so that further mistakes and failures can be avoided (Mitsuru Yamamoto 1974: 184–188).

Opposition parties in the Diet play an important role in the Japanese policy-making process in spite of the LDP's dominance. Their key role, as veteran LDP member Motoji Suganuma suggested, is "to stabilize politics and to let various opinions be heard"; therefore, "together with the ruling party, they are two wheels of a cart."[10] This is especially true with regard to the informal aspect in Japan's political life. Therefore, informal mechanisms can play a catalytic function in promoting more pluralistic policymaking in Japan.

Nevertheless, the "fragmented opposition," the term used by Taketsugu Tsuru-tani (1977: 170–173), has significantly limited the role of opposition parties in the Diet regarding the formation of foreign policy. As Richard Samuels (1990: 51) observes, "a divided and periodically discredited opposition cannot win power."

One wheel of the cart—the ruling party—has a much stronger influence over the policymaking process than the other (the combined opposition parties). There are other limitations to the role played by opposition parties. Haruo Okada, a veteran Socialist Diet member and former vice-president of the National Diet, gave his explanation when he talked about the declining role of opposition parties in terms of the formation of China policy. First, in many aspects, the differences in opinion between opposition parties and the LDP have greatly narrowed, especially with regard to the China policy. Second, the establishment of official channels since normalization between Japan and China has given the ruling party and bureaucracy the upper hand. Third, some opposition parties, such as the DSP and CGP, have lost several Diet seats during the last one or two decades, thereby weakening their political positions. Finally, because organized business (which supports the LDP) has worked hard to cultivate relations with China, the influence of opposition parties, which have mainly represented the interests of the small- and medium-sized businesses, has gradually decreased.[11]

Another development from the early 1970s is the increasing participation in politics by scholars, specialists, and the press, as well as interest groups. In the postwar democracy, there has been no governmental censorship except during the occupation period, and "all the major newspapers and TV networks have been avowed guardians of democracy" (J. Watanuki 1977: 26). Intellectuals and "think-tanks," as shown in the cases of Sino-Japanese rapprochement and Japan's aid policy to China before and after Tiananmen, have begun to participate in policy-oriented forums and activities.[12]

The Japanese experience of political development shows the extent of Western influence on Japan. Yet, Western political systems cannot be entirely transplanted into Japan, and it must adopt to "Japanese traditions and circumstances" (T. Fukutake 1981: 159). Over the years in the postwar period, the Japanese have developed their own policymaking mechanisms—informal mechanisms. The informality in Japan's political life can be traced back to a period long before World War II. Indeed, the words used in this study such as *tsukiai*, *kuromaku*, and *nemawashi* have existed for a long time. But the phenomenon of full-scale democratization and pluralization came into being arguably only after the 1947 constitution. Without this basic political foundation and without structures receptive to democratic principles, informal mechanisms would not have fully developed in Japan.

The breakup of bureaucratic dominance, the rise of the LDP's influence, and the increasing activities of interest groups and the business community have created what Ellis Krauss (1982: 110) has called "an expansion in the size, scope, and diversity of the real decision-making elite in Japan." This development has further strengthened political pluralization, which is a foundation for Japan's informal mechanisms. On the other hand, as Eva Etzioni-Halvey (1983: 44) points out, a political system is pluralist not only in its being subject to a plurality of pressures but also in its very structure. The complexity of the state structure affords interest groups multiple access points at which to exert their influence. In providing this access, informal mechanisms have supported pluralistic development in Japan. This fact refutes the plausible argument that the appearance of pluralism in Japan is deceptive because of extensive informal activities in the policymaking process. As Samuel Kernell (1991a: 370) argues, the informal mechanism of political control in Japan "does not mean that the constitutional order has been corrupted or that policymaking has become less democratic."

Informal practice is only one characteristic of Japan's political life. In many cases political operation in Japan is quite formal, open, and public. Yet, the informal aspect of Japan's policymaking has not been systematically examined. The development of the informal mechanisms model in Japan has provided an alternative basis of study for political scientists as well as Asian specialists. It has broad implications beyond Japan's domestic politics and foreign policymaking. The impact of a "Japan model" on other East Asian societies, such as South Korea and Taiwan, has remained an intriguing research topic for scholars to pursue.

INTERNATIONAL COMPARISONS

This study would not be complete without making international comparisons between Japan and other societies. As the interdependence between nations increases, the need for mutual understanding also increases. Misunderstanding will more likely become a primary cause for international conflicts. As a global economic (and a potential political) superpower, Japan plays and will continue to play a significant, and arguably a leading, role in world affairs. There is an increasing need to understand Japan in the international community, not only in general terms, but also the Japanese way of policymaking in comparative terms. Nevertheless, this book is not intended as a full-fledged comparative study. Since Japan is a society influenced by both the East and West, this comparison will focus on the informal aspects of Japanese politics and policymaking against the backgrounds of East Asian societies and the United States.

The broader implications for the informal mechanisms model suggest that there are similar patterns of political development in other non-Western societies, especially those of East Asia, where rapid economic and political changes have been taking place. On the path to modernization and democratization, each society has its own historical legacy which includes political structure and traditional culture. Therefore, each has its own norms and patterns for development. Yet, nations may learn from one another in terms of modernization. The Japanese experience of political development is believed to have special significance to Japan's East Asian neighbors.

As an East Asian society, Japan shares common cultural legacies—Confucianism, for example—with China, Korea, Singapore, Taiwan, Hong Kong, and Vietnam. In studying East Asian politics, many believe that cultural differences are "important contributions to distinctive patterns" of these societies (B. Richardson 1974: 2–4). It is not enough, however, to emphasize only cultural traditions. Political institutions and social structures should also be taken into account.

The move toward modernization and democratization in East Asia began as early as the nineteenth century, but actual development in many East Asian nations began only in the 1960s, and reached a high in the 1980s. We can see bold economic reforms and periodic political turmoils in China, democratization marked by a dynamic opposition party movement in Taiwan, and a political realignment which created a LDP-type conservative coalition in 1990 and continuing mass demonstrations in South Korea. These changes in East Asia differ in the means, scope, and strategies of interest groups and ruling elites. One commonality is the basic trend and popular desire for economic development and political democratization.

In this sense, both internal conditions and the international environment for most East Asian societies are at a favorable juncture, providing a golden opportunity for every country in the region to achieve economic and political progress. The Japanese experience is useful to political development in other East Asian societies. For example, the establishment of South Korea's conservative coalition (the Democratic Liberal Party) in early 1990 with the merger of three political parties (despite its controversial nature), was arguably modeled on Japan's ruling Liberal Democratic Party. The LDP model, one big party dominance while allowing the existence of opposition parties, has increasingly attracted attention from Japan's neighbors such as South Korea and Taiwan.

When we compare the Japanese with the Chinese political and economic systems, we see obvious differences between capitalist and socialist systems.[13] However, we also see similarities in the policymaking mechanisms between the two societies, particularly the informal aspects of the policymaking processes.

A number of China specialists have emphasized informality in China's political life. Andrew Walder (1986: 76–80), for example, in his study of China's social structure and workers' politics, emphasizes the importance of an informal network in Chinese society. Walder claims that "informal relationships are the real arena for the pursuit of interests." Indeed, social connections and network are as important in Chinese politics as they are in Japan. *Guanxi* is a widely used term referring to social networking and is arguably the equivalent of the Japanese term *tsukiai*.[14] In China, *guanxi* is regarded as a catalyst to increase one's social network and to get things done. Without *guanxi* one would hardly have any significant influence in China's political arena.

Tsou Tang (1986: 98) has conducted a specific study on informal groups in Chinese Communist party politics. He analyzes "informal rules, groups and processes" and how they are transformed into formal ones, and he describes this practice as "one of the most interesting phenomena in the dynamics of bureaucracy and the political system." Evidence of informality in Chinese politics is abundant. Other than *guanxi*, the counterpart of *tsukiai* discussed above, there is also a Chinese type of *kuromaku*, behind-the-scenes influential political figures who may not necessarily hold formal positions; and a Chinese-style *nemawashi* emphasizing informal contacts for preparation of decisions. While the Japanese and Chinese styles are not entirely the same,[15] there are striking similarities in

East Asian political structures and cultures that influence political mechanisms. Looking at the recent experience and the developmental patterns of Japan. China, Korea, Taiwan, and other societies, we may wonder that, in spite of different economic and political systems, the direction of development for the East Asian societies may become even more politically pluralistic, though perhaps in an informal way.

The Japanese political system resembles that of other advanced industrial democracies, as T. J. Pempel (1992: 8–9) points out, "in most of its political and social institutions and behavioral traits, but it emerges from a non-Western cultural tradition." Hence, Pempel further argues, Japan has become "a good case study for examining ideal conceptions of democracy in contrast to practical democratic realities." In neither Japan nor the United States is there a single source of authority and concentration of power in the sense of the absolutist state. The most striking similarity between the two countries is their democratic and pluralistic societies. The institutionalization of political leadership, the determination to form a government with popular consent through elections, and the citizens' basic political rights such as freedom of expression and freedom of association have made both Japan and the United States different from authoritarian states. The setting of the democratic political system in both countries has permitted interest groups to voice their demands, which in turn influence the policymaking process. The role of organized farmers in the case of Japan's raw silk protectionism is similar to that of many lobbying activities in the United States.

Before turning to differences between Japan and the United States, I should make it clear that comparing a presidential system such as that in the United States and a parliamentary system like Japan's is like comparing an apple with an orange. Despite similarities in terms of the democratic nature of the regimes, there are many differences between the two nations, particularly with regard to institutional functions and the policymaking process. A Brookings book *Parallel Politics: Economic Policymaking in Japan and the United States* (S. Kernell, 1991b) has made an extensive comparison between the two countries' political systems and the policymaking process. In Samuel Kernell's concluding chapter (pp. 325–378), he discussed in detail similarities and differences with regard to the party system, elections, the legislature, executive leadership (presidents versus prime ministers, etc.), and the governmental bureaucracy. Since this book is not intended to provide a comprehensive comparison between the two political systems and I do not want to repeat general arguments presented by previous studies, here I will only discuss a few points related to the informal aspect of the policymaking.

Informal practice is an inherent feature of Japan's political life. It has a prominent role in Japan's legislative politics partially because of the structural limitation of the Japanese Diet. The government provides only two or three congressional aides for Diet members, so that Diet members have to rely heavily on informal channels and advisory groups in conducting policy research, and on bureaucracy in drafting legislation. In contrast, members of the U.S. Congress have enough funds from the government to hire both administrative and legislative aides. The average number of aides a senator has, for example, is about twenty-five or more, and it may reach seventy-five. Many legislative aides have higher academic degrees, often Ph.D.s, in their field and write drafts for legislation without outside help. There are additional staff on the committees and subcommittees. Even when the White House initiates legislation (and asks individual senators or congressmen to sponsor it), it often relies on the help of congressional aides in drafting the legislative proposals. Instead of relying on the bureaucracy as Japanese politicians do, American politicians rely on congressional staff.

Many of the differences between the U.S. and Japanese political systems can be attributed to the informality of Japanese politics. The prominent role played by the special social network, informal political actors and organizations, and personal contact for preparing consensus demonstrate distinct mechanisms in exercising political influence. There are differences in terms of attitudes toward authority: acceptance of *informal* authority as well as *legal* authority is much greater in Japan than in the United States. In Japan, informal channels are widely used to help the ruling party and government bureaucracy apparatus coordinate different interests in preparing policies. Through these informal and nonlegislative means, it is relatively easy for the Japanese to reach a consensus among themselves, whereas in the United States, highly publicized political debates and a powerful legislative branch have made some highly sensitive policy issues more visible.

To be sure, there is also an informal aspect in American politics. In Washington, for example, some so-called super lawyers are politically influential but often exercise their power quietly without appearing in the press. After-work dinners for cultivating political ties are also popular in Washington, and one constantly hears behind-the-scenes bargaining, negotiations, and compromise at Capitol Hill and other political battlegrounds. The "old boy connections" of Ivy League graduates on the East Coast, who enjoy similar socioeconomic backgrounds, are also important in Washington politics. In this sense, there are similarities between Tokyo and Washington even in the aspect of informal politics.

But when we examine Japan's policymaking mechanisms, such as social network (*tsukiai*), informal political actors and organizations (*kuromaku*), and behind-the-scenes consensus-building (*nemawashi*), we can sense a difference in scope and degree. For example, although both countries have *gakubatsu*, or a "school clique," within the government bureaucracies, there is a much higher degree of concentration in Japan in a single university (the University of Tokyo) than in the United States. Furthermore, the differences in policymaking mechanisms may often become sources of misunderstanding between the two countries. For example, as Robert Christopher (1989: 32) points out, Americans are apt to regard the *nemawashi* process as "inordinately time consuming," or even as "a deliberate delaying tactic or mechanism for deceit."

Informal diplomacy and politics behind politics are not unique to Japan of course, but are common to all political systems. One hears of "under-the-table-politics" all the time in Tokyo, as well as in Western democracies such as Washington and London.[16] If informal politics simply means that many informal groups (that is, groups without legal jurisdiction over an issue) are involved, then every nation has informal politics. But Japan's informal mechanism, a tripartite policymaking device, does have its own characteristics. When we look closely at how widely *kuromaku*, *tsukiai*, and *nemawashi* are used in the policymaking process as shown in the four case studies of the formation of Japanese foreign policy, we can discern a distinct Japanese way of policymaking. Use of social connections for political influence and mobilization is "a common phenomenon in Japan, perhaps a more visible or a more frequent activity there than in any other industrialized country" (B. Richardson 1991: 338). In other words, with regard to informal politics, there is a difference in degree of intensity between Japan and the Western democracies.

In sum, compared to the United States, policymaking in Japan often appears less institutionalized and more ambiguous, and more dependent on informal means such as social network and personal connection. Rather than the fundamental difference in the democratic nature of politics, the differences between the two are mainly in the areas of structure and the decision-making process, the political mechanism for policy formation, and the working style and method.

NOTES

1. For detailed discussions on the functions and status of the Japanese Diet, see Hans Baerwald's *Party Politics in Japan* (1986). In the concluding chapter, Baerwald asked and answered a question: Is the national assembly (Diet) supreme? (pp. 154–158).

2. For a detailed account of informal contacts between Japan and China, see Yukio Besshi, "Informal Contact-Makers in Japan-China Relations," in *Informal Channels in Japanese Diplomacy* (Tokyo: Japan Association of International Relations, 1983), pp. 89–113.

3. The original idea of the 1955 political system was first raised by Masumi in his *Seiji taisei*, published in *Shiso* in June 1964. The idea was later elaborated in his *Postwar Politics in Japan, 1945–1955* (1985: 329–342).

4. Robert Delfs, "Japan: Seeds of Change," *Far Eastern Economic Review*, July 23, 1992, pp. 21–22.

5. Excellent research on this issue has been done in David Held's *Models of Democracy* (1987).

6. Interview with Michihiko Kunihiro, assistant vice minister of the MOFA, June 4, 1986, Tokyo.

7. An excellent study on one-party dominant democracies is presented in *Uncommon Democracies: The One-party Dominant Regimes*, edited by T. J. Pempel (1990).

8. Robert Delfs, "Missing Links: Ministry Realizes It Cannot Function in a Vacuum," *Far Eastern Economic Review*, July 18, 1991, pp. 20–21.

9. Interview with Yukio Nakamaru, staff member of the Division of Foreign Affairs, LDP's Policy Affairs Research Council, August 28, 1986, Tokyo.

10. Interview with Motoji Suganuma, former president of the Tokyo Municipal Assembly, March 6, 1986, Tokyo.

11. Interview with Haruo Okada, February 27, 1986, Tokyo.

12. For a detailed elaboration of the development of the think-tank in Japan, see Quansheng Zhao, "Xuezhe he Zhinongtuan" [Scholars and think-tanks] (1986).

13. For a detailed account of the Chinese foreign policymaking system, see Quansheng Zhao (1992), "Domestic Factors of Chinese Foreign Policy: From Vertical to Horizontal Authoritarianism."

14. There are some subtle differences between the Chinese *guanxi* and the Japanese *giri* and *tsukiai*. According to Lucian Pye (1982: 91), *giri* implies a more explicit sense of indebtedness and obligation than the diffusely binding Chinese concept of *guanxi*, which may have made the Japanese wary of getting too close to the Chinese. The Japanese are much more sensitive to the potential dangers of backlash by a people whose wishes for dependency cannot be gratified.

15. K. John Fukuda, for example, has analyzed the differences between the Chinese and the Japanese in terms of managerial style. Fukuda (1988: 133) argues that "the Chinese pattern of leadership emphasizes rational commitment to the leader, rather than emotional ties as generally found in Japan. Therefore, any attempts at creating a more informal effective atmosphere on the part of subordinates, especially those who do not belong to the clan, are interpreted by Chinese leaders as efforts to undercut leaders' prerogatives.
. . . Unlike Japanese leaders who admit their dependence on subordinates, Chinese leaders attempt to achieve goals through fostering competition among subordinates."

16. One useful account of Washington's political life, for example, is Charles Peter's *How Washington Really Works* (1980).

Bibliography

BOOKS AND ARTICLES

Abegglen, James, and George Stalk. 1985. *Kaisha: The Japanese Corporation.* New York: Basic Books.

Akita, George. 1967. *Foundations of Constitutional Government in Modern Japan.* Cambridge, Mass.: Harvard University Press.

Allison, Graham. 1971. *Essence of Decision: Explaining the Cuban Missile Crisis.* Glenview, Ill.: Scott, Foresman & Co.

Almond, Gabriel. 1956. "Comparative Political Systems." *Journal of Politics* 18 (3): 391–409.

Almond, Gabriel, and Sidney Verba. 1965. *The Civic Culture.* Boston: Little, Brown.

Anchordoguy, Marie. 1989. *Computers Inc.: Japan's Challenge to IBM.* Cambridge, Mass.: The Council on East Asian Studies, Harvard University.

Angel, Robert C. 1991. *Explaining Economic Policy Failure: Japan in the 1969–1971 International Monetary Crisis.* New York: Columbia University Press.

Apter, David, and Nagayo Sawa. 1984. *Against the State: Politics and Social Protest in Japan.* Cambridge, Mass.: Harvard University Press.

Arnold, Walter. 1985. "Japan and China." In *Japan's Foreign Relations: A Global Search for Economic Security,* ed. by Robert Ozaki and Walter Arnold. Boulder, Colo.: Westview Press, p. 114.

Baerwald, Hans. 1974. *Japan's Parliament.* New York: Cambridge University Press.

———. 1986. *Party Politics in Japan.* Boston: Allen & Unwin.

———. 1989. "Japan's House of Councilors Election: A Mini-Revolution?" *Asian Survey* 29, no. 9 (September): 833–841.

Barnard, Chester. 1938. *The Functions of the Executive.* Cambridge, Mass.: Harvard University Press.

Barnett, A. Doak. 1977. *China and the Major Powers in East Asia.* Washington, D.C.: Brookings Institution.

Beardsley, Richard, John Hall, and Robert Ward. 1959. *Village Japan.* Chicago: University of Chicago Press.

Beasley, W. G. 1975. "Modern Japan: An Historian's View." In *Modern Japan: Aspects of History, Literature and Society*, ed. by W. C. Beasley. Berkeley: University of California Press, pp. 13–23.

Befu, Harumi. 1986. "Gift-Giving in a Modernizing Japan." In *Japanese Culture and Behavior*, ed. by Takie Lebra and William Lebra. Honolulu: University of Hawaii Press, pp. 158–170.

Ben-Ari, Eyal, Brian Moeran, and James Valentine, eds. 1990. *Unwrapping Japan*. Honolulu: University of Hawaii Press.

Benedict, Ruth. 1946. *The Chrysanthemum and the Sword: Patterns of Japanese Culture*. New York: New American Library.

Benjamin, Roger, and Kan Ori. 1981. *Tradition and Change in Postindustrial Japan*. New York: Praeger.

Besshi, Yukio. 1983. "Informal Contact-Makers in Japan-China Relations." In *Informal Channels in Japanese Diplomacy*. Tokyo: Japan Association of International Relations.

Bestor, Theodore. 1989. *Neighborhood Tokyo*. Stanford, Calif.: Stanford University Press.

Blaker, Michael. 1977. *Japanese International Negotiating Style*. New York: Columbia University Press.

Bowen, Roger. 1992. "Japan's Foreign Policy." In *PS: Political Science and Politics* 35 (1): 57–73.

Brenkman, John. 1987. *Culture and Domination*. Ithaca, N.Y., and London: Cornell University Press.

Bunge, Frederica, ed. 1983. *Japan: A Country Study*, 4th ed. Washington, D.C.: Department of the Army.

Bureau of Silkworm and Horticulture of MAFF. 1986. *Saikin no sanshi gyō-o meguru jōhō* [Recent development of raw silk production]. Tokyo.

Burks, Ardath. 1981. *Japan: Profile of a Postindustrial Power*. Boulder, Colo.: Westview Press.

Butow, Robert. 1954. *Japan's Decision to Surrender*. Stanford, Calif.: Stanford University Press.

Calder, Kent. 1988. *Crisis and Compensation: Public Policy and Political Stability in Japan, 1949–1986*. Princeton, N.J.: Princeton University Press.

Campbell, John. 1977. *Contemporary Japanese Budget Politics*. Berkeley: University of California Press.

———. 1984. "Policy Conflict and Its Resolution Within the Government System." In *Conflict in Japan*, ed. by Ellis Krauss, Thomas Rohlen, and Patricia Steinoff. Honolulu: University of Hawaii Press, pp. 294–334.

———. 1992. *How Politics Change: The Japanese Government and the Aging Society*. Princeton, N.J.: Princeton University Press.

Campbell, John, ed. 1981. *Parties, Candidates, and Voters in Japan*. Ann Arbor, Mich.: Center for Japanese Studies.

Christopher, Robert. 1983. *The Japanese Mind: The Goliath Explained*. New York: Linden.

———. 1989. "Culture Dimensions of the U.S.-Japan Relations." In *Destinies Shared: U.S.-Japanese Relations*, ed. by Paul Lauren and Raymond Wylie. Boulder and London: Westview Press, pp. 27–40.

Clapp, Priscilla, and Morton Halperin, eds. 1974. *United States-Japan Relations in the*

1970's. Cambridge, Mass.: Harvard University Press.

Cohen, Bernard, and Scott Harris. 1975. "Foreign Policy." In *Handbook of Political Science Vol. 6: Policies and Policymaking*, ed. by Fred Greenstein and Nelson Polsby. Reading, Mass.: Addison-Wesley, pp. 381–438.

Cohen, Warren. 1989. "China in Japanese-American Relations." In *The United States and Japan in the Postwar World*, ed. by Akira Iriye and Warren Cohen. Lexington: University Press of Kentucky, pp. 36–60.

Corporation in the Stabilization of Raw Silk and Sugar Price (CSRSSP). 1986. *Sanshi satō rui kakaku antei jigyō dan hō kankei hōki binran* [Guiding-book of related statutes on the stabilization of raw silk and sugar prices]. Tokyo.

Curtis, Gerald. 1971. *Election Campaigning Japanese Style*. New York: Columbia University Press.

———. 1975. "Big Business and Political Influence." In *Modern Japanese Organization and Decision-making*, ed. by Ezra Vogel. Berkeley: University of California Press, pp. 33–70.

———. 1988. *The Japanese Way of Politics*. New York: Columbia University Press.

Dahl, Robert. 1956. *A Preface to Democratic Theory*. Chicago and London: University of Chicago Press.

———. 1989. *Democracy and Its Critics*. New Haven, Conn.: Yale University Press.

Destler, I. M., Haruhiro Fukui, and Hideo Satō. 1979. *The Textile Wrangle: Conflict in Japanese-American Relations, 1969–1971*. Ithaca, N.Y.: Cornell University Press.

DeVos, George, and Takao Sofue. 1984. *Religion and the Family in East Asia*. Berkeley: University of California Press.

Domhoff, William. 1983. *Who Rules America Now?* Englewood Cliffs, N.J.: Prentice-Hall.

Dore, Ronald. 1986. *Flexible Rigidities: Industrial Policy and Structural Adjustment in the Japanese Economy 1970–80*. Stanford, Calif.: Stanford University Press.

———. 1987. *Taking Japan Seriously*. Stanford, Calif.: Stanford University Press.

Dougherty, James, and Robert Pfaltzgraff. 1990. *Contending Theories of International Relations*. New York: Harper & Row.

Drifte, Reinhard. 1990. *Japan's Foreign Policy*. New York: Council on Foreign Relations Press.

Duus, Peter. 1969. *Feudalism in Japan*. New York: Alfred A. Knopf.

———. 1976. *The Rise of Modern Japan*. Boston: Houghton Mifflin Co.

———. 1989. "Introduction." In *The Japanese Informal Empire in China, 1895–1937*, ed. by Peter Duus, Ramon Myers, and Mark Peattie. Princeton, N.J.: Princeton University Press, pp. xi–xxix.

Eckstein, Harry. 1975. "Case Study and Theory in Political Science." In *Handbook of Political Science Vol. 7: Strategies of Inquiry*, ed. by Fred Greenstein and Nelson Polsby. Reading, Mass.: Addison-Wesley Co., pp. 79–138.

Editorial Department. "Tanaka seiken to zaikai no mitsugetsu [Honeymoon between the Tanaka government and the Zaikai]." 1972. *Sekai* (September): 158–161.

Ellison, Herbert, ed. 1987. *Japan and the Pacific Quadrille*. Boulder, Colo., and London: Westview Press.

Encarnation, Dennis J. 1992. *Rivals Beyond Trade: America versus Japan in Global Competition*. Ithaca, N.Y., and London: Cornell University Press.

Etō, Shinkichi. 1972. "Nihon ni okeru taigai seisaku katei" [Decision-making of Japanese foreign policy]. A paper presented at the Autumn Conference of the Association for International Law, Tokyo, October 7.

Etzioni-Halevy, Eva. 1983. *Bureaucracy and Democracy*. London and Boston: Routledge & Kegan Paul.

Fenno, Richard. 1973. *Congressmen in Committee*. Boston: Little, Brown.

Fisher, Glen. 1980. *International Negotiation*. Chicago: Intercultural Press.

Flanagan, Scott. 1991. "Mechanisms of Social Network Influence in Japanese Voting Behavior." In Scott Flanagan, Shinsaku Kohei, Ichirō Miyake, Bradley Richardson, and Joji Watanuki, *The Japanese Voter*. New Haven, Conn., and London: Yale University Press.

Flanagan, Scott, Shinsaku Kohei, Ichirō Miyake, Bradley Richardson, and Jōji Watanuki. 1991. *The Japanese Voter*. New Haven, Conn., and London: Yale University Press.

Friedman, David. 1988. *The Misunderstood Miracle: Industrial Development and Political Change in Japan*. Ithaca, N.Y.: Cornell University Press.

Fukai, Shigeko, and Haruhiro Fukui. 1992. "Elite Recruitment and Political Leadership." In *PS: Political Science and Politics* 35 (1): 25–36.

Fukuda, K. John. 1988. *Japanese-Style Management Transferred: The Experience of East Asia*. London and New York: Routledge.

Fukui, Haruhiro. 1970. *Party in Power: The Japanese Liberal-Democrats and Policy-Making*. Berkeley and Los Angeles: University of California Press.

————. 1972. "Economic Planning in Postwar Japan: A Case Study in Policy Making." *Asian Survey* 7, no. 4 (April): 327–348.

————. 1977. "Tanaka Goes to Peking: A Case Study in Foreign Policymaking." In *Policymaking in Contemporary Japan*, ed. by T. J. Pempel. Ithaca, N.Y., and London: Cornell University Press, pp. 69–102.

Fukutake, Tadashi. 1981. *Japanese Society Today*. Tokyo: University of Tokyo Press.

Furukawa, Mantaro, 1981. *Nitchū sengo kaikei shi* [The History of postwar Japan-China relations]. Tokyo: Hara shobō.

Geertz, Clifford. 1973. *The Interpretation of Cultures*. New York: Basic Books.

George, Alexander. 1972. "The Case for Multiple Advocacy in Making Foreign Policy." *American Political Science Review* 66, no. 3 (September): 751–795.

George, Aurelia. 1986. "The Politics of Agricultural Protection in Japan." In *The Political Economy of Agricultural Protection*, ed. by Kym Anderson and Yujirō Hayami. Sydney: Allen & Unwin, pp. 91–110.

————. 1988. "Rice Politics in Japan." *Political Economic Papers*, no. 159. Canberra: Research School of Pacific Studies, Australian National University.

Guo, Zhongxin, and Bi Zhiheng. 1986. "Yatai diqu de maoyi ji chanye tiaozheng [Trade in the Asian Pacific area and industrial adjustment]." *Riben Wenti* [Japan Issues] 4 (August); 19–22. Beijing: Institute of Japan Studies, Chinese Academy of Social Sciences.

Hall, John, and G. John Ikenberry. 1989. *The State*. Minneapolis: University of Minnesota Press.

Hall, John Whitney. 1965. "Changing Conceptions of the Modernization of Japan." In *Changing Japanese Attitudes Toward Modernization*, ed. by Marius Jansen, Rutland, Vt., and Tokyo: Charles Tuttle, pp. 7–41.

Halperin, Morton. 1974. *Bureaucratic Politics and Foreign Policy*. Washington, D.C.: Brookings Institution.

Hammer, Derrel. 1974. *USSR: The Politics of Oligarchy*. Hinsdale, Ill.: Dryden.

Hane, Mikiso. 1986. *Modern Japan*. Boulder, Colo., and London: Westview Press.

Haruhara, Akihiko, et al. 1986. *Japan's Mass Media*. Tokyo: Foreign Press Center.

Hashikawa, Bunso. 1980. "Japanese Perspectives on Asia: From Dissociation to Coprosperity." In *The Chinese and the Japanese*, ed. by Akira Iriye. Princeton, N.J.: Princeton University Press, pp. 328–355.

Held, David. 1987. *Models of Democracy*. Stanford, Calif.: Stanford University Press.

Hellmann, Donald. 1969. *Japanese Foreign Policy and Domestic Politics: The Peace Agreement with the Soviet Union*. Berkeley and Los Angeles: University of California Press.

———. 1974. "Japan and China: Competitors in a Multipolar World?" In *United States-Japanese Relations*, ed. by Priscilla Clapp and Morton Halperin. Cambridge, Mass.: Harvard University Press, pp. 164–182.

———. 1988. "Japanese Politics and Foreign Policy: Elitist Democracy Within an American Greenhouse." In *The Political Economy of Japan Volume 2: The Changing International Context*, ed. by Takashi Inoguchi and Daniel Okimoto. Stanford, Calif.: Stanford University Press, pp. 345–380.

Henderson, Dan. 1968. "Introduction: Perspectives on the Japanese Constitution After Twenty Years." In *The Constitution of Japan: Its First Twenty Years, 1947–67*, ed. by Dan Henderson. Seattle: University of Washington Press, pp. xi–xv.

Hendry, Joy. 1987. *Understanding Japanese Society*. London and New York: Groom Helm.

Herring, Pendleton. 1965. *The Politics of Democracy*. New York: W. W. Norton.

Hilsman, Roger. 1967. *To Move a Nation*. Garden City, N.Y.: Doubleday & Co.

Hirose, Michisada. 1981. *Hojokin to seikento* [Government Subsidies and the Party in Power]. Tokyo: Asahi shimbunsha.

Hong, Song Yook. 1977. *The Sino-Japanese Fisheries Agreements of 1975*. Baltimore: University of Maryland School of Law.

Hornby, A. S. 1963. *Oxford Advanced Learner's Dictionary of Current English*. London: Oxford University Press.

Hosoya, Chihiro, and Jōji Watanuki, eds. 1977. *Taigai seisaku kettei katei no nich-bei hikaku* [A comparison of foreign policy making-process between Japan and the United States]. Tokyo: Tokyo Daigaku Shuppankai.

Hough, Jerry. 1972. "The Soviet System: Petrification or Pluralism." *Problems of Communism*, no. 21 (March-April): 25–45.

———. 1977. *The Soviet Union and Social Science Theory*. Cambridge, Mass.: Harvard University Press.

House of Representatives of Japan (72nd Cong.). 1974. *Records of the Hearings of the Foreign Affairs Committee* 15 (March).

———. 1974. *Records of the Joint Hearings of the Foreign Affairs Committee and the Transportation Committee* 1 (May).

Hrebenar, Ronald. 1986. *The Japanese Party System: From One-Party Rule to Coalition Government*. Boulder, Colo., and London: Westview Press.

Hsiao, Gene. 1977. *The Foreign Trade of China*. Berkeley and London: University of California Press.

Huntington, Samuel. 1968. *Political Order in Changing Societies*. New Haven, Conn.: Yale University Press.

———. 1987. "The Goals of Development." In *Understanding Political Development*, ed. by Myron Weiner and Samuel Huntington. Boston: Little, Brown, pp. 3–32.

Ijiri, Hidenori. 1987. "The Politics of Japan's Decision to Normalize Relations with China, 1969–72." Ph.D. diss., University of California, Berkeley.

Ike, Nobutaka. 1972. *Japanese Politics: Patron-Client Democracy*. 2nd ed. New York: Alfred A. Knopf.

————. 1978. *A Theory of Japanese Democracy*. Boulder, Colo.: Westview Press.

Inglehart, Ronald. 1990. *Culture Shift in Advanced Industrial Society*. Princeton, N.J.: Princeton University Press.

Inoguchi, Takashi. 1983. *Gendai nihon seiji keizai no kōzu* [Contemporary Japanese political economy]. Tokyo: Toyo Keizai Shinpposha.

————. 1985. *Kokusai kankei no seiji keizaigaku* [Political economy of international relations]. Tokyo: Tokyo Daigaku Shuppankai.

Inoguchi, Takashi, and Tomoaki Iwai. 1987. *"Zoku giin" no Kenkyū* [Research on "Zoku Diet members]." Tokyo: Nihon Keizai Shimbunsha.

Inoguchi, Takashi, and Daniel Okimoto. 1988. *The Political Economy of Japan Volume 2: The Changing International Context*. Stanford, Calif.: Stanford University Press.

Iriye, Akira, ed. 1980. *The Chinese and the Japanese*. Princeton, N.J.: Princeton University Press.

Iriye, Akira, and Warren Cohen, eds. 1989. *The United States and Japan in the Postwar World*. Lexington: University Press of Kentucky.

Ishida, Eiichirō. 1974. *Japanese Culture*. Honolulu: University Press of Hawaii.

Ishida, Takeshi. 1983. *Japanese Political Culture: Change and Continuity*. New Brunswick, N.J.: Transaction Books.

Ishida, Takeshi, and Ellis Krauss, eds. 1989. *Democracy in Japan*. Pittsburgh: University of Pittsburgh Press.

Ishikawa, Tadao. 1974. "The Normalization of Sino-Japanese Relations." In *United States-Japanese Relations*, ed. by Priscilla Clapp and Morton Halperin. Cambridge, Mass.: Harvard University Press, pp. 147–163.

Itō, Masaya. 1982. *Jimintō sengokushi* [History of the LDP warring period]. Tokyo: Asahi Sonorama.

Iwanaga, Kenkichirō. 1985. *Sengo nihon no seitō to gaikō* [Postwar Japan's political parties and diplomacy]. Tokyo: Tokyo Daigaku Shuppankai.

Jain, R. K. 1981. *China and Japan 1949–1980*. Oxford, England: Martin Robertson.

Jan, George. 1969. "Japan's Trade with Communist China." *Asian Survey* 9, no. 12 (December): 900–918.

Jansen, Marius. 1975. *Japan and China, From War to Peace 1894–1972*. Chicago: Rand McNally.

Japan Association of International Relations, ed. 1983. *International Relations—Informal Channels in Japanese Diplomacy*. Tokyo: Japan Association of International Relations.

Japan-China Economic Association. 1975a. *Nitchū keizai kyōkai ho* [Bulletin of Japan-China Economic Association].

————. 1975b. *Nitchū bōeki shin tenkai ka no shomondai* [Problems of the new development of Japan-China trade]. Tokyo.

————. 1975c. *Nitchū oboegaki (kakusho) no jūichi nen* [Japan-China's eleven years of memorandum trade]. Tokyo.

————. 1976. *Nitchū bōeki kakudai kinkō e no shiren* [Experiment for expanding and balancing Japan-China trade]. Tokyo.

————. 1977. *Nitchū bōeki chōki antei no jitsugen o mezashite* [Aiming on long-term stability of Japan-China trade]. Tokyo.

————. 1979. *Nitchū bōeki, aratana hiyaku e no kadai* [New development in Japan-China trade]. Tokyo.

————. 1980. *Chōseika ni sōgoizon no shinten o motomete* [Search on the new development of interdependence under adjustment]. Tokyo.

————. 1981. *Byōdo gokei to sōgoizon no jitsumu kankei-o* [Develop a mutual benefit, interdependent and realistic relationship]. Tokyo.

————. 1982. *Jitsumu kyōryoku e no kiso gatameo mezashite* [Aiming on a solid foundation for a mutual-help and realistic relationship]. Tokyo.

————. 1986. *1985 nen no chūgoku nōgyō* [Chinese agriculture in 1985]. Tokyo.

————. 1987a. *Chūgoku no unyu sangyō* [China's export industry]. Tokyo.

————. 1987b. *Chūgoku otorimaku kokusai seiji keizai kankei* [China's international political and economic relations]. Tokyo.

————. 1987c. *Kinkō kaifuku to sōgo rikai e no doryoku* [Aiming on recovering balance and mutual understanding]. Tokyo.

Japan External Trade Organization (JETRO). 1972. *How to Approach the China Market.* New York.

Japan Newspaper Publishers and Editors Association. 1973. *The Japanese Press.* Tokyo: Nihon Shimbun Kyōkai.

Jeremy, Michael, and M. E. Robinson. 1989. *Ceremony and Symbolism in the Japanese Home.* Honolulu: University of Hawaii Press.

Jiyūminshutō (Liberal Democratic Party), ed. 1977. *Nihon no seitō* [Political parties in Japan]. Tokyo: Jiyūminshutō Kōhō Iinkai Shuppan Kyoku.

Johnson, Chalmers. 1982. *MITI and the Japanese Miracle.* Stanford, Calif.: Stanford University Press.

————. 1985. "Political Institutions and Economic Performance: The Government Business Relationship in Japan, South Korea, and Taiwan." In *Asian Economic Development—Present and Future,* ed. by Robert Scalapino, Seizaburō Satō, and Jusuf Wanandi. Berkeley: Institute of East Asian Studies, University of California at Berkeley, pp. 63–89.

————. 1986. "Tanaka Kakuei, Structural Corruption, and the Advent of Machine Politics in Japan." *Journal of Japanese Studies* 12, (1) 1–28.

Kabashina, Ikuo, and Jeffrey Broadbent. 1986. "Referent Pluralism: Mass Media and Politics in Japan." *Journal of Japanese Studies* 12, no. 2 (Summer): 329–361.

Kamei, Katsuichirō. 1958. "Return to the East." In *Sources of Japanese Tradition,* compiled by Ryusaku Tsunoda, W. T. Bary, and Donald Keene. New York: Columbia University Press, pp. 900–906.

Kaplan, Eugene, J. 1972. *Japan—The Government-Business Relationship.* Washington, D.C.: Department of Commerce.

Keesing, Felix. 1958. *Cultural Anthropology: The Science of Custom.* New York: Holt, Rinehart & Winston.

Kernell, Samuel. 1991a. "The Primacy of Politics in Economic Policy." In *Parallel Politics: Economic Policymaking in Japan and the United States,* ed. by Samuel Kernell. Washington, D.C.: Brookings Institution.

————, ed. 1991b. *Parallel Politics: Economic Policymaking in Japan and the United States.* Washington, D.C.: Brookings Institution.

Kim, Paul. 1988. *Japan's Civil Service System.* Westport, Conn.: Greenwood Press.

Kim, Young C. 1981. *Japanese Journalists and Their World*. Charlottesville: University Press of Virginia.

Kingdon, John. 1981. *Congressmen's Voting Decisions*. New York: Harper & Row.

Kishima, Takako. 1991. *Political Life in Japan: Democracy in a Reversible World*. Princeton, N.J.: Princeton University Press.

Kishimoto, Kōichi. 1988. *Politics in Modern Japan*. 3rd ed. Tokyo: Japan Echo.

Koh, B. C. 1989. *Japan's Administrative Elite*. Berkeley and Los Angeles: University of California Press.

Koppel, Bruce, and Michael Plummer. 1989. "Japan's Ascendancy as a Foreign-Aid Power: Asian Perspective." *Asian Survey* 29, no. 11 (November): 1055.

Kosaka, Masataka, ed. 1989. *Japan's Choice*. London and New York: Pinter Publishers.

Krauss, Ellis. 1974. *Japanese Radicals Revisited*. Berkeley: University of California Press.

—————. 1982. "Japanese Parties and Parliament: Changing Leadership Role and Role Conflict." In *Political Leadership in Contemporary Japan*, ed. by Terry Mac-Dougall. Michigan Papers in Japanese Studies, no. 1. Ann Arbor: University of Michigan, p. 93–114.

Krauss, Ellis, Thomas Rohlen, and Patricia Steinhoff, eds. 1984. *Conflict in Japan*. Honolulu: University of Hawaii Press.

Krauss, Ellis, and Muramatsu Michio. 1988. "Japanese Political Economy Today: The Patterned Pluralist Model." In *Inside the Japanese System*, ed. by Daniel Okimoto and Thomas Rohlen, Stanford, Calif.: Stanford University Press, pp. 208–210.

Kubota, Akira. 1969. *Higher Civil Servants in Postwar Japan*. Princeton, N.J.: Princeton University Press.

Kuroda, Yasumasa. 1974. *Reed Town, Japan: A Study in Community Power Structure and Political Change*. Honolulu: University of Hawaii Press.

Kusuda, Minoru. 1975. *Shuseki hishokan: satō sōri tono jūnenkan* [Chief secretary: ten years with Prime Minister Satō]. Tokyo: Bungei Shunjusha.

Kusumoto, Mitsuo. 1976. *Shimbun no sugao* [The true face of newspapers]. Tokyo: Kobundō.

Kuwabara, Takeo. 1983. *Japan and Western Civilization*. Tokyo: University of Tokyo Press.

Kyōgoku, Jun-ichi. 1987. *The Political Dynamics of Japan*. New York: Columbia University Press.

Longdon, Frank. 1973. *Japan's Foreign Policy*. Vancouver: University of British Columbia Press.

—————. 1978. "Japanese Liberal Democratic Factional Discord on China Policy." *Pacific Affairs* (Fall).

—————. 1983. *The Politics of Canadian-Japanese Economic Relations 1952–1983*. Vancouver: University of British Columbia Press.

Lebra, Takie, and William Lebra eds. 1986. *Japanese Culture and Behavior*. Revised ed. Honolulu: University of Hawaii Press.

Lee, Chae-Jin. 1976. *Japan Faces China*. Balitmore and London: Johns Hopkins University Press.

—————. 1984. *China and Japan, New Economic Diplomacy*. Stanford, Calif.: Hoover Institution Press.

Lee, Chong-sik. 1985. *Japan and Korea: The Political Dimension*. Stanford, Calif.: Hoover Institution Press.

Lee, Jung Bock. 1985. *The Political Character of the Japanese Press*. Seoul: Seoul National University Press.

Lewellen, Ted. 1983. *Political Anthropology*. South Hadley, Mass.: Bergin & Garvey Publishers.

Lin, Biao. 1965. *Renmin zhanzheng shengli wansui* [Long live the victory of people's war]. Beijing: Foreign Language Press.

Lincoln, Edward. 1987. *Japan's Economic Role in Northeast Asia*. Lanham and New York: University Press of America.

Lindsay, A. D. 1943. *The Modern Democratic State*. London: Oxford University Press.

Lowi, Theodore. 1964. "American Business, Public Policy, Case-studies, and Political Theory." *World Politics* 16, no. 4 (July): 677–715.

MacDougall, Terry, ed. 1982. *Political Leadership in Contemporary Japan*. Ann Arbor, Mich.: Center for Japanese Studies, University of Michigan.

Maki, John. 1962. *Government and Politics in Japan*. New York: Praeger.

Makin, John, and Donald Hellmann, eds. 1989. *Sharing World Leadership? A New Era for America and Japan*. Washington, D.C.: American Enterprise Institute.

Malone, Giggord. 1988. *Political Advocacy and Cultural Communication*. Lanham and New York: University Press of America.

Mason, R.H.P., and J. G. Caiger. 1972. *A History of Japan*. New York: Free Press.

Masumi, Junnosuke. 1985a. *Gendai seiji* [Contemporary politics]. Tokyo: Tokyo daigaku shuppankai.

———. 1985b. *Postwar Politics in Japan, 1945–1955*. Berkeley: Institute of East Asian Studies, University of California.

McCraw, Thomas, ed. 1986. *America Versus Japan*. Boston: Harvard Business School Press.

McNelly, Theodore. 1984. *Politics and Government in Japan*. 3rd ed. Lanham and New York: University Press of America.

Mendel, Douglas. 1961. *The Japanese People and Foreign Policy*. Berkeley: University of California Press.

Mente, Boye De. 1987. *Japanese: Etiquette and Ethics in Business*. 5th ed. Lincolnwood, Ill.: Passport Books.

Minami, Hiroshi. 1971. *Psychology of the Japanese People*. Toronto: University of Toronto Press.

Misawa, Shigeo. 1973. "An Outline of the Policy-Making Process in Japan." In *Japanese Politics—An Inside View*, ed. by Hiroshi Itoh. Ithaca, N.Y.: Cornell University Press, pp. 12–48.

Miyagawa, T., ed. 1987. *Seiji Handobukku* [Handbook of Politics]. Tokyo: Seiji Kōhō Sentā.

Miyoshi, Osamu, and Shinkichi Etō. 1972. *Chūgoku hōdō no henkō o tsuku* [Criticism on the changing report about China]. Tokyo: Nisshin Hōdō.

Moeran, Brian. 1986. "Individual, Group and Seishin: Japan's Internal Cultural Debate." In *Japanese Culture and Behavior*, ed. by Takie Lebra and William Lebra. Honolulu: University of Hawaii Press, pp. 62–79.

Moerman, Michael. 1988. *Talking Culture*. Philadelphia: University of Pennsylvania Press.

MOFA, ed. 1970. *Waga gaikō no kinkyō* [Recent situation of our country's diplomacy]. 1969 ed. Tokyo.

Moore, Wilbert E. 1946. *Industrial Relations and the Social Order*. New York: Macmillan.

Morrison, Charles. 1985. *Japan, the United States and a Changing Southeast Asia.* Lanham and New York: University Press of America.

Mouzelis, Nicos. 1967. *Organization and Bureaucracy.* Chicago: Aldine Publishing Co.

Mueller, Peter, and Douglas Ross. 1975. *China and Japan—Emerging Global Powers.* New York: Praeger.

Murakawa, Ichirō. 1989. *Jimintō no seisaku kettei shisutemu* [The system of LDP's decision-making]. Tokyo: Kyōikusha.

Muramatsu, Michio. 1981. *Sengo nihon no kanryōsei* [Bureaucratic system in postwar Japan]. Tokyo: Toyo keizai shinposha.

Muramatsu, Michio, and Ellis Krauss. 1985. "The Ruling Coalition and Its Transformation." Paper presented at the Japan Political Economy Conference, Honolulu, January 7–11.

Nakajima, Mineo. 1982. "Hori shokan wa watashi ga kaita [I wrote the Hori Letter]. *Bungei shunjū* (October).

Nakamura, Takafusa. 1981. *The Postwar Japanese Economy.* Tokyo: University of Tokyo Press.

Nakane, Chie. 1970. *Japanese Society.* Berkeley: University of California Press.

————. 1972. *Human Relations in Japan.* Tokyo: Ministry of Foreign Affairs.

————. 1986. "Criteria of Group Formation." In *Japanese Culture and Behavior*, ed. by Takie Lebra and William Lebra. Honolulu: University of Hawaii Press, pp. 171–187.

Neustadt, Richard. 1960. *Presidential Power.* New York: John Wiley & Sons.

Nicholls, David. 1975. *The Pluralist State.* London: Macmillan.

Odom, William. 1976. "A Dissenting View on the Group Approach to Soviet Politics." *World Politics* 28, no. 4 (July): 542–567.

Ogata, Sadako. 1977. "The Business Community and Japanese Foreign Policy: Normalization of Relations with the People's Republic of China." In *The Foreign Policy of Modern Japan*, ed. by Robert Scalapino. Berkeley: University of California Press, pp. 175–203.

————. 1988. *Normalization with China: A Comparative Study of U.S. and Japanese Processes.* Berkeley: Institute of East Asian Studies, University of California, Berkeley.

Ōhira, Masayoshi. 1979. *Brush Strokes: Moments from My Life.* Tokyo: Foreign Press Center.

Okada, Akira. 1983. *Mizutori gaikō hiwa* [Secret story of water bird diplomacy]. Tokyo: Chūō kōronsha.

Okimoto, Daniel. 1988. "Political Inclusivity: The Domestic Structure of Trade." In *The Political Economy of Japan Volume 2: The Changing International Context*, ed. by Takashi Inoguchi and Daniel Okimoto. Stanford, Calif.: Stanford University Press, pp. 305–344.

Ōkubo, Tasuku. 1986. *China and Japan: Financial Aspects.* Tokyo: Sophia University.

Ornstein, Norman, and Shirley Elder. 1978. *Interest Groups, Lobbying and Policymaking.* Washington, D.C.: Congressional Quarterly Press.

Orr, Robert. 1990. *The Emergence of Japanese Foreign Aid Power.* New York: Columbia University Press.

Park, Yung. 1975. "The Politics of Japan's China Decision." *Orbis* 19, no. 2 (Summer): 562–590.

———. 1986. *Bureaucrats and Ministers in Contemporary Japanese Government.* Berkeley, Calif.: Institute of East Asian Studies, University of California at Berkeley.

Pempel, T. J. 1982. *Policy and Politics in Japan, Creative Conservatism.* Philadelphia: Temple University Press.

———. 1987. "The Unbundling of 'Japan, Inc.' " *Journal of Japanese Studies* 13, no. 2 (Summer): 271–306.

———. 1990. "Introduction." In *Uncommon Democracies: The One-Party Dominant Regimes,* ed. by T. J. Pempel. Ithaca, N.Y., and London: Cornell University Press, pp. 1–32.

———. 1992. "Japanese Democracy and Political Culture: A Comparative Perspective." In *PS: Political Science and Politics* 35 (1): 5–12.

Pempel, T. J., ed. 1977. *Policymaking in Contemporary Japan.* Ithaca, N.Y., and London: Cornell University Press.

Peter, Charles. 1980. *How Washington Really Works.* Reading, Mass.: Addison-Wesley.

Pharr, Susan. 1981. *Political Women in Japan.* Berkeley: University of California Press.

———. 1984. "Status Conflict: The Rebellion of the Tea Pourers." In *Conflict in Japan,* ed. by Ellis Krauss, Thomas Rohlen, and Patricia Steinhoff. Honolulu: University of Hawaii Press, pp. 214–240.

———. 1990. *Losing Face: Status Politics in Japan.* Berkeley: University of California Press.

Pollack, David. 1986. *The Fracture of Meaning.* Princeton, N.J.: Princeton University Press.

Polsby, Nelson. 1980. *Community Power and Political Theory.* 2nd ed. New Haven, Conn., and London: Yale University Press.

Pye, Lucian. 1965. "Introduction: Political Culture and Political Development." In *Political Culture and Political Development,* ed. by Lucian Pye and Sidney Verba. Princeton, N.J.: Princeton University Press, pp. 3–26.

———. 1982. *Chinese Commercial Negotiating Style.* Cambridge, Mass.: Oelegeschlager, Gunn & Hain, Publishers.

———. 1985. *Asian Power and Politics: The Cultural Dimensions of Authority.* Cambridge, Mass.: Harvard University Press.

———. 1990. "Political Science and the Crisis of Authoritarianism." *American Political Science Review* 84, no. 1 (March): 3–19.

Pyle, Kenneth. 1989. "The Burden of Japanese History and the Politics of Burden Sharing." In *Sharing World Leadership?: A New Era for America and Japan,* ed. by John Makin and Donald Hellmann. Washington, D.C.: American Enterprise Institute for Public Policy Research, pp. 41–77.

Reed, Steven. 1986. *Japanese Prefectures and Policymaking.* Pittsburgh: University of Pittsburgh Press.

Reischauer, Edwin. 1988. *The Japanese Today.* Cambridge, Mass.: Harvard University Press.

Richardson, Bradley. 1974. *The Political Culture of Japan.* Berkeley: University of California Press.

———. 1991. "Social Networks, Influence Communications, and the Vote." In Scott Flanagan, Shinsaku Kohei, Ichirō Miyake, Bradley Richardson, and Jōji Watanuki, *The Japanese Voter*. New Haven, Conn., and London: Yale University Press, pp. 332–366.

Richardson, Bradley, and Scott Flanagan. 1984. *Politics in Japan*. Boston: Little, Brown & Co.

Roethlisberger, F. J., and W. J. Dickson. 1941. *Management and the Worker*. Cambridge, Mass.: Harvard University Press.

Rosenbluth, Frances M. 1989. *Financial Politics in Contemporary Japan*. Ithaca, N.Y., and London: Cornell University Press.

Rowe, David Nelson. 1975. *Informal "Diplomatic Relations": The Case of Japan and the Republic of China, 1972–1974*. Hamden, Conn.: Shoe String Press.

Rozman, Gilbert. 1992. *Japan's Response to the Gorbachev Era, 1985–1991*. Princeton, N.J.: Princeton University Press.

Ryū, Shintarō. 1961. "Seifu to shimbun" [The government and newspapers]. *Asahijin* (June).

Sahlins, Marshall. 1976. *Culture and Practical Reason*. Chicago: University of Chicago Press.

Samuels, Richard. 1982. "Power Behind the Throne." In *Political Leadership in Contemporary Japan*, ed. by Terry E. MacDougall. Ann Arbor, Mich.: Center for Japanese Studies, University of Michigan, pp. 127–146.

————. 1983. *The Politics of Regional Policy in Japan*. Princeton, N.J.: Princeton University Press.

————. 1990. "Japan in 1989: Changing Times." *Asian Survey* 30, no. 1 (January): 42–51.

Satō, Seizaburō. 1984. "Political Institutionalization and Democracy in Japan: Emergence of Predominant Party System." Paper presented for the Project on Development, Stability and Security in the Pacific-Asian Region, Berkeley, March 19–21.

Satō, Seizaburō, and Tetsuhisa Matsuzaki. 1986. *Jimintō Seiken* [Politics and power of the LDP]. Tokyo: Chūō Kōronsha.

Scalapino, Robert, ed. 1977. *The Foreign Policy of Modern Japan*. Berkeley: University of California Press.

Scalapino, Robert, and Junnosuke Masumi. 1962. *Parties and Politics in Contemporary Japan*. Berkeley and Los Angeles: University of California Press.

Schmitter, Philippe, ed. 1979. *Trends Towards Corporatist Intermediation*. Beverly Hills, Calif.: Sage Publications.

Seekins, Donald. 1983. "The Political System." In *Japan: A Country Study*, 4th ed., ed. by Frederica Bunge. Washington, D.C.: Headquarters, Department of the Army, pp. 245–298.

Seiznick, Philip. 1961. "Foundations of the Theory of Organization." In *Complex Organizations*, ed. by Amitai Etzioni. New York: Holt, Rinehart & Winston.

Shinohara, Hajime. 1971. *Nihon no seiji* [Japanese politics]. Tokyo: Iwanami Shoten.

Smith, Robert. 1983. *Japanese Society: Tradition, Self and Social Order*. Cambridge: Cambridge University Press.

————. 1989. "Presidential Address: Something Old, Something New—Tradition and Culture in the Study of Japan." *Journal of Asian Studies* 48, no. 4 (November): 715–723.

Sofue, Takao. 1986. "Continuity and Change in the Japanese Personality." In *Asian Peoples and Their Cultures*, ed. by Sang-bok Han. Seoul: Seoul National University Press, pp. 259–276.

Steinbruner, John. 1974. *The Cybernetic Theory of Decision: New Dimensions of Political Analysis*. Princeton, N.J.: Princeton University Press.

Stockwin, J.A.A. 1982. *Japan: Divided Politics in a Growth Economy*. London and New York: W. W. Norton.

————. 1988. "Dynamic and Immobilist Aspects of Japanese Politics." In *Dynamic and Immobilist Politics in Japan*, by J.A.A. Stockwin, et al. Honolulu: University of Hawaii Press, pp. 1–21.

Story, Greg. 1987. *Japan's Official Development Assistance to China*. Canberra, Australia: Research School of Pacific Studies, Australian National University.

Suzuki, Takao. 1986. "Language and Behavior in Japan: The Conceptualization of Personal Relations." In *Japanese Culture and Behavior*, ed. by Takie Lebra and William Lebra. Honolulu: University of Hawaii Press, pp. 142–157.

Szajkowski, Bogdan, ed. 1986. *Marxist Local Governments in Western Europe and Japan*. London: Frances Printer.

Tagawa, Seiichi. 1972. "Hori kanjichō no seii o tou [Questioning the sincerity of Secretary General Hori]." *Sekai* (March): 202–212.

————. 1973. *Nitchū kōsho hiroku* [The secret records of Japan-China contacts]. Tokyo: Mainichi Shimbunsha.

————. 1983. *Nitchū kōryū to jimintō ryōshūtachi* [Japan-China exchanges and the LDP leaders]. Tokyo: Yomiuri Shimbunsha.

Takabatake, Michitoshi. 1978. *Gendai nihon no seiji 72–77* [Contemporary Japanese politics 1972–1977]. Tokyo: San-ichi Shobō.

Tanaka, Akihiko. 1985. "Bei-chū-so no aide de" [Surrounded by the U.S., China, and the USSR]. In *Sengo nihon no taigai seisaku* [Postwar Japanese foreign policy], ed. by Akio Watanabe. Tokyo: Yūhikaku, pp. 220–253.

Tanaka, T. 1971. *Nihon no kokyō* [Japan's hometown]. Tokyo: Nōkyō Kyōkai.

Taylor, Jared. 1983. *Shadows of the Rising Sun*. New York: William Morrow & Co.

Taylor, Robert. 1985. *The Sino-Japanese Axis*. London: Athlone Press.

Thayer, Nathaniel. 1969. *How the Conservatives Rule Japan*. Princeton, N.J.: Princeton University Press.

Tocqueville, Alexis de. 1969. *Democracy in America*. Garden City, N.Y.: Doubleday & Co.

Trezise, Philip. 1990. "U.S.-Japan Economic Issues." In *The United States and Japan*, ed. by the Atlantic Council of the United States. Lanham and New York: University Press of America, pp. 15–35.

Tsou, Tang. 1986. *The Cultural Revolution and Post-Mao Reforms*. Chicago: University of Chicago Press.

Tsou, Tang, Tetsuo Najita, and Hideo Ōtake. 1978. "Sino-Japanese Relations in the 1970s." In *China and Japan: Search for Balance Since World War I*, ed. by Alvin Coox and Hilary Conroy. Santa Barbara, Calif.: ABC-Clio, pp. 401–431.

Tsuneishi, Warren. 1966. *Japanese Political Style*. New York: Harper & Row.

Tsurutani, Taketsugu. 1977. *Political Change in Japan*. New York: David McKay Company.

Tsūshinsha, Jiji Seijibu, ed. 1972. *Dokyumento: nitchū fukkō* [Documents: The restoration of Japan-China diplomatic relations]. Tokyo.

Upham, Frank. 1987. *Law and Social Change in Postwar Japan*. Cambridge, Mass.: Harvard University Press.

U.S. Congress. House and Senate. Committee on Foreign Affairs, Committee on Foreign

Relations. 1986. *Legislation on Foreign Relations Through 1985*, vols. 1 and 2. Washington, D.C.: Government Printing Office (April).

Valeo, Francis, and Charles Morrison, eds. 1983. *The Japanese Diet and the U.S. Congress*. Boulder, Colo.: Westview Press.

Verba, Sidney. 1965. "Comparative Political Culture." In *Political Culture and Political Development*, ed. by Lucian Pye and Sidney Verba. Princeton, N.J.: Princeton University Press, pp. 512–560.

Verba, Sidney, et al., eds. 1987. *Elites and the Idea of Equality: A Comparison of Japan, Sweden, and the United States*. Cambridge, Mass.: Harvard University Press.

Viotti, Paul, and Mark Kauppi. 1987. *International Relations Theory*. New York and London: Macmillan.

Vogel, Ezra. 1963. *Japan's New Middle Class*. Berkeley: University of California Press.

Walder, Andrew. 1986. *Communist Neo-Traditionalism: Work and Authority in Chinese Industry*. Berkeley: University of California Press.

Waltz, Kenneth. 1959. *Man, the State and War*. New York: Columbia University Press.

Wan, Feng. 1981. *Riben Jindaishi* [Modern history of Japan]. 2nd ed. Beijing: Zhongguo shehui kexue chubanshe.

Ward, Robert. 1978. *Japan's Political System*. 2nd ed. Englewood Cliffs, N.J.: Prentice-Hall.

Watanabe, Akio, ed. 1985. *Sengo nihon no taigai seisaku* [Postwar Japanese foreign policy]. Tokyo: Yūhikaku.

Watanuki, Jōji. 1977. *Politics in Postwar Japanese Society*. Tokyo: University of Tokyo Press.

————. 1991. "Social Structure and Voting Behavior." In *The Japanese Voter*, ed by Scott Flanagan, Shinsaku Kohei, Ichirō Miyake, Bradley Richardson, and Jōji Watanuki. New Haven, Conn., and London: Yale University Press, pp. 49–83.

Weber, Max. 1968. *On Charisma and Institution Building*. Chicago: University of Chicago Press.

Wen, Tianshen. 1990. "Silk Country." *China Today* 39, no. 1 (January): 24–26.

Westney, D. Eleanor. 1987. *Imitation and Innovation: The Transfer of Western Organizational Patterns to Meiji Japan*. Cambridge, Mass.: University of Harvard Press.

Whiting, Allen. 1989. *China Eyes Japan*. Berkeley: University of California Press.

————. 1992. "China and Japan: Politics Versus Economics." *The Annals* (AAPSS) 519 (January): 39–51.

Wildavsky, Aaron. 1986. *Budgeting, A Comparative Theory of Budgetary Processes*. Revised ed. New Brunswick, N.J.: Transaction.

Wolferen, Karel van. 1989. *The Enigma of Japanese Power*. New York: Alfred A. Knopf.

Woronoff, Jon. 1986. *The Japanese Syndrome*. New Brunswick, N.J.: Transaction Books.

Yamamoto, Mitsuru. 1974. *Jishu gaikō no gensō* [Fantasy of independent diplomacy]. Tokyo: Chūō Kōronsha.

Yamamoto, Taketoshi. 1989. "The Press Club of Japan." *Journal of Japanese Studies* 15, no. 2 (Summer): 371–388.

Yamamura, Kōzō. 1982. "Success That Soured: Administrative Guidance and Cartels in Japan." In *Policy and Trade Issues of the Japanese Economy*, ed. by Kōzō Yamamura. Seattle and London: University of Washington Press, pp. 77–112.

Yamamura, Yoshiharu, and Tsuyoshi Yamamoto. 1972. "Mitsubishi gurūpu no kareinaru tenshin [The Mitsubishi Group's magnificent turnabout]." *Chūō Kōron*, no. 10 (October): 222–231.

Yano, Ichirō, ed. 1986. *Nihon kokuseizu* [Survey of Japan's national development]. Tokyo.

Yasuhara, Yōko. 1986. "Japan, Communist China, and Export Controls in Asia." *Diplomatic History* 10 no. 1 (Winter): 75–90.

Yoshino, M. Y., and Thomas Lifson. 1986. *The Invisible Link: Japan's Sōgō Shōsha and the Organization of Trade.* Cambridge, Mass.: MIT Press.

Yu, Qingao, Hua Jue, et al., eds. 1984. *Xiandai riben mingren lu* [Dictionary of famous people in contemporary Japan]. Beijing: Shishi chubanshe.

Zhao, Quansheng. 1986. "Xuezhe he zhinongtuan" [Scholars and think-tanks]. *Riben Wenti* [Japan Issues] 9 (October): 68–70.

———. 1988. "The Making of Public Policy in Japan: Protectionism in Raw Silk Importation." *Asian Survey* 28, no. 9 (September): 926–944.

———. 1989. " 'Informal Pluralism' and Japanese Politics: Sino-Japanese Rapprochement Revisited." *Journal of Northeast Asian Studies* 8, no. 2 (Summer): 65–83.

———. 1990. "Politics of Japan-China Trade Negotiations." *Asian Profile* 18, no. 2 (April): 97–115.

———. 1992. "Domestic Factors of Chinese Foreign Policy: From Vertical to Horizontal Authoritarianism." *The Annals* (the American Academy of Political and Social Sciences) 519 (January), special editor, Allen Whiting, pp. 159–176.

Zhao, Quansheng, and Robert Sutter, eds. 1991. *Politics of Divided Nations: China, Korea, Germany and Vietnam.* Balitmore: University of Maryland School of Law.

SELECTED JOURNALS AND NEWSPAPERS

American Political Science Review. (Journal in English)
Asahi jarʔru. (Journal in Japanese).
Asahi shimbun. (Newspaper in Japanese).
Asian Profile. (Journal in English).
Asian Survey. (Journal in English).
Beijing Review. (Journal in English).
Bungei shunjū. (Journal in Japanese).
China Business Review. (Journal in English).
The China Quarterly. (Journal in English).
China Today (formerly *China Reconstructs*). (Journal in English).
Chūō kōron. (Journal in Japanese).
Comparative Politics. (Journal in English).
Diplomatic History. (Journal in English).
Far Eastern Economic Review. (Journal in English).
Guoji Maoyi [International Trade]. (Journal in Chinese).
Japan Times. (Newspaper in English).
Journal of Asian Studies. (Journal in English).
Journal of Japanese Studies. (Journal in English).
Journal of Northeast Asian Studies. (Journal in English).
Journal of Political Science Review. (Journal in English).
New York Times. (Newspaper in English).
Nihon keizai shimbun. (Newspaper in Japanese).

Pacific Affairs. (Journal in English).
Pacific Community. (Journal in English).
The Pacific Review. (Journal in English).
Renmin Ribao. (Newspaper in Chinese).
Riben Wenti [Japan Issues]. (Journal in Chinese).
World Politic. (Journal in English).

Index

Abe, Shintarō, 50, 55, 56
administrative guidance, 88, 149
Afro-Asian Problems Study Group, 74, 76, 98
ahiru gaikō (duck diplomacy), 12, 80, 81, 83, 92, 108, 186, 187, 190
amakudari (descent from heaven), 52, 123
American occupation, 25, 42, 129
anthropological theory, 186
anti-Japanese demonstrations, 169, 179
Asanuma, Inejirō, 93, 94
Asian Affairs Bureau (AAB) 77, 78, 80, 131
Asian Development Bank, 162
Asian Problems Study Group, 73, 74
Association of Southeast Asian Nations (ASEAN), 174
authoritarian rule, 20, 22, 42, 193, 200

Barnard, Chester, 67
Barnett, A. Doak, 24, 83
Beardsley, Richard, 7
Beasley, W. G., 8
Benjamin, Roger, 196
Bestor, Theodore, 9, 155
bureaucracy, 9–12, 20, 22, 23, 34, 37, 39, 41–44, 49–54, 57, 59, 67, 75–77, 79, 83, 88, 91, 92, 102, 105, 107, 121–126, 138, 143, 145, 149, 154, 187–191, 193–197, 200, 201; breakup of bureaucratic dominance, 44, 197; bureaucratic dominance, 11
Bush, George, 56, 172, 174, 175, 177
business community, 8, 12, 27, 79, 83, 85, 88–92, 108, 130, 134, 138, 140, 148–151, 154, 167, 195, 197
Butow, Robert, 138

Calder, Kent, 9, 191
Campbell, John, 3, 6, 9, 67
case studies, 5, 9–11, 13, 63, 65, 161, 185, 186, 189, 190, 202
catalytic and valve functions, 88, 107
Chiang, Kai-shek, 26, 79, 139, 140, 168
China (PRC), 5, 9–13, 23–34, 38, 39, 47, 50, 52, 53, 55, 56, 59, 63, 65, 66–85, 88–99, 101–108, 117–124, 127–133, 138–154, 159, 161–180, 187–191, 193, 195, 197, 198, 199, 200; Beijing's strategy, 83; Cultural Revolution, 27, 68, 69, 152, 153; domestic political development in, 68; lifting of martial law, 172, 175, 178; position of, 94, 151; Tiananmen, 10, 12, 13, 144, 159, 161–163, 165–171, 173–175, 177–180, 187, 190, 191, 196, 197
China Council for the Promotion of International Trade, 26, 91, 118, 150, 151

About the Author

QUANSHENG ZHAO is Director of the Institute of Asian Studies, Chairman of the Asian Studies Committee, and faculty member in political science at Old Dominion University. He is co-editor of *Politics of Divided Nations: China, Korea, Germany, and Vietnam* (1991) and has authored articles published in *Asian Survey, Asian Profile, The Annals of the AAPSS, Journal of Northeast Asian Studies, The Pacific Review,* and *World Outlook.*